Sports Tourism

Sports Tourism

Participants, policy and providers

Mike Weed and Chris Bull

ELSEVIER
BUTTERWORTH
HEINEMANN

AMSTERDAM BOSTON HEIDELBERG LONDON NEW YORK OXFORD
PARIS SAN DIEGO SAN FRANCISCO SINGAPORE SYDNEY TOKYO

Elsevier Butterworth-Heinemann
Linacre House, Jordan Hill, Oxford OX2 8DP
200 Wheeler Road, Burlington MA 01803

First published 2004

British Library Cataloguing in Publication Data
A catalogue record for this book is available from the British Library

Library of Congress Cataloguing in Publication Data
A catalogue record for this book is available from the Library of Congress

ISBN 0 7506 5276 4

For information on all Elsevier Butterworth-Heinemann
publications visit our website at www.books.elsevier.com

Typeset by Genesis Typesetting Ltd, Rochester, Kent, UK
Printed and bound in Great Britain

Contents

Figures

Tables

Boxes

Acknowledgements

In addition to our respective partners, to whom we owe a large debt of gratitude for their support and patience over a considerable period of time, we would also like to thank various other people for their help and support in the writing of this text. Considerable thanks must go to Dr Guy Jackson, formerly of the Institute of Sport and Leisure Policy at Loughborough University, now Marketing Manager for Loughborough Sport, who was initially going to be involved in the authorship of this text. Guy put his considerable 'archive' of sports tourism research and materials at our disposal, and provided valuable advice about the direction and nature of the text. We would also like to acknowledge the contribution made by the various Masters and Doctoral students whose work is quoted throughout this text, and specifically the contribution of Dr Martin Reeves's doctoral research. Thanks are also due to Mick Green and Professor Barrie Houlihan at Loughborough University for guidance on international sports policy structures.

Finally, we would like to express our appreciation to the various staff at Butterworth-Heinemann, in particular Sally North, for their continued support for this project and the help they have provided.

Prologue: the study of sports tourism

In 1966, Don Anthony wrote a paper entitled 'Sport and tourism' for the Central Council of Physical Recreation in the UK (Anthony, 1966). This appears to be one of the earliest writings on the links between sport and tourism and, although the paper simply reviewed the role sport played in holiday tourism, it is an important landmark in the development of the study of sports tourism.

Almost forty years on from Anthony's landmark paper, the field of sports tourism is still struggling in many quarters for academic legitimacy, with Gammon and Kurtzman (2002: v) noting how: 'those writing and researching in the area have been accused of clumsily diluting two already established disciplines in order to profit from professional precedence and thus committing the indefensible crime of academic triviality'.

Such accusations may partly be due to the fragmented nature of the field, with many papers at academic conferences and in peer-reviewed journals being isolated studies of impacts that do little to contribute to the advancement of knowledge or theory in the field. This was recognized by Gibson in 1998, who identified a number of problems that are still salient today:

> the field suffers from a lack of integration in the realms of policy, research and education. At a policy level, there needs to be better co-ordination among agencies responsible for sport and those responsible for tourism. At a research level, more multi-disciplinary research is needed, particularly research which builds upon existing knowledge bases in both sport and tourism. In the realm of education, territorial contests between departments claiming tourism expertise and those claiming sport expertise need to be overcome. (Gibson, 1998: 45)

A central question, therefore, might relate to how the study of sports tourism has developed in the last forty years given that it is still struggling for legitimacy in the eyes of some academics. As such it is perhaps useful to take a brief look at the development of the area since Anthony's paper.

The first point to note is that Anthony's paper in 1966 did not stimulate a great deal of further interest, and while De Knop (1990) argued that academic interest in sports tourism began in the 1970s (e.g. Baker and Gordon, 1976; Schreiber, 1976), it is really Glyptis's (1982) study of sport and tourism in five European countries that marks the beginning of a growth of literature on the links between sport and tourism. Further work by Glyptis (1991a) and subsequently the report commissioned by the GB Sports Council on the interrelationship between sport and tourism (Jackson and Glyptis, 1992) were also some of the earliest substantive works in the area. Other valuable reviews of the field have been carried out by De Knop (1990), Standeven and Tomlinson (1994), Gibson (1998), Weed (1999a) and Jackson and Weed (2003). Different facets of the interrelationship between sport and tourism have also been researched (e.g. Collins and Jackson, 1999; Jackson and Reeves, 1998; Redmond, 1991; Reeves, 2000; Vrondou, 1999; Weed, 1999b). In addition, commercial analysts have reviewed the volume and value of this emerging sector of the leisure industry (Leisure Consultants, 1992; Mintel, 1999).

More recently, a number of complete texts focusing on sports tourism have been published. The first of these was the 1999 offering from Standeven and De Knop which, like the later publication from Robinson, Gammon and Jones (2003), provides a relatively introductory overview, focusing to a large extent on the impacts of sports tourism. The text by Turco, Riley and Swart (2002) approaches the subject from a management perspective, providing an introduction to sports tourism operations and marketing. In contrast, the forthcoming text by Hinch and Higham (Channel View Publications) promises a more advanced overview of development aspects of sports tourism. Each of these books are, as noted later in this prologue, very different from the material presented in this text.

Sports tourism is now relatively well represented on the international conference circuit. However, one of the earliest conferences to include a sports tourism theme was the GB Sports Council's 1986 Recreation Management Seminar, which included a consideration of the role of sport within tourism, practically illustrated by a session on Birmingham's Olympic bid (Sports Council, 1986). More recently, sports tourism has been a specific theme of the 2001 Leisure Studies Association Conference (see Gammon and Kurtzman, 2002) and the 2002 European Association of Sport Management Congress (see Laaksonen et al., 2002). Further examples are provided by TEAMS in the USA, an annual congress which held its first session in 1997, and the Illinois Sport Tourism Conference in the mid-1990s. However, most significant among these, in terms of the profile of the organizations involved, was the joint International Olympic Committee (IOC)/World Tourism Organization (WTO) Conference held in February 2001 (see WTO, 2002).

This 'First World Conference on Sport and Tourism' was held in Barcelona and was attended by the then President of the International Olympic Committee, Juan Antonio Samaranch. However, as with much of the academic work in the field, the conference focused largely on impacts and management considerations. Two reports were prepared for this conference: the first, an introductory report (Keller, 2001) which did not draw to any great extent on previous research in the area; and the second, a case study of the sports tourism preferences of the Dutch, the Germans and the French (IPK International, 2001).

There has been no evidence of any further collaboration between the IOC and WTO in relation to sports tourism since this conference.

The joint IOC/WTO conference might be seen as representative of some of the problems that the field of sports tourism has experienced. First, the conference was largely limited to considerations of impacts, management and marketing, with much of the content lacking theoretical insight. Second, the two reports that informed the conference showed, in the case of the introductory report, a lack of appreciation of previous research in the area and presented, in the case of the IPK report, case studies of the preferences of an arbitrary group of North Europeans. Finally, the conference did not lead to any further strategic alliances between policy agencies for sport and for tourism.

Among the participants in the IOC/WTO conference were representatives of the Sport Tourism International Council (STIC). This organization, initially named the Tourism Sport International Council, was formed in 1990 to: establish a professional association for sports tourism, to foster research on the role of sports tourism, and to interlink tourism and sport organizations, groups and other sectors directly and indirectly related to the sports tourism industry'. (STIC website)

In 1995, the Sport Tourism International Council formed a research unit, and subsequently launched an online *Journal of Sports Tourism*. In the early years much of the content of this journal was very introductory in nature and, although recent issues have improved, it is hoped that its launch as a 'hardcopy' journal with Routledge in 2003 will result in a journal that can provide the international showcase for sports tourism research that the field needs.

The STIC has now turned its attention to curriculum concerns in relation to sports tourism, and the development of a Certification Programme that will allow people to be accredited as Certified Sports Tourism Managers. However, while specific sports tourism degrees exist (e.g. BSc Sports Tourism at the University of Luton in the UK), there is a question as to the extent to which specialist sports tourism degrees are required. Gibson (1998: 69) suggests that any growth in such degrees is likely to be driven by the financial concerns of universities, which might see the provision of sports tourism degrees as a lucrative strategy. The development of curricula for sports tourism is something that will be re-examined in the epilogue to this book.

Notwithstanding some of the more negative elements of the above discussion, the field of sports tourism has clearly developed significantly during the last decade. However, the extent to which academics working in the sports tourism field around the world are often unaware of each other's work (Gibson, 1998; 2002) is starting to be reflected in an unnecessary duplication of research efforts. The studies quoted in the early part of this prologue have, *inter alia*, established that there are significant links between sport and tourism and the broad nature of such links and their impacts, and as such they need not be replicated. Consequently, this text does not devote a great deal of its content to the impacts of linking sport and tourism; rather it focuses, as the title suggests, on the three main groups of actors involved in sports tourism: participants, policy-makers and providers.

The material presented in this book is not merely an agglomeration of secondary research, the discussions of participants, policy-makers and providers are derived from primary empirical studies at Masters, Doctoral and Post-

Doctoral level at Loughborough University and Canterbury Christ Church University College over the last decade. As such, the theoretical concepts discussed and the models presented are grounded in empirical research, and extracts from this are presented where appropriate throughout the text. However, a wide range of perspectives from secondary sources are also included, both in setting the context for the study of sports tourism in the first part of the book, and in supplementing, complementing and substantiating the primary research that underpins Parts Two, Three and Four.

The book is organized into five parts, each of which is introduced by a brief preface. Part One (Context) comprises Chapters 1 and 2, which trace the historical growth of sports tourism and provide an international overview of the effects of linking sport and tourism respectively. The second part of the book focuses on sports tourism participants and comprises Chapters 3, 4 and 5. Chapter 3 attempts to conceptualize the sports tourist, discussing definitional concerns, place experience and the motivations of sports tourists, while Chapter 4 discusses and describes sports tourist profiles, examining the behaviours of a range of sports tourist types. Chapter 5 draws on the material in the previous two chapters to develop a Sports Tourism Participation Model, which can be used to understand both sports tourist behaviour and, as discussed later in the text, the strategies of sports tourism providers. Part Three comprises two chapters which focus on sports tourism policy, highlighting and examining the general lack of strategic liaison between policy-makers for sport and for tourism around the world.

In these chapters theoretical perspectives from policy studies are used, alongside previous primary empirical work in the sports tourism area, to develop a model of cross-sectoral policy development. In addition, the Policy Area Matrix for Sport and Tourism (Weed, 1999b; Weed and Bull, 1997a) is used to illustrate those areas in which it might reasonably be expected that sport and tourism agencies should collaborate. The fourth part of the book examines sports tourism providers, with Chapter 8 outlining the features of the supply side of the market for sports tourism. From the discussions in Chapter 8 a model of Sports Tourism Types is developed which is used, alongside the Sports Tourism Participation Model developed in Chapter 5, to examine sports tourism provision strategies in Chapter 9. The final part of the book comprises four case study chapters that illustrate the issues discussed in earlier parts of the book in relation to sports tourism as a diversification strategy, urban sports tourism, outdoor activity sports tourism and skiing, in relation to Malta, Sheffield, Wales and the European Alps respectively. Finally, an epilogue discusses and speculates on the future development of the field of sports tourism. A key theme throughout the book is that sports tourism as an area of study produces a range of issues that cannot be analysed and addressed via a simple amalgamation of approaches previously applied to the individual sectors of sport and tourism. As such, sports tourism is conceptualized as a social, economic and cultural phenomenon that arises from the unique interaction of activity, people and place.

A final introductory comment prior to the main text is perhaps needed in relation to terminology. A detailed discussion of definitions and concepts is provided in Chapter 3, but some clarification is useful at the outset in relation to the use of the terms 'sports tourism', 'sport tourism' and the 'sport-tourism link'. The term 'sport-tourism link' refers to a broad concept that, in addition to tourism involving some element of sports related activity, also embraces liaison between the sport and tourism areas on issues such as resources and funding, policy and planning, and information and research. As such, it is a useful term to use in discussions of policy, and in any discussion seeking to examine the effects of linking sport and tourism. The use of the terms 'sports tourism' and 'sport tourism' is more problematic, and is the basis of some debate among academics in the area. Gibson (2002: 115), along with many others in the field (e.g. Delpy, 1999; Standeven and De Knop, 1999), argues that the term 'sport tourism' should be used because 'sport' refers to the broader social institution of sport, while 'sports' refers to a collection of activities that have come to be defined as such. Consequently, the term 'sport tourism' encompasses 'a wider analysis of sport as a social institution rather than the micro-view of individual sports' (Gibson, 2002: 115). However, the use of the term 'sport tourism' for these reasons implies a reliance on sport as a social institution to define and delimit the area of 'sport tourism'. Given that one of the precepts of this text is that sports tourism is a unique area of study derived from the interaction of activity, people and place, a dependence on the social institution of sport to characterize the area would be somewhat incongruous. Furthermore, the concept of sport can in many cases be a misnomer in that it implies coherence where none exists and detracts from the heterogeneous nature of sporting activities. As one of the unique aspects of sports tourism is that the interaction of people and place with the activities in question expands rather than limits heterogeneity, in this text the term 'sports tourism' is used, along with the focus on diverse and heterogeneous activities that the term implies.

Notwithstanding the above discussion, the wider social institution of sport does play a role in determining policy responses to the sport-tourism link. However, as discussed above, in relation to areas such as policy development, where the impact of cultural and social assumptions about the scope and nature of sport are important considerations, the broader term 'sport-tourism link' can be employed.

Abbreviations

AALA	Adventure Activities Licensing Authority
AIS	Australian Institute of Sport
AOC	Australian Institute of Sport
ASC	Australian Sports Commission
ATC	Australian Tourism Commission
BBC	British Broadcasting Corporation
CABR	Centre for Applied Business Research
CC	Countryside Commission
CRRAG	Countryside Recreation Research and Advisory Group
CTC	Canadian Tourism Commission
DCMS	Department for Culture, Media and Sport
DGE	Directorate Generale for Enterprise
DoE	Department of the Environment
ETB	English Tourist Board
EU	European Union
FA	Football Association
GIR	government–industry relations
IGR	intergovernmental relations
IOC	International Olympic Committee
IVV	Der Internationale Volksport-verband
MCC	Marylebone Cricket Club
MINOS	Mountain International Opinion Survey
NTO	National Tourist Organization
RTB	Regional Tourist Board
RYA	Royal Yachting Association
STIC	Sport Tourism International Council
TEAMS	Travel, Events and Management in Sports
TIAA	Travel Industry Association of America
USOC	United States Olympic Committee
USTTA	United States Travel and Tourism Association
WTB	Wales Tourist Board
WTO	World Tourism Organization
YHA	Youth Hostels Association
YMCA	Young Men's Christian Association

Part One: Context

Preface

Many of the published texts on sports tourism focus much of their attention on the nature of its impacts, with significant emphasis often being placed on its economic impacts. The Standeven and De Knop (1999) text, for example, takes this approach presenting, after several introductory and context-setting chapters, chapters on economic, sociocultural, environmental and health impacts. In other cases particular subsectors of sports tourism are addressed. Hudson's (2000) book, *Snow Business*, falls into this category, as does his edited collection (Hudson, 2003a) which contains chapters by a range of authors on sport events, winter sport, marine, golf and adventure tourism.

In contrast to much else published in the field, the aim of this text is not to focus on an analysis of sports tourism impacts, but to examine the behaviours of those involved in sports tourism, namely, the actual participants, the policy-makers, and the providers. However, an important context for this analysis is material related to the development, nature and impacts of sports tourism which is provided by the next two chapters.

Chapter 1 traces the development of sports tourism over time, focusing particularly on developments related to travel for sport rather than revisiting material on the history of sport and of tourism that is covered in much greater detail in other sources. While some of this material is international in nature, the historical overview is presented from a British perspective for two related reasons. First, because a completely international history would be almost impossible given the diverse historical development of sport, tourism and sports tourism around the world and, second, given that any history will be derived from a particular perspective, the British perspective has been taken because it is the one with which the authors are most familiar and therefore best equipped to comment on. As such, the historical issues raised will, in some cases, be illustrative of the development of sports tourism rather than directly relevant in every country. Chapter 2 is the longest in the book and is designed as a comprehensive overview of the nature and impacts of sports tourism. While some of the situational and statistical material may change over time, many of the issues are likely to remain salient for some years to come.

1

Tracing interest in sports tourism

Early examples of sports tourism

The earliest documented example of sports tourism is that of the Olympic Games which date from 776 BC. However, the pan-Hellenic games at Olympia were but the most prestigious of more than a hundred such festivals (Finley and Pleket, 1976). Athletic games were an essential part of Greek life and every self-respecting city had its own stadium (Davies, 1997). However, the touring element was an important part of the sport. The participants were professional sportsmen and toured in order to win prizes; as Davies (1997: 127) points out 'athletes were not amateurs, being accustomed to arduous training and expecting handsome rewards'. In addition, thousands of spectators travelled to support their athletes and the prestige of their city, possibly in similar fashion to modern-day football supporters travelling to support their team. The games at Olympia may have attracted as many as 40 000 people from all parts of Greece (Van Dalen and Bennett, 1971) and 'there was probably no other occasion in the ancient world when as many people were on the road (or on the sea) for the same destination at the same time' (Finley and Pleket, 1976: 53). Unlike provision for modern-day tourists, there was little accommodation and visitors slept in tents or in the open air, although a hostel was established at Olympia in the fourth century

(Baker, 1982, quoted in Standeven and De Knop, 1999). The tourism aspect of the games was further emphasized by its wider political aims. It is often advocated that both sport and tourism may help to bring different peoples and cultures closer together, and a key aim of the ancient games was to bring 'a strong sense of cultural unity to a politically divided country' (Davies, 1997: 127).

The Romans continued the travel element associated with sport, although in different forms. Athletic activity 'became more health and socially oriented' (Standeven and De Knop, 1999: 15) and less competitive and, as such, the related tourist activity was no longer significant. The gladiatorial combats and chariot races which replaced athletics as the principal spectator event were essentially home-grown affairs, at least as far as the spectators themselves were concerned. One activity that did involve travel was the penchant for bathing, although how active this pursuit happened to be and thus how far it deserves to be considered as sport is no doubt open to debate. While bathing was also primarily a local activity (Rome had almost 900 baths) the ease of travel and the spread of the empire had led to a number of foreign towns such as Spa in Belgium, Baden-Baden in Germany, Tiberias in Israel and Bath in England becoming fashionable resorts for travelling Roman officials because of their bathing facilities (Standeven and De Knop, 1999).

The other influence on sports tourism which Standeven and De Knop (1999) attribute to the Romans is that of the survival of ball games. The Romans' disposition to travel enabled the ideology of games as a means of fitness to be disseminated throughout Europe, and it is argued that, but for this, ball play would probably have disappeared due to its association with pagan customs.

It is important to highlight these ancient antecedents because they demonstrate that sports tourism is not a totally modern phenomenon; that some of the motivations which may influence current activity could have been present several thousand years earlier. Despite these earlier examples, however, there is relatively little evidence of much sports tourism occurring between the Roman period and relatively recent times.

Standeven and De Knop (1999) discuss connections between sport and tourism in the Middle Ages and Renaissance period but little is provided in terms of real sports tourism other than jousting tournaments and real tennis, and even these are rather limited. In the case of the former, professional knights would tour as a way of making their living and there would thus seem to be some similarities here between the knights and the athletes of ancient Greece, although the early tournaments were unregulated, warlike and 'there was no provision for spectators and few spectators were present' (Guttmann, 1992: 148). Eventually between the twelfth and sixteenth centuries the tournament was 'civilized' and transformed into both an elegant sport and a spectacle but only for aristocrats and upper ranks of society. Similarly, real tennis, for which international games are recorded, became popular in the sixteenth century but was also purely the preserve of aristocrats.

As modest improvements in transportation from the sixteenth century onwards enabled people to travel more easily, there is no doubt that opportunities for sports tourism also increased. One key tourism phenomenon which has received much coverage in the literature is the European Grand Tour (see, e.g., Towner, 1985; 1996; Withey, 1997) which began in the sixteenth century and lasted until the nineteenth, and involved the wealthy in society travelling to various destinations in Europe. Towner (1996: 96) describes the Grand Tour as 'a re-emergent form of cultural tourism which had existed in the ancient world' and thus we have yet another key link with the touring behaviour of the ancient Greeks and Romans. The essential influence according to Towner (1996) was the development of a 'travel culture' deriving its inspiration from the cultural and intellectual movements of the Renaissance and, then, later the Enlightenment. While sport may not have been the principal motive, certainly in the early phases of the Tour, it did feature to some extent in later periods. While formal education was more important for the early Grand Tourists, social skills became more prominent in the seventeenth century and these included, among other things, such physical pursuits as riding and fencing; and one seventeenth-century writer (quoted by Towner) clearly lists 'exercise' as one of the motives for the Tour. In addition, as Baker (1982: 61, quoted in Standeven and De Knop, 1999) has suggested, it is likely that 'young gentleman (may have been) more active than contemplative and physically adroit as well as learned'.

While it is possible to identify some examples of sport associated with this tourism phenomenon, it is the broader influences of the Grand Tour which have real significance for sports tourism. The Grand Tour provided an early model for the tourist industry in general, in terms of specific itineraries and the eventual development of a limited tourist infrastructure. While it was still primarily associated with the upper classes, this development laid the foundations for the eventual growth of mass tourism in later centuries. More specifically in relation to sports tourism, the Grand Tour also opened up the Alps as a tourist destination. The earlier 'classical Grand Tour', linked to galleries, museums and high cultural artefacts, eventually shifted to the 'romantic Grand Tour' which saw the emergence of 'scenic tourism' and a new taste for mountain scenery (Towner, 1996). This change in tastes and the development of centres in the Alpine region thus paved the way for the subsequent growth of sports activities such as climbing and skiing which are so prominent today.

The development of sports tourism in the Industrial Age

One of the key constraints on the development of sports tourism prior to the nineteenth century was the lack of suitable transport. As indicated above there were incremental improvements from the fifteenth century onwards involving more comfortable coaches and, in the eighteenth century, greatly improved roads, at least in Britain if not everywhere in Europe. But transport was primarily slow and costly. For example, the journey time from London to Bath in 1680, a distance of 107 miles, was around sixty hours. Vastly improved roads had cut this time to ten hours by 1800 (McIntyre, 1981) but the time and cost still meant that only the wealthy in society could travel substantial distances. It was not until the development of the railways in the nineteenth century that a relatively cheap and efficient form of transport was afforded to the population at large, enabling sports tourism to develop beyond the small and exclusive upper class activity that had existed hitherto. As Vamplew (1988: 11) points out the railways 'revolutionized sport in England by widening the catchment area for spectators and by enabling participants to compete nationally'.

5

The railways were the product of industrialization which along with the associated urbanization had profound implications for sports tourism. The impact of new factory working regimes, urban living conditions and urban middle-class attitudes on the nature and development of leisure in general and sport in particular are well documented (Bailey, 1987; Clark and Critcher, 1985; Cross, 1990; Cunningham, 1975; Lowerson and Myerscough, 1977; Mason, 1989; Myerscough, 1974; Walton and Walvin, 1983) and there would seem little point in reiterating much of that story. Similarly, much has been written on the gradual development of tourism from the latter part of the nineteenth century (Gregory, 1991; Inglis, 2000; Ousby, 1990; Pimlott, 1947; Towner, 1996; Walton 1981; 2000; Withey, 1997). What is important here is the influence of urban industrialization on the specific activity of sports tourism and, in this respect, two clear trends can be discerned: the development of sports requiring the participants themselves to travel and the development of sporting activity involving travelling spectators.

In relation to participant sports tourists, two very different groups emerge at this time: those who travel to participate in competitions and those who travel in order to use particular facilities or resources which may not be available to them in their own locality. The nineteenth century was a particularly important era in the development of competitive sport as attempts were made to transform various forms from unorganized, rowdy traditional games into rationalized activities involving the establishment of rules and governing bodies. As Cross (1990: 147) points out: 'These organizations replaced the muddle of contradictory regulations that customarily governed play in the village or school and made possible contests at the national and even international level.'

Nowhere was this more evident than in the case of soccer, which took root in the new urban communities of industrialized society (Horne, Tomlinson and Whannel, 1999). The establishment of the Football Association (FA) in 1863 introduced a national code of rules and other key developments followed shortly afterwards, such as the refereeing of games in the 1870s. By 1871, rules appeared to be sufficiently standardized for the southern-based FA to travel to play a game against the Sheffield Football Club (Horne, Tomlinson and Whannel, 1999) and a Challenge Cup was inaugurated in 1872. Another fundamental development at this time was the growth of professionalism, which provoked intense debates within the sport (Mason, 1980; Tischler, 1981). Football had originally been a popular folk activity but had been 'civilized' by the urban middle classes in the nineteenth century as part of the wider attack on popular culture and the diffusion of 'rational recreation' (Bailey, 1987; Cross, 1990). But the amateur ethos and related values which had been part of this transformation in the public schools were challenged by the eventual necessity to pay players. What had become briefly the sport of gentlemen soon returned to its popular roots as club teams sprang up in many of the growing urban centres. As increasing numbers of ordinary working men began playing for these teams, 'they often required financial support to pay for the time lost from work and for long-distance travel to matches' (Cross, 1990: 150). However, the extent of soccer tourism at this time was wider than this. Horne, Tomlinson and Whannel (1999: 42) cite the example of the Blackburn Olympic side who, prior to winning the FA Cup in 1883, had 'spent a week in Blackpool for preparation and training before the semi-final against Old Carthusians'. Thus, improved transport, the widespread adoption of a national code of rules, the emergence of the professional player and the growth of intense competition and rivalry all combined to establish the beginnings of one of the most significant forms of sports tourism.

While soccer may be the best example of competitive sport involving inter-urban and inter-regional travel, it was by no means unique. Cricket was another sport which involved such travel. The basic rules of the game had been codified as early as 1787 by the Marylebone Cricket Club (MCC) but for almost another century it remained essentially a localized activity involving country-house cricket and London-based matches among the aristocracy and local village contests involving the gentry, shopkeepers and craftsmen as well as the aristocracy (Horne, Tomlinson and Whannel, 1999). As with football, it was not until the second half of the nineteenth century that cricket tourism began to emerge, first, due to an all-England professional touring team that took cricket to virtually every part of the kingdom (Sandiford, 1994) and, second, and more enduringly, the establishment of county cricket which involved nine counties in 1873 and sixteen by the end of the century. Both developments were aided by the railways and the growing importance of the sporting press, the latter being especially important in a number of sports for encouraging 'fan'-consciousness (Cross, 1990).

In addition to inter-county competition, cricket is also associated with relatively early international touring. Standeven and De Knop (1999) cite the example of the Surrey (England) Cricket Club, attempting to visit Paris in 1789, as possibly the first touring team of any sport, even though it was prevented from reaching its destination due to the French Revolution. Quoting Green (1982) they report that overseas touring by an English cricket team commenced with visits to North America in 1859 and Australia in 1861–62, aided by the newly established passenger steamship services. English cricketers regularly visited Australia after 1861 and by the end of the century teams were touring all parts of the empire (Holt, 1989).

The development of commercialized and professional sport also required a further ingredient, however, and that was the emergence of a sizeable body of spectators. By the second half of the nineteenth century some of the wealth creation of industrialization was beginning to trickle down to the working classes, as evidenced by a discernible increase in real wages which rose by 91 per cent between 1860 and 1913 (Myerscough, 1974). Probably for the first time significant numbers of working people were beginning to acquire disposable incomes which could be spent on leisure, and this, along with the increased leisure time and the ease of travel brought about by the railways, provided the means for the growth of spectator sport. By the 1880s and 1890s soccer was becoming commercialized with the establishment of limited companies and investment in stadiums which were attracting several thousand paying spectators to Saturday afternoon games. Football competition was also encouraging inter-urban rivalries, and improved transport allowed a number of loyal fans to travel to support their teams. 'Railway specials to selected sports events soon joined the seaside excursions as part of working class leisure' (Vamplew, 1988: 11). And the ability to travel to away games involved more than simply the opportunity to support the team but also offered the attractive experience of the travel itself. As Holt (1988: 81) points out:

7

For Northern fans, who made up the great majority of spectators at professional football before 1914, the chance to go to London for a big game was the experience of a lifetime. Thousands of men would go together on specially hired trains, singing and shouting as they spilled out along the London streets.

The cricket tours referred to above, and horse racing, were other sports which attracted large crowds. The railways made a major breakthrough in the transport of horses and, together with the easier access they provided for racegoers, led to racing becoming a genuine national sport rather than one pursued only at a local or regional level (Vamplew, 1988). By the 1890s race crowds of 10 000 to 15 000 were not unusual with perhaps 70 000 to 80 000 at major Bank Holiday events.

The second major area of participant sports tourism to emerge at this time was that involving people travelling to use particular resources or facilities, with skiing, climbing and hiking being particularly important examples. As already mentioned in the previous section, later developments of the Grand Tour involved an attraction to mountain scenery in areas such as Switzerland and 'by the 1890s the new sport of Alpine skiing was finding favour among a few adventurous visitors' (Withey, 1997: 217). Travel was aided by tourist operators such as Thomas Cook and Henry Lunn, and by the early decades of the twentieth century Switzerland had acquired a significant sports tourism industry.

> In Switzerland clusters of ski resorts to the east and west of the country, many with their own rail links, had emerged by the 1920s with Davos (nearly 6000 beds) and St Moritz (6000 beds) in the east and Villars (2000 beds) and Leysin (2800 beds) forming major resort centres.
> (Towner, 1996: 250)

Similarly, climbing and mountaineering was also stimulated by the changed attitudes towards mountain environments and, as with skiing, it was the Alpine districts of Switzerland which became one of the most important destinations for the sport, primarily because Switzerland possessed the highest mountains in Europe. Two Britons had unsuccessfully attempted to climb the Jungfrau in 1827 and it was also young British visitors who between 1854 and 1872 made thirty-one of the thirty-nine first ascents of the highest European Alpine peaks (Standeven and De Knop, 1999). Withey's (1997: 207) account of the development of mountaineering in Switzerland highlights the links with education and the ideals of rational recreation that influenced so many sporting activities in the Victorian era:

> The Britons who took up mountain climbing were primarily middle class professionals, many of them educated at Oxford and Cambridge, where sports and the competitive spirit were an essential part of their education and manliness was associated with endurance and courage. Climbing offered both sport and danger, as well as competition against the forces of nature (especially appealing for those who did not excel at team sports – with mountain climbing it was individual strength and determination that counted). The public school and university experience also encouraged these men to be joiners, so it was no surprise that a group of them banded together in 1857 to form the Alpine Club.

The Alpine Club aimed, among other things, to promote climbing as sport and, along with similar clubs which were created in several other Western European countries, played a significant role in developing this form of sports tourism. By the last quarter of the nineteenth century tourism had become a mainstay of the Swiss economy and by the first decade of the twentieth century Switzerland was indeed 'the playground of Europe' (Withey, 1997: 219). And, while many tourists to Switzerland came to enjoy the scenery, sport was nevertheless a major ingredient in the overall tourism product and was to become even more important later in the century (see Chapter 13).

Skiing and mountaineering were entirely the preserve of the wealthy upper and middle classes at this time, but so too were less adventurous sports such as hiking and cycling. Hiking depended on people's financial capability to travel to remoter rural areas and pay for suitable accommodation, and the cost of bicycles was beyond the means of ordinary working people until the twentieth century. Apart from financial barriers, social class barriers were also important. Various clubs formed at this time to encourage and facilitate participation in a range of sports barred the working class from membership. According to Bailey (1987: 140) 'the barring of mechanics, artisans and labourers was . . . standard policy for the Amateur Rowing Association and the Bicycle Union', as well as other clubs such as the Amateur Athletics Association, the justification being that those whose work involved physical labour would enjoy unfair advantage in competition. There were some attempts to encourage a broader social mix in relation to hiking. For example, Tomlinson and Walker (1990) cite a number of organizations such as the Co-operative Holidays Association and the Manchester Young Men's Christian Association (YMCA) Rambling Club which organized walking holidays for those of humbler origins. Nevertheless, those who travelled to participate in these resource-based sports during the nineteenth century were almost exclusively upper and middle class.

A final key issue arising from nineteenth-century industrialization which needs to be highlighted is that of colonization and the associated cultural diffusion of sport from its 'homelands' to distant parts of the world (Holt, 1989). This in itself, of course, was not sports tourism, as those involved in the playing or watching of the sport did not necessarily travel. Cricket, for example, was now being played in many parts of Africa, the Antipodes and the Indian subcontinent, as a result of British imperialism, and did not of itself involve people having to travel, the games were simply being played in different parts of the world by those who lived there. Nevertheless, such cultural diffusion was to have enormous significance for the future of sports tourism as it provided the basis for international competition. As has been indicated above, such competition was already under way in a modest form in the nineteenth century but it was to become a major aspect of sport in the twentieth.

Sports tourism in the twentieth century

The previous section has illustrated how nineteenth-century urban industrialization provided the necessary conditions for significant development of many forms of sports tourism and, while it still remained elitist and exclusive in character, essentially involving the upper and middle classes, the foundations were laid for subsequent expansion in the twentieth century which would embrace all sections of society in a great many different forms. To begin with this growth essentially involved incremental change but eventually in the second half of the century, and especially in the 1980s and 1990s, the expansion of sports tourism was extremely dramatic. Unlike in the previous sections where substantial detail about the nature of the contemporary sports tourism has been highlighted, it is not possible to provide such detail here as there is so much. This detail would require an entire text to itself and, in any case, much of the remainder of this book provides essential insights into what has happened in the last few decades of the twentieth century. What this final section is intended to do is to provide a brief discussion of key factors that were to shape this development. Some simply involved a continuation of developments which had already begun to influence change in the previous century – such as increasing wealth, increasing leisure time and improving transport, although they were still to have revolutionary impacts at certain times, especially during the latter part of the twentieth century. Other influences, such as those associated with attitudes and values, globalization, corporate capitalism and the media were primarily of more recent relevance.

In relation to leisure time, while the working week only reduced gradually over the twentieth century, the increase in holiday time was far more dramatic. The century began with the movement to provide holidays with pay, which was achieved for most workers by the 1920s and was regularized for everyone in the Holidays With Pay Act 1938. The vast majority of people could now take a modest holiday, such as a week at the seaside, and thus the opportunity to travel away from home for more than a brief excursion was no longer the preserve of the wealthy classes. But even more significant were the changes in the last quarter of the century which provided most people with four or five weeks' holiday. By then leisure time and holiday entitlement were seen as essential components of everybody's lifestyle with significant implications for sports tourism. Not only did ordinary people now have the time to travel further afield to watch sport, and in the latter part of the century they began to do so in substantial numbers, they could also participate in physical activities away from their local area. At its simplest level this might merely involve playing sport on holiday on a relatively casual basis but, as holidays became an established part of normal life, such sports participation as a tourist became especially important. Alternatively, it also meant that ordinary people acquired the time to travel to participate as 'amateurs' in sports competitions or go on specific sports holidays (e.g. golf or cycling), often in addition to an 'ordinary' holiday. Furthermore, the latter part of the twentieth century also witnessed substantial sports tourism activity associated with retirement. Not only were people living longer once retired, due to increased life expectancy arising from improved health care, but also substantial numbers of people were able to take early retirement. With campaigns to encourage the 'elderly' to remain active, sports tourism has become an important pursuit for certain sections of this particular group, golfing and walking holidays being especially significant.

The twentieth century also produced a substantial increase in affluence for most people and, although the increases were relatively modest to begin with, by the late 1950s full employment and a booming economy ensured incomes were both secure and rising, and there was plenty of disposable income available for leisure. Not only did people have the time for leisure and travel; they also had the economic means to use it. Throughout the last four decades of the twentieth century people's expenditure on leisure continued to rise such that, by the end of the century, households in Britain were for the first time spending more on leisure than on food, housing or transport (OPCS, 1999). Expenditure on tourism generally has involved an inexorable growth, and sports tourism has been an important part of this development.

The expansion of sports tourism in the twentieth century has also been subsequently influenced by further developments in transportation. Just as the railways revolutionized travel in the nineteenth century, so the automobile and then aeroplanes produced even more dramatic changes in the twentieth. The significance of the car in the development of sport and tourism generally has attracted considerable coverage (see, e.g., Page, 1999; Patmore, 1983; Shaw and Williams, 2002) and it has had no less an impact on sports tourism specifically. Although originally invented towards the end of the nineteenth century, it started to become a mass form of transport in the 1920s in the USA and rather later in Britain. Apart from its convenience and flexibility, the car has the additional advantages of affording access to many areas not served by public transport, as well as allowing the easy transport of luggage and equipment. As a result, it was invaluable for the development of many forms of sports tourism but especially those such as hiking, climbing, cycling, and various forms of water sport which require the transportation of people and equipment to relatively remote locations. The introduction of air transport with its ability to transport people thousands of miles within a few hours has also had a huge impact on sports tourism. Although expensive to begin with, the development of cheap air travel in the 1960s, linked to charter flights and package holidays, revolutionized international tourism and allowed many forms of sports tourism to flourish, such as the growth of international competitive sport, involving both participants and spectators, the expansion of winter sports and the development of various forms of sports holiday, especially those linked to activities like golf, walking, tennis and water sports in attractive locations such as the Mediterranean.

The expansion of reasonably priced, good quality hotel accommodation associated with tourism growth generally has also facilitated the growth of sports tourism, but the specific demand for certain types of sports tourism has also produced some peculiar forms of accommodation which, once established, have encouraged subsequent growth. Holiday camps are sometimes cited as examples of this, especially those developed in 1930s Germany with their emphasis on health and fitness (Standeven and De Knop, 1999). Another example would be the establishment of Youth Hostels in Britain, also dating from the 1930s, which provided the opportunities for many people to ramble and cycle in the countryside. While more recently the term 'holiday camp' has been dropped and replaced by terms such as 'centre', 'village' or 'holiday world' (Urry, 2002), a totally new type of holiday centre, with artificial environments where sport, especially water sport, is of paramount importance, has been pioneered by Center Parcs. Originating in the Netherlands, several Center Parcs villages now exist in various parts of Europe and other companies such as Rank are establishing similar facilities.

In addition to these more tangible influences, a number of other factors have also played a prominent role on the development of sports tourism. A key characteristic of the twentieth century was a fundamental change in values and attitudes, which, not surprisingly given its influence on so many other things, also influenced the development of sports tourism. One important change was that of democratization. The elitism that had characterized both sport and travel gradually gave way to a process of wider involvement so that by the end of the twentieth century, not only were the means available to enable most people to participate, but so too was the expectation. The wider involvement in sport was promoted through the schools and through various government promotional campaigns, at first primarily for extrinsic reasons linked to improving health and fitness and for reasons of moral welfare and social control, and then, eventually, for people's individual wellbeing and leisure. While some sports have retained a certain class bias (e.g. participation in golf is still dominated by the middle classes and polo by the upper classes) most sports are no longer socially exclusive.

In addition to acceptance that sport and travel could be available to anyone, the other key value change was that sport and travel became central aspects of people's lives. While western nations may not have fully embraced the leisure society that some pundits were proclaiming in the 1970s, there is no denying the weakening of the work ethic and the increased importance placed on pleasure and hedonism by the end of the twentieth century. Furthermore, sport and tourism were important for many different reasons, very much in keeping with postmodern values. For some, sport was still pursued for the traditional motives of fitness, health, competition and achievement, but now many participated simply for fun and pleasure or indulged in sports for reasons of body image and fashion. Similarly, holidays were also to become an important part of many people's lifestyles. As Urry (2002: 5) has pointed out, 'it is a crucial element of modern life that travel and holidays are necessary' and by the latter part of the 1980s travel was estimated to be occupying 40 per cent of people's free time. For an increasing number of people the lifestyle choice came to involve both sport and travel combined. This is illustrated in particular by two types of sports tourism: outdoor pursuits and international sporting mega-events. The former is linked to a range of motives and values relating to health, fitness, image, excitement and, even, fashion, while the latter is associated with experience and spectacle (see below for further discussion on this).

The development of sports mega-events is a product of additional influences which have played a key role in the growth of sports tourism in the twentieth century, those of commercialization and globalization. Commercialization was present in the previous century but its impact was relatively minor compared with what has occurred in recent times, largely as a result of global developments. While much sport is still organized through voluntary clubs on an amateur basis, many sports have become increasingly commercialized, especially elite sport. This can be seen particularly in the development of international sport which as Horne, Tomlinson and Whannel (1999: 277) argue 'is a product of the jet, television and corporate capitalism'. Horne, Tomlinson and Whannel highlight the fact that, whereas in 1950 there were 5 million television sets worldwide with television only available in Great Britain, the USA and USSR, by 1970 there were 250 million sets in 130 countries and, since the early 1970s, television has spread rapidly to most of the developing world. Television is a major global business and sport is one of many phenomena that can be commodified and sold to an ever-growing audience. Now sport can be watched round the clock on several different television channels. At first sight it might seem odd that television would influence sports tourism, as it allows people to watch sport without ever having to leave their home. However, its great significance is that it has popularized a great many sports and highlighted their benefits and spectacle to a mass audience and this, in turn, has encouraged international exchange in sport and the expansion of international sporting competitions (Tomlinson, 1996; Whannel, 1985). Not only has this led to many athletes travelling to participate in such competitions but also encouraged many people to travel to watch such events. At the same time that satellite television was allowing test match cricket from the Antipodes or the West Indies to be watched live in Britain, the English cricket team was attracting a growing and vociferous band of 'home-grown' spectators at the actual matches. By highlighting, if not exaggerating, the excitement and drama at such events, television has persuaded many people to want to experience such spectacle at first hand. International competitions such as the Olympic Games, the Commonwealth Games, the football World Cup and continental cup football competitions, cricket test matches, Wimbledon and Grand Prix motor racing meetings have become major tourist attractions in their own right, attracting not just the traditional fans and enthusiasts but also those searching, in true postmodern fashion, for the spectacular tourist experience. Furthermore, the investment of corporate capital in the merchandising of team products and the global marketing of sportswear may also enhance the tourist experience linked to the need to dress or parade in the appropriate attire and to collect souvenirs.

While it is clear that private businesses have played a major role in the development of sports tourism, the role of government has not been entirely absent. As already outlined, sport has been encouraged by governments for a host of extrinsic reasons, and tourism has similarly been supported in recent times due to its economic contribution, especially in relation to employment. However, the realization that certain forms of sport can attract tourists, especially the mega-events referred to above, has led many governments in the latter part of the twentieth century to be especially proactive in seeking to host such competitions. Several cities have found their economies and environments significantly transformed as a result of such events with the stimulus of sports tourism producing far wider benefits for both tourism generally and the wider economy (see Chapter 11).

Conclusion

As was demonstrated at the outset of this chapter, sports tourism possesses a long history and it is rather symbolic that the century which witnessed the most substantial growth and development of sports tourism was heralded by the revival of the modern Olympic Games in Athens in 1896. Such symbolism can be further extended when looking at the Olympic Games today, in that they clearly reflect the importance and significance of contemporary sports tourism, involving many of the influences and characteristics discussed above. While the earlier examples of sports tourism do not constitute the principal concerns of this text, it is nevertheless useful to have established the broader context from which contemporary sports tourism has developed. With entire texts devoted to the history of both sport and tourism, the historical analysis presented here has been inevitably brief. Nevertheless, some important points have emerged. It is clear that various factors which have influenced sports tourism in earlier times are still relevant today and it would appear that whenever people have obtained the means and opportunities to participate they have tended to exploit them. The history of the development of sports tourism in the twentieth century has been largely about overcoming various constraints to enable such opportunities to be widened to involve most people rather than just a privileged few. As both this and the next chapter show, sports tourism in its many different forms is now a substantial activity and one of tourism's most significant market niches. The remainder of this text thus seeks to examine the phenomenon through an analysis of the various participants, the policy-making process and the providers, with related issues being further explored through a series of specific case studies. First, however, the next chapter continues to set the context for this analysis by providing an overview of the implications and impacts of linking sport and tourism.

2

An overview of the sport-tourism link

The previous chapter, in tracing the increasing interest in sports tourism over time, has provided a useful historical backdrop for the contemporary overview of the links between sport and tourism given in this chapter. In fact, while the title of the book refers to sports tourism, it is perhaps useful in providing this overview to consider the broader concept of the sport-tourism link (see discussions in the Prologue) which, in addition to sports holidays, also embraces liaison between the two areas on issues such as resources and funding, policy and planning, and information and research (see Chapter 7 for more detail on these areas). However, much of the previous work on the links between sport and tourism has concentrated on the narrower area of sports tourism – holidays involving sport either as a spectator or as a participant. This is not surprising as this area is the most obvious area of the sport-tourism link. Jackson and Glyptis (1992) delineate two types of sports-related tourism: the first, where sport is consciously used by destinations seeking to develop their tourism profile, and the second, where tourism has emerged more or less spontaneously as a result of sports activity. As this chapter will highlight, sports tourism is a large area, not just of the sport-tourism link but of the tourism industry as a whole. Yet, taking this one-dimensional approach to the sport-tourism link indicates that the only benefits of such links are in the use of sport in the promotion of tourism and that there would be little that might interest the sports lobby in promoting greater collaboration. However, this is far from the case as worldwide evidence suggests that there are wide-ranging benefits for both the sport and tourism industries in encouraging greater links.

Tourism can aid the sports world in its push for greater levels of facility provision and in its efforts to increase participation. Sports facilities on tourist sites could be opened up to the local community in off-peak periods, or throughout the year through a membership system. Conversely, the tourist market can help sustain local sports facilities, possibly making provision viable where local demand is insufficient to do so. There is also considerable potential for tourism to aid sports development as a great deal of sports participation takes place while on holiday. In the 1980s it was estimated that 55 per cent of those people who take part in sailing do so only on holiday (Veal, 1986). Holidays can provide an entry route to sports participation through access to coaching and facilities not available in the tourists' home area. There is a great deal of potential here to convert these brief holiday flirtations into long-term sustained participation in the tourists' home area (Weed, 2001b).

It would therefore appear that there are sufficient mutual advantages in linking sport and tourism to make greater co-operation attractive to both sectors. However, while commercial providers have been quick to recognize and capitalize on the links between sport and tourism to which consumers have responded, public sector policy-makers in these areas appear to be more than reticent to work together (this is discussed in greater detail in Chapters 6 and 7). This chapter seeks to give an overview of the sport-tourism link – a concept that is, as highlighted above, broader than sports tourism, which is usually taken to mean sports holidays. This broader area is perhaps best explored by examining the effects of linking sport and tourism in a wide range of areas, and by specifically examining who benefits from such a linkage. In conducting such an examination the chapter seeks to provide a contemporary context for the analysis of the sports tourism phenomenon, and to act as a springboard for the analysis that follows in the remainder of the book.

The effects of linking sport and tourism

There are perhaps three identifiable strands of literature relating to the sport-tourism link. The first, and by far the largest strand, focuses on advocacy, simply attempting to establish that there is a link between sport and tourism, and to establish it as a legitimate field worthy of consideration by both academics and providers. While this strand has been useful in the preliminary development of work in this area, it provides little in the way of empirically substantiated research or conceptual understanding, as it has tended to focus on speculative areas for liaison or isolated case studies. A second, smaller, body of work has attempted to quantify the links between sport and tourism, establishing the volume and value of sports tourism and the spending patterns and profiles of different types of sports tourists. This strand has been useful in evidencing the sport-tourism link, although, the isolated nature of many such studies means that the statistical evidence produced is rarely comparable over time or across national borders. Finally, there is a very limited range of material comprising the third strand of research relating to the response of policy-makers to the sport-tourism link. Each of these areas are used in this overview, while the remainder of the book seeks to develop the area further in establishing a conceptual understanding of sports tourists, developing the material on policy responses and understanding the rationales of providers.

In conducting a detailed analysis of the effects of linking sport and tourism it is useful to organize the discussion under the following five headings:

1 Benefits to the sports participant.
2 Benefits to the tourist.
3 Mutual benefits to sports participants and tourists.
4 Economic and community development.
5 Negative aspects of the sport-tourism link.

Benefits to the sports participant

The major benefit of linking sport and tourism for the local resident sports participant is in the provision of facilities (Jackson and Weed, 2003), which is specifically highlighted in the Sheffield case study in Chapter 11. As Bone (1995) identifies, the overarching benefit is that of economies of scale, the combined market of the tourist and the local resident allowing the provision of better facilities for all. In Britain, the Sports Council (now split into two organizations and renamed Sport England and UK Sport) recognized the potential in this area, when its 1988 strategy 'Sport in the Community: Into the Nineties' advocated collaboration with tourist boards on facility development in tourist areas. However, it appears that this initiative was not carried forward, as in 1992 Jackson and Glyptis reported on the need for sports agencies to: 'Identify, evaluate and disseminate examples of good practice in policy and facility development of benefit to both residents and tourists which might be replicated elsewhere' (Jackson and Glyptis, 1992: 112).

There are three ways in which local sports participants can benefit from tourism. First, in the opening up of tourist-based facilities for local resident use (dual use); second, in the support the tourist market can provide for local sports provision; and third, in the case of potential rather than actual participants, contributing to the development of sports participation and healthy lifestyles.

Dual use of tourist facilities

There are valid reasons why both sport and tourism policy-makers should support this type of initiative. In Britain sport and leisure policy-makers have long advocated the dual use of sports facilities on school sites. As long ago as 1973 the House of Lords Select Committee on Sport and Leisure concluded: 'Dual use of school recreational facilities offer enormous benefits which must be tapped. No school should be built without consideration being given at the earliest stage to the possibilities of dual use to meet the needs of both school and the local community' (House of Lords, 1973: cxxvi).

There would appear to be no reason why this principle should not also be applied to tourist sites. In fact the Select Committee recommended a wider application of the dual use principle: 'Apart from educational establishments other facilities are susceptible to dual use . . . Recreation Departments should set themselves the task of identifying facilities and projects where dual use can be introduced or where existing use can be widened' (House of Lords, 1973: cix).

Such campaigns for dual use of schools have continued up to the present day, with the publication of documents such as *Sharing Does Work* (Sports Council, 1988) and *Community Use of Sports Facilities on School Sites* (Sports Council, 1994) in Britain and reviews of best practice in this area in Australia by Richardson (2000) and Ewin (2000). However, to date the House of Lords' recommendation of extending dual use to other sites has not been followed, although Reeves (1995) comments on the implications of dual use for the training of sports instructors and wardens employed in recreational parks, while Redmond (1991) makes a similar point in relation to Canada's National Parks.

In an analysis of the non-economic benefits of tourism for local residents, Schroeder (1993) identifies access to recreational facilities as a major consideration. However, it is also important that tourism developments are socially acceptable to local residents (Marsh, 1987). There is an increased emphasis on community involvement and a growing relationship between recreation and tourism. Local resident attitudes towards tourists result from a reaction to tourist numbers and behaviour rather than stemming from a cultural gap (Ap and Crompton, 1993; Toh, Khan and Lim, 2001; Weaver and Lawton, 2001). Personal costs and benefits are also a major factor in locals' reaction to tourism (Clements, Schultz and Lime, 1993). The need is for balanced development in the interests of local residents as well as tourists (Standeven and Tomlinson, 1994). It is important, therefore, that the tourist agencies support the balanced development of tourist-based sports facilities, advocating the incorporation of the needs of local residents in any plans.

In order for major sports facilities built for mega-events to be sustainable in the long term, they need to be adaptable for local community use. One of the legacies of the World Student Games in Sheffield is the Ponds Forge International Sports Centre which comprises a 50-metre swimming pool, a diving pool with full diving facilities, a leisure pool and an indoor sports centre (Times, 1988). This facility is one of the most flexible in the world, the pools having movable floors and bulkheads which make it adaptable for a large range of community uses (Swimming Times, 1990). In fact, Bramwell (1997a) describes the provision of new sport and recreation facilities for the long-term use of Sheffield residents as a key objective for the hosting of the World Student Games (see the Sheffield case study in Chapter 11 for more details). The city of Victoria in Canada took a sustainable view of the Commonwealth Games it hosted in 1994. Rather than building on a large grandiose scale, Victoria developed facilities that could be easily adapted after the event for community use, simply erecting temporary seating and spectator accommodation for the duration of the Games (Center for South Australian Economic Studies, 1992), an approach which is becoming increasingly common (Devetta, 2002). Another approach is to permanently adapt facilities for long-term use. For example, the athletics stadia erected for the 1996 Atlanta Olympics and the 2002 Commonwealth Games were modified after the Games for long-term use as a baseball stadium by the Atlanta Braves and a football stadium by Manchester City Football Club respectively.

It is important to note, however, that many facilities built for major games may not be best suited to ongoing community use, either for participation or spectating. Furthermore, Getz (2003) notes the tendency, particularly in North America, for the public sector to pay for facilities that generate mostly private benefits to professional sports clubs. In relation to ongoing use, Whitson and MacIntosh (1993; 1996) quote the luge and bobsled track and ski-jump towers built for the 1988 Calgary Winter Olympics as examples of facilities that have been very costly to maintain, requiring refrigeration and snow-making capacity. Furthermore, along with the indoor speed skating oval – a world-class facility by any standard – these facilities have required significant ongoing subsidy and have not attracted, or in some cases have not been adaptable for, local community use. Yet, as an indication of the variability in the sustainability of such facilities, the Canmore Nordic Ski Centre attracted 40 000 cross-country skiers in its first year of post-Olympic operation.

In a continued drive for custom, and in adapting themselves to the modern domestic tourism market, many traditional British 'holiday camps' are installing a wide range of sport and leisure facilities (McKoy, 1991; Reeves, 2000). Many of these facilities, by the very nature of the holiday camp market, will lay dormant for a large proportion of the year. There is therefore great potential for this spare capacity to be filled by the local resident market at off-peak times.

Tourist support of local sports provision

Evidence of the role that tourism could play, particularly in coastal or rural areas where population may be dispersed, in supporting standards of sports facilities that would not otherwise be available to local residents was identified by Jackson and Glyptis (1992). There is a range of evidence of tourist support of the upkeep of recreational parkland and sports facilities in rural communities in North America (Donnelly et al., 1998), Australia (Johansson, 2000) and, even, Thailand (Tananone, 1991). This concept was also supported, albeit briefly, by the British government in its planning policy guidance on sport and recreation (DoE/Welsh Office, 1991). The guidance calls for 'local plan policies to take into account the recreational needs of tourists and where appropriate encourage the development of facilities that benefit both visitors and residents' (DoE/Welsh Office, 1991: 4).

In many cases, facility developers find it essential to account for the recreational needs of tourists (Grcic-Zubcevic, 2001). In order to maximize potential economic activity, a leisure pool development must attract a high proportion of visitors from outside the immediate area (Woodward, 1990). It is also important to ensure that these visitors spend money both inside and outside the facility. Woodward (1990) notes that without this visitor support many leisure developments are simply not viable.

Many urban regeneration initiatives use sport and tourism, and other leisure sectors (e.g., arts, culture and heritage), as tools for regeneration. In this context, the local community will often gain facilities otherwise beyond their reach, through the support of the tourist industry (see later discussion of economic and community development). Here, as the priority of these initiatives is the local community, residents' needs in the majority of cases, quite rightly, take precedence.

19

Hotel leisure facilities provide an interesting case study. Hotels are now almost required to install leisure facilities to keep pace with their competitors (Meler, 2001). Furthermore, if they aspire to the valuable business and conference markets, then these facilities need to be of the highest standard (Dillard, 1995; Law, 1993). However, in many cases hotels need to open up their facilities at off-peak times to local residents in order to make them viable. Such arrangements are often on a membership basis (Goring, 1987) and facilities can be of the highest standard, far beyond that which the local community alone could hope to support. For example, the Stena Hotel in Frederikshaven, Denmark, has a 10 000 square metre water leisure centre with a sauna, a solarium and an extensive fitness suite (Fache, 1990).

The final consideration here is the market for sports training which was initially exploited by tour operators in response to demands for team training abroad where better facilities and climatic conditions prevail (Glyptis, 1982; and see the Malta case study in Chapter 10). In many countries, such training weekends, with high-profile coaches, are increasingly taking place in the domestic context and are becoming increasingly popular in a number of sports as diverse as golf, swimming and archery (Jackson and Weed, 2003). In initiatives such as this, Glyptis (1982) suggests that coaching and instruction for tourists could be provided by local sports clubs in exchange for greater access to facilities. In addition to training camps, many low-key sports events are often staged (e.g. marathons, 10-kilometre races, swim meets) which, although aimed at attracting competitors from outside the local area, also provide opportunities for the local sports enthusiast to compete (Bratton, 1988).

Sports development and health promotion

It has been noted by a range of authors (Bull and Weed, 1999; Jackson and Glyptis, 1992; Reeves, 2000) that sports tourism has the potential to contribute to sports participation development and health promotion goals. As such, this is a benefit to the 'latent' or potential sports or recreation participant. Since the mid-1960s many countries have promoted national campaigns aimed at stimulating participation in sport, largely with health and lifestyle goals (e.g. 'Sport for All' in the UK, 'Life Be In It' in Australia, 'Moving Together' in Malaysia, 'Be Active – Be Alive' in Ireland and 'Active Living' in Canada), yet little recognition has been made of the role sports opportunities on holiday might play in such campaigns. Holidays often represent a period of time when families and individuals are brought into close contact with, have time for and are willing to participate in new or lapsed sports or recreational activities. In such cases, evidence suggests (Weed, 2001b) that it is possible to convert brief holiday flirtations into long-term activity in the tourists' home area.

Agne-Traub (1989) outlines the German concept of 'Volkssports', which translates as 'people's sports' or 'life sports'. Volkssports are family-orientated active recreations which originated in Germany, Austria and Switzerland in the early 1960s. The American Volkssports Association, which co-ordinates over 500 clubs in the USA, promotes the activities – walking, cycling, swimming and cross-country skiing – as sports that anyone can participate in with friends and family throughout his or her life. The concept is now found in over twenty countries around the world under the auspices of 'Der Internationale Volksport-verband' (IVV). However, as Agne-Traub (1989) describes, their increasing international popularity means that they can easily be incorporated into business or pleasure travel. Furthermore, and significantly for sports development, 'Volkssports Tours' are not limited to organized volkssporters, but often attract tourists who are in the area for a traditional holiday but learn of Volkssports during their stay. Due to the social element of the activities, Agne-Traub (1989: 7) claims that 'once hooked they often look for an active club in their home area to continue their participation'.

There is great potential for similar stimulation of sporting activity in a range of other areas and, because such activities lend themselves to universal participation, they can be linked to health promotion and active living programmes. Sports holidays also provide the opportunity for 'recreational training' or 'advanced instruction' (Weed, 2001a). Reeves (2000) undertook a brief pilot study of a squash training week at Club La Santa in Lanzarote, organized by the Priory Rackets Club in Edgbaston, UK. The participants in this study felt that the actual playing standard of an individual did not affect the enjoyment or benefit to be gained from such a holiday.

Benefits to the tourist

Tourists stand to benefit from the sport-tourism link in the range and quality of sports participation opportunities available on holiday. Glyptis (1982) notes that tourist sports activity may be either primary (the main purpose of the trip) or incidental (on holidays where sport is not the prime purpose). Furthermore, sports activities may be either participative or non-participative (i.e. as spectators).

Sports spectating

Jackson and Weed (2003) describe the significant growth in sports event tourism as both demand and commercial suppliers have developed. Such growth provides significant opportunities for the many tourists for whom, both domestically and internationally, sports spectating has become a primary reason for holiday trips (Getz, 2003). Major and hallmark events (Olympic, Commonwealth and Pan-American Games, and World and European Championships in individual sports) provide opportunities for tourists to take a holiday based solely around high-class sports spectating, or to incorporate sports spectating into their holiday (Cha, McCleary and Uysal, 1995; Tourism Canada, 1993). Some spectator-orientated sports with 'world tours' are capable of generating major sports spectacles in each of a series of countries which host major or grand prix tournaments (e.g. tennis, golf and motor racing), and travel to a vast array of sports events is now possible, enabled by both traditional and new specialist tour and travel companies (Jackson and Glyptis, 1992). At a less spectacular level, the weekly leagues in a range of sports, although mostly football, in a range of countries around the world provide for regular domestic sports-spectating day trips (Jones, 2000). However, as football becomes more popular and competitions such as the European Champions' League develop, such trips become international and in the vast majority of cases involve at least one overnight stay. The economic impact of such trips in proportion to their length is significant.

21

A large proportion of sports spectators are often present as guests of corporate sponsors, and Brown (2000) highlights the economic importance to host areas of sports-spectating hospitality trips co-ordinated through complementary promotions with the tourist organizations of the host area. Furthermore, Brown (2000) claims that tourism organizations can play an important role in attracting sponsors to sports events, and in achieving positive economic outcomes for the host community. In fact, much of the literature on major events focuses on their economic impact and, as such, this will be dealt with later as part of a general discussion on economic impacts.

However, sports spectating is not limited to major events and professional sports. Much spectator tourism involves travel to watch a family member or friend compete. The spectator following of events such as the London or New York marathons and, indeed, many smaller mass participation events illustrate this point (Destination Sheffield, 1995; Getz, 1997b), as do the large numbers (mainly parents and family) who turn up to watch junior sports tournaments and events (SCF, 1994). See the Sheffield and Malta case studies in Chapters 10 and 11 for an illustration of this.

Participation opportunities
In its 1987 tourism strategy, *A Vision for England*, the English Tourist Board identified three major trends that still show no signs of change:

1 A spreading concern for healthy living.
2 A strongly developed market for theme- and activity-based holidays.
3 A massive growth in demand for short breaks and second holidays.

These factors are coupled with an increasing propensity to view holidays (especially short breaks or second holidays) not as time for relaxation and recuperation, but as an opportunity to 'do something' (Jackson and Glyptis, 1992). In fact, at the beginning of the last decade De Knop (1990) quoted recent research as showing that the choice of destination for camping holidays, which are in themselves inherently active, was based in 35 per cent of cases on the presence of possibilities for sport and recreation.

The activity holiday sector is diverse; a large number of small-scale operators provide an equally large number of activities. With notable exceptions (e.g. PGL) there are few large-scale operators. The providers can vary from farms looking to diversify into tourism, to hotels looking to increase off-season occupancy or educational establishments aiming to make use of facilities during vacations. The consumer profile is equally diverse – independent adults, parents and families, school parties or groups of children at summer camps (Broek, 1997; McKie, 1994; Reeves, 2000). Activity holidays are rarely taken as a main holiday, with many consumers seeing them as an extra break, taken outside the traditional holiday period (KPMG/Tourism Company, 1994; Mintel, 1999). Aligned to the activity holiday market is the German concept of 'Volkssports' described earlier. Volkssporting events – of which walking is the most popular – are scheduled to attract day-tripping tourists (Landes, 1989). More recent equivalents would be the range of events established and calendared by local and municipal authorities to attract visitors and their spending, as well as providing a recreational, sometimes elite, performance event, for the benefit of the local population, and sometimes to promote the city or area (Jackson and Weed, 2003). British examples would be events such as the London Marathon (and others), the Great North Run, the Scarborough Cricket Festival and the Worthing Bowls Festival.

Purpose-built sports-leisure orientated holiday villages now provide considerable opportunities for holiday sports participation. Center Parcs, modelled on the Danish concept of a year-round sport and leisure holiday, is the most obvious example (Larner, 1994) and the company now runs twelve clubs in four countries with an almost unheard of year-round occupancy rate of over 90 per cent (Mintel, 2002a). In the UK, following the purchase of Oasis from Bourne Leisure, there are now four Center Parcs villages. These parks, set in scenic forest locations, offer high standard facilities for a wide range of sports, and an advanced climatically controlled 'subtropical' leisure pool – 'A British holiday the weather can't spoil' (Seward, 1994: 37). Internationally, Club Med has been providing luxurious sports-leisure resort holidays since 1950, albeit without the necessity for a simulated subtropical pool. Club Med divides its operations into Europe, Africa, America, Asia/India and Atlantic Ocean, and now operates Club Med hotels, cruise ships and, a less expensive option, Club Aquarius. Undoubtedly, Club Med set the standard for this type of holiday, and it is a clear forerunner of the Center Parcs product (Standeven and De Knop, 1999).

Of course, many traditional package holidays involve some element of sports participation, often cycling or walking, or water sports such as surfing, windsurfing, water-skiing or scuba-diving. In fact, De Knop (1990) claimed that only one-third of German holiday-makers do not spend any time on sports activities. However, some evidence suggests (Keynote, 2001; Reeves, 2000) that sports facilities (particularly those in hotels), while playing an important role in the marketing mix, are actually used by surprisingly few guests. German research comparing British and German visitors to Corfu indicated that, although providers aggressively promoted sports opportunities, both in their travel literature and on site, actual take-up was surprisingly low (Tokarski, 1993). If swimming and walking are excluded, only three out of ten Britons and two out of ten Germans participated in sports. It should be noted that this research is now over ten years old, but in the absence of more recent studies the current situation can only be the subject of speculation.

At the higher end of the market, conference and business tourists now have high-class, prestigious facilities made available to them as competition increases for their custom. Manchester, for example, used its Olympic bids to spearhead its push for the conference market (Tourism Marketplace, 1993) and its successful bid and hosting of the 2002 Commonwealth Games was used in a similar way. Sports facilities are now seen as almost essential in attracting the conference market (Meler, 2001; Stevens, 1987), as noted previously with reference to hotel based leisure facilities. In addition to providing for the conference market, many 'country-house' hotels cater for the 'up-market' sports tourist. Activities such as golf, angling, shooting and other countryside sports are provided alongside the most luxurious standards of accommodation (Standeven and Tomlinson, 1994). Weed (2001a) notes that it is often the quality of the facilities and the luxurious nature of the accommodation rather than the activities on offer that define this product as up-market. In fact, in many cases this market is provided for by the addition of five-star accommodation to long-established and well-renowned facilities. However, while for the up-market sports tourist it is the nature of the facilities and accommodation rather than the activities themselves that are important, for enthusiasts of the activities who cannot afford such hotels, many farms have diversified into tourism and provide similar activities for those on a tighter budget (Busby and Rendle, 2000; Fitzgerald, 1993; Holloway, 1995).

Finally, mixed developments with retail outlets are increasingly providing opportunities for the sports tourist (Delpy-Neirotti, 2003), with Harrison (1990: 14) concluding that 'any large retail scheme without leisure facilities will soon be seen as incomplete'. The sheer size of these developments, perhaps most notably West Edmonton Mall in Canada, mean they are major tourist attractions (Canadian Geographer Special Edition, 1991), in fact the Metrocentre in Gateshead counts much of Scandinavia among its target market (Chesterton Chartered Surveyors, n.d). Many such mixed developments are often located within marina or waterfront developments, and are discussed in greater detail in the next section.

Mutual benefits to the sports participant and the tourist

There are some areas of the sport-tourism link where the interests and needs of sports participants and tourists are virtually inseparable. In the countryside it is almost impossible to distinguish between tourist and sports participant; in many cases the two are one and the same. In addition, marina and dockland developments serve and benefit both market sectors. Liaison on funding, research and information is also of benefit to both tourists and sports participants.

Countryside recreation
Many developments benefiting both local sport and recreation participants and tourists or day-trippers have taken place in the countryside in a range of countries across the world. The National Parks in Britain, Canada, the USA and Australia have all been promoted to local and tourist alike for sports and recreation activity. However, this has not been without objection from some quarters, with Redmond (1991) describing how some conservationists, perhaps particularly in North America, see this as a 'deplorable trend'. However, to many others, particularly sports tourists, it is seen as a natural growth (Walter, 2002).

Long before the Calgary Winter Olympics of 1988 were held in the area there were attempts to secure them for Banff National Park, first in 1968 and then in 1972. These bids failed due, in large part, to the objections of conservationists who argued that the Games and their associated facilities were contrary to the original purpose of National Parks, although Nelson and Scace (1968) saw this as a somewhat dubious proposition given the variety of recreational amenities introduced in the Banff Park since its establishment in the 1880s. Redmond (1991) describes the 'active promotion' of Canadian National Parks for profitable tourism, and shows how sport and recreation has played a large part in such promotion, while Galloway (2002) examines, among others, recreational use as a market segment. In Australia, D'Abaco (1991) sees the Victoria

Tourism Commission's 'Melbourne Now' campaign as a prime example of the effective marketing of parks and recreational facilities as tourism attractions.

Evidence from Britain in the early 1990s indicated that eight out of ten people visited the countryside at least once a year, the vast majority for informal pursuits such as walking or horse riding (CPRE, 1991). In this climate, the Sports Council (1992) produced a policy document, *A Countryside for Sport*, while the English Tourist Board (ETB), in co-operation with the Countryside Commission (CC), issued *Principles for Tourism in the Countryside* (ETB/CC, 1993). Although the central concern of these documents is the environmentally sensitive sustainable development of the countryside, a secondary concern of both statements is to establish sport and tourism respectively as legitimate countryside land uses. Continued access for these interests in a time of considerable change in the countryside is also an important concern.

While the philosophy and role of National Parks and informal countryside areas varies internationally (Reeves, 1995), it is almost undeniable that the interests of sport and tourism with regard to the countryside are startlingly similar. Therefore, it is quite surprising that, to date, there have been very few examples of liaison between sport and tourist agencies around the world in this respect. It would appear to be in the interests of both the sports participant and the tourist that the respective agencies engage in a co-operative marketing campaign and joint lobbying to ensure their interests regarding the countryside are safeguarded while also ensuring the simultaneous protection of the countryside as a recreational resource.

Examples of the effective but sustainable use of, often very fragile, countryside resources for sport and recreation exist. Jackson (1999) notes the environmentally friendly nature of cycling as an activity in National Parks in America, while in Crete and Thrace 'soft' forms of sports tourism, such as walking, hiking, orienteering and cycling have been promoted in rural areas (Vrondou, 1999). In this Greek case, these soft forms of sports tourism have been seen as having the potential to diversify tourism beyond the traditional 'mass' product for which Greece is known. Sports tourism is seen as sustainable tourism that might 'minimize negative effects and maximize social, environmental and economic benefits' (Regional Programme for Crete, 1994–1999, quoted in Vrondou, 1999) while also having the potential to promote local cultures as the activities involved result in greater access to alternative routes and localities, with distinct natural and cultural characteristics. This is something which the WTO (1988) has recognized, commenting that the sport and recreation dimension can enrich the tourism experience by allowing greater integration with destinations and a fuller appreciation of the social and cultural life of local communities.

Marina/dockland development

In 1986 it was stated that sophisticated indoor leisure facilities and waterside complexes, as part of marinas, docklands or canal developments would dominate the next generation of tourist attractions (Trollope, 1986). Seventeen years on, marina and dockland developments characterize the increasingly pervasive sport-tourism link, both in restructuring port cities and inland centres with river or canal fronts, but also in developing coastal economies which are highly reliant on tourism, such as Mediterranean Europe or the Caribbean. These developments provide water sports, broader leisure facilities and

25

sometimes event venues, alongside hotel complexes, nightclubs, casinos, cinemas and retail centres, designed largely to attract high-spending tourists, but also catering for residents

The link between sport and tourism in areas with thriving waterfront developments is not, as Anderson and Edwards (1998) highlight, a new phenomenon. They provide examples of marina-based sports leisure developments both in areas that have a maritime tradition and those attempting to use the sport-tourism link as part of a newly established waterfront area. Amarcal and Corrough (1994) discuss the use of marine parks and marinas as tourism stimulators in Brazil while an evaluation of the success of the Wellington Waterfront in New Zealand is provided by Doorne (1998). What is common to the vast majority of such projects is their desire to be sustainable through their use of land recycling and the environmentally sensitive balancing of natural and constructed environments (Edwards, 1996). Marina developments are popular as a result of the impressive array of facilities that they provide (Jennings (2003). The Mission Inn Golf and Tennis resort in Howey-in-the-Hills, Florida features two golf courses, a full service tennis complex, sailing and water sports, and retail and restaurant outlets, all set among natural hills and wetlands (Travel and Leisure, 1995). Britain's largest marina is located in Brighton and provides 2000 berths, water sports provision, a large hypermarket, pubs and restaurants, and a multi-screen cinema. This, along with several smaller marinas on the south coast, is considered to contribute considerably to the region's identity as a venue for sailing and water sports (Standeven and Tomlinson, 1994).

London Docklands provides Britain's most prominent dockland development. Initiated as an industrial and residential development (Page, 1988), the tourism and leisure element has since attracted considerable interest. The Docklands Sailing Centre provides for sailing, sailboarding and canoeing, while the Surrey Docks Water Sports Centre offers sailing, boardsailing, canoeing, subaqua, fishing and rowing. The London Wetbike Club was one of the first clubs in Britain to offer both the new personal watercraft sports of wetbiking and jet-skiing (Tyrer, 1990). Although the docklands is capable of attracting tourists from a considerable distance, these activities are also well patronized by local residents.

Marina developments, however, are often motivated by local political considerations. Wilson (1991), supported by Bennet (1991) in his discussion of Expos, describes how proposals for sports tourism events and attractions are used in a relatively precise and premeditated way by local elites as land development projects to regenerate and recapitalize decaying waterfront land left derelict as a result of the long-term worldwide decline of the shipping industry. This was one of the most significant outcomes of the 1992 Barcelona Olympics, which created a whole new affluent community alongside a waterfront sport and leisure development (Jackson and Weed, 2003). The negative side of such developments, however, can often be the displacement or break-up of indigenous communities, which is discussed later under negative aspects of the sport-tourism link.

Funding, information and research
The involvement of both sport and tourism agencies in developments linking the two spheres can often open up additional sources of funding (Weed and Bull,

1997a). While there are funds available for leisure from the European Union, the structure of these funds towards regenerative projects and the tourism industry means that sports projects often need to apply through the tourism directorate, which requires partnerships with tourism organizations (Persey, 1995). In the USA, Knopf (1998) outlined proposals to the US government as to how funding mechanisms might be used to stimulate closer co-operation, particularly on information and research, between sport and tourism systems. The British National Lottery has no fund for tourism, but through partnership with organizations in other areas of leisure such as sport and heritage, tourism organizations can tap into Lottery funding. Specifically, for sports facilities on tourist sites, the tourism industry can bid, through Sport England, into the National Lottery Sports Fund (Dowling, 1996). As these and other examples are reviewed, it becomes apparent that greater liaison on this issue can realize significant additional funding that stands to benefit both sectors in the long run. However, to capitalize fully on such 'cross-funded' benefits, the exchange of development advice between agencies is essential. Such exchange can help ensure that sports facilities on tourist sites are built to the correct specification for the most flexible use, while advice on tourism potential can help ensure that local sports provision built on the basis of tourist use is appropriate to the tourist industry, and specifically tourist visitor numbers, in a particular area (Padfield, 1995).

Gunn (1990) believes that although the sport and tourism sectors in many countries have historically grown from separate roots and been supported by separate organizations, they share planning and management considerations, are often influenced by similar areas of economic performance and resource allocation mechanisms, and have similar promotional emphases and research needs. Furthermore, Jackson and Glyptis (1992) see Gunn's observations as holding true throughout the world. Gunn (1990) cites an example of collaboration between the Tourism Agency and the Recreational Planning Agency in South Africa on a joint research programme to identify tourism strengths in relation to sports and recreation facilities and resources, although more recently Swart (1998) has been more sceptical about the potential for liaison in South Africa. In Victoria, Australia, the Ministry of Tourism, Recreation and Culture produced a best practice guide for local authorities wishing to develop a sports tourism strategy (Barnard, 1988), and in Britain the establishment of a Major Events Group within UK Sport and the British Tourist Authority's Sports Tourism section indicates a move towards a more strategic approach, although practical examples of liaison are, as yet, limited (Weed, 2002c; 2003c).

Finally, there would appear to be significant scope for collaboration in producing and distributing the sources of information used by both tourists and sports participants. In the UK, the network of tourist information centres has the potential to be used as an integrated information resource for sport, recreation and leisure opportunities for both tourists and local communities (Jackson and Weed, 2003). The same might be said of National Park Information Points. Research in the USA, which highlighted the attraction of National Parks for international tourists, investigated the sources of information used by visitors from a range of European countries, and highlighted the scope for collaboration between recreation and tourism organizations in reaching and informing international visitors, both at their points of origin and at the destination areas (Uyssal, McDonald and Reid, 1990).

27

Economic and community development

Literature dealing directly with the sport-tourism link that examines economic impacts and links studies across time and national borders is rare. It has tended to be in the areas of mega-events and major arenas that impact studies have been most prevalent. Both Jackson and Reeves (1996) and Collins and Jackson (1999) bemoan the lack of statistical sources that can provide a comprehensive assessment of the volume and value of sports tourism. The latter emphasize the continuing 'inability of tourism statistics accurately to profile the behaviour of tourists, which has long been noted' (Collins and Jackson, 1999: 173).

Research in various countries has attempted to quantify the number of activity holidays by domestic and international tourists within their borders, but the inconsistent posing of questions and the varying definitions used means that international comparisons are rendered useless. Some figures estimated by Smith and Jenner (1990) from around twelve years ago highlight this point, with estimates of holiday-makers motivated by sporting activities varying from 8.4 per cent to 56 per cent across Europe (see Table 2.1).

Table 2.1 Holiday-makers motivated by sporting activities

Country	Percentage
Switzerland	56.0
Cyprus	52.0
Scotland	21.0
Britain	14.0
Germany	10.0
Sweden	8.4

Source: Smith and Jenner (1990).

More recently, Jackson and Reeves (1996) provided a 'guesstimate' that figures of 10–15 per cent of domestic holidays in Northern Europe having a sports orientation are not unreasonable, but call for a more specific and consistent focus on this area in tourism statistic collection. In 1999 Collins and Jackson attempted to synthesize a range of previous economic impact studies in disparate disciplines to present an overview of the economic impacts of the sport-tourism link in the UK. In doing so they commented that their work could only be considered 'indicative of the overall economic impact because of the inconsistent and invariably incompatible nature of the available data' (Collins and Jackson, 1999: 175). Their 'conservative' estimates for the overall value of sports tourism in the UK are illustrated in Table 2.2 which suggests an overall value of over £2.5 billion annually.

Other studies are sketchy, or do not provide statistical evidence. Lee (1999), for example, comments on the 'immense' economic impact of outbound golf and ski tourism from Japan that is stimulating aggressive promotion by many operators in this market. In relation to outdoor recreation in Scotland, Higgins (2000) claims that previous economic analyses have underestimated the contribution of this area to the Scottish economy. He claims that at least £600–800

Table 2.2 The economic impact of sports tourism in the UK

	£ million
Sport as a prime activity on domestic holidays	1640
Sport as a prime activity by overseas visitors	142
Sport as a prime activity on day trips	831
Total	2611

Source: Collins and Jackson (1999).

million of Scotland's tourist income, much of which is in rural areas and extends the traditional tourist season, is derived from outdoor recreation.

These analyses aside, many studies exist that focus on either sport or tourism. Many of these are relevant to this analysis, particularly those examining sports events or regeneration initiatives, and are discussed below.

Sports events

The obvious direct benefits of major sporting events (new facilities and visitor spending) are supplemented in most cases by a post-event tourism boost (Collins, 1991; Getz, 2003; Kolsun, 1988). Resulting publicity and the positive influence on local tourism are clear advantages of staging such events (Ritchie, 1984). Getz (1991) identified six reasons why cities may bid for these events:

1 To attract people into the area.
2 To attract people outside the main season.
3 To create media attention and raise the profile of the area.
4 To add animation and life to existing facilities.
5 To encourage repeat visits.
6 To assist regeneration.

Ritchie (1990) found that Calgary's visibility and image had increased in Europe and the USA as a result of hosting the 1988 Winter Olympic Games. Furthermore, Melbourne's reputation as a city with a capacity to host major sports events has become a tourist asset and, as a result, it is able to attract virtually guaranteed full houses to its major sports events (Downey, 1993). More recently, Rozin (2000) noted how the image of Indianapolis as a 'sports venue' has helped it attract a number of corporate headquarters to the city.

Since the commercial success of the Los Angeles Games in 1984, there has been considerable competition for the privilege of being the host city for the Olympic Games. The act of winning the Olympic Games is a catalyst for bringing forward general infrastructure investments that may have been on the drawing board for a number of years (Hughes, 1993). As a result of the 1992 Olympic Games, Barcelona gained a ring-road, a new airport and the redevelopment of an area of derelict waterfront for the Olympic Village (Law, 1993). The worldwide publicity and infrastructure investment that the Olympic Games brings should enable a host city to attract further general investment, future events and more tourists (Getz, 2003). Even a failed Olympic bid can attract a large amount of public and private sector investment to provide some facilities and infrastructure (Kitchen, 1994) – Manchester gained a world-class velodrome from its Olympic bid. In addition the spirit of community collectivism that a bid can engender cannot be undervalued (Law, 1993). Whitson and Macintosh (1993) identified the concept of 'boosterism' as a major advantage of hosting major sports events. Because major games provide 'place identity', local political and business leaders join forces in a 'corporate civic project' to boost their city (Critcher, 1991). It is claimed that boosterism benefits the whole community – for example, Centre for Applied Business Research (CABR, 1986) figures show that 87 per cent of Fremantle residents would welcome another event like the Americas Cup, while 85–88 per cent of Calgary residents supported the Winter Olympics (Ritchie, 1988). Getz (1997b; 2003) supports this view, describing how major games can aid in community development and enhance the host population's way of life, economy and environment. Major sports events can give an unattractive area a tourism focus or can spread the use of accommodation facilities into off-peak times (Collins, 1991). The level of public investment is usually justified along these lines (Schumacher, 2000), with Whitson and Macintosh (1996) describing the importance that cities attach to establishing an identity as a 'world-class city' in the circuits of international culture and tourism. At city level a major motivator may be the significant level of central government funding that can often be attached to such projects. In fact, the group responsible for initiating Victoria's successful bid for the 1994 Commonwealth Games cite the infusion of federal funds into the city as one of the most important reasons for going after the Games.

Having staged a major games, Collins (1991) identifies the need for cities to seek to attract a string of future events. Subsequent events can be staged at a fraction of the cost of the original event as the infrastructure is already in place. However, the promotional image and economic effects still persist. In this vein, Bramwell (1997a) discusses the use of the 1991 World Student Games in Sheffield as part of a sustainable development strategy that promoted, and continues to promote, economic efficiency, social equity and environmental integrity in the city of Sheffield. The continued legacy of these games is reflected in Sheffield's ongoing major sports events strategy (SCCSDEU, 1995; and see Sheffield case study in Chapter 11) that has attracted events such as Euro 96 and the World Masters Swimming Championships to the city (Dobson and Gratton, 1997).

However, as Dobson and Gratton (1997) discuss, it is not only large-scale events that can generate economic benefits for local communities. Work by Bale (1989) indicates that retail outlets near soccer grounds can increase their revenue by up to 500 per cent on match days, while an analysis in America of the Peterborough Church League Atom Hockey Tournament in the early 1980s showed that even a junior tournament can generate a considerable visitor spend of $165 165 (Marsh, 1984). In similar research in the late 1980s, Yardley, MacDonald and Clarke (1990) examined visitor spending and behaviour at a veterans tournament in Canada and found that an average family attending a three-day 'Old Timers' hockey tournament spent between 200 and 300 Canadian dollars.

It is important, however, that economic impact studies take a long-term view of an event's impact, assessing post-event tourism and economic activity. It is unfortunate that few studies are able to take this longitudinal approach (Jackson and Glyptis, 1992). In addition, it is also important that assessments take into account the wider 'public goods' generated by sports stadia and events in order to obtain the complete picture concerning their impact (Baade and

Dye, 1988; Stevens and Wootton, 1997). However, Crompton and Lee (2000) discuss the 'mischievous manipulation' of many economic impact studies to inflate economic impacts as studies are often conducted by organizations retained by organizing committees who need to justify their spending. This American research suggests that a large number of participants and spectators is not necessarily an indication of large economic impacts. Economic impact figures for 'non-elite' sport of $55 per person per day for a youth tournament, and around $100 per person per day for an adult tournament are proposed as realistic expectations. Work from Dobson and Gratton (1997) on non-elite sports events in Britain estimates the impact as higher than this American research, but in the British case many more overnight stays were generated.

Community (re)generation initiatives

Sports tourism has played a significant part in a number of countries in the generation of community identity and pride and in the economic and social regeneration of decaying urban areas (Schumacher, 2000). In addition, its economic potential has been harnessed in many rural areas to support the local economy and services. In the immediate aftermath of apartheid in South Africa, Nelson Mandela spoke of the role of the 1995 Rugby World Cup, hosted and won by South Africa, in 'national building' after the years of internal turmoil and international isolation the country had suffered. Both in Britain and the USA, sports-related tourism initiatives have been at the forefront of urban regeneration programmes, while the role of 'soft' sports tourism (discussed earlier in the Greek context) in contributing to the rural economy is evident in a range of countries across the world.

In *Climber* magazine, Wright (2000) describes how the use of the countryside by climbers and mountaineers can contribute to the economies of rural communities, specifically highlighting the generation of additional economic activity that assists in supporting local services such as shops, post offices and public houses. Furthermore, climbing is a particularly good example of environmentally sustainable sports tourism, as the 'canons' and expected behaviours that are subscribed to by most climbers regard the defacing of mountain areas or rock faces as 'cheating'. Other countryside pursuits, such as hiking, orienteering, fell-running and cycling all contribute to the rural economy in a similar way, but perhaps the latter has received the most attention in the literature. For example, a range of papers from 'Velo-city', the Eleventh International Bicycle Planning Conference held in Austria in 1999, highlight, through a range of worldwide case studies, the benefits of cycle tourism to rural economies throughout the world. Earlier research in the USA by Schuett and Holmes (1996) suggests the construction of an entire regional marketing plan for the Adirondack North Country Region of New York State based on the opportunities it offers for cycle tourism. Such a plan would bring together local businesses, tourism organizations and bicycle-related firms and organizations in seeking to use such tourism to develop local economies. Other work by Schutt (1998) focuses on another area of 'soft' sports tourism provision, namely rural trails. He highlights the economic potential of this seemingly insignificant area of provision, and suggests that trail development is incorporated within local economic development strategies as it has the ability to both strengthen and diversify rural economies for the benefit of all citizens.

In urban areas, the use of sport within tourism by local government for regenerative purposes is well documented (Buckley and Witt, 1985; Gratton and Henry, 2001; Law, 1992; Lilley, 1991; SCLG, 1994). In Scotland, for example, Glasgow developed the Scottish Exhibition and Conference Centre in 1985, which provided a major venue in the city. This was followed by the conversion of the Kelvin Hall into an indoor sports arena, which became one of Britain's premier indoor athletics venues. It was estimated by Friel (1990) that Glasgow spent £90 million on events and infrastructure, but that this investment generated £300 million in income for the city.

The use of sports tourism within such urban regeneration strategies has been part of the programmes of successive British governments for almost twenty years now. In 1985 the British government produced a report, *Pleasure, Leisure and Jobs: The Business of Tourism* (Cabinet Office, 1985) which noted the economic importance of tourism and the role sports and recreation facilities can play within this, particularly in terms of creating employment. Further to this, in 1990, five objectives were identified for urban regeneration schemes (DoE, 1990):

1 To foster enterprise and business activity.
2 To improve job prospects.
3 To improve inner city environments.
4 To make the area attractive to residents and inward investors.
5 To enhance safety and make it an attractive area in which to live, work and recreate.

In assessing these objectives, the Department of the Environment (DoE, 1990) conducted a cost–benefit (other than direct financial surplus) analysis of several tourism-based grant-assisted urban regeneration projects some of which include sport and recreation facilities:

1 Employment generation at the facility.
2 Employment generation elsewhere.
3 Spending elsewhere.
4 Environmental benefits.
5 Changing attitudes and image.
6 Morale boosting.
7 Health benefits.

These benefits are substantiated by evidence identified by Jackson and Glyptis (1992), and more recently in Gratton and Henry (2001), of major sports projects being included in urban regeneration schemes. In these cases the dual aims are the enhancement of quality of life for residents, and the attraction of visitors, associated revenue and increased investment as a direct result of the high standards of leisure facilities available (SBMR, 2000). In the last five years in Canada there has been a similar emphasis on policy which has focused more specifically on sports tourism. The Canadian Tourism Commission has been involved, since 1996, in a programme designed to promote community and tourism industry interest in the development of sports tourism as a viable contributor to the economic wellbeing of local communities (CTC, 1999). While this work has been in both rural and urban areas, it is perhaps in the latter that the largest number of projects has been established.

Further North American research by Chapin (1996), and more recently by Rosentraub (2000), discusses the incredible surge in the number of new sports and entertainment facilities – largely aimed at staging sports events, concerts, conventions, conferences, exhibitions and any other events requiring a facility with a capacity of around 20 000 people – built in the USA and Canada in the mid-1990s. The prime objective identified in almost all of these cases has been economic development and revitalization (Rozin, 2000; SBMR, 2000). Chapin (1996) specifically reviews the varying strategies of three facilities: the Key Arena in Seattle, the Rose Garden in Portland and the GM Palace in Vancouver. The construction of the Key Arena in Seattle was part of a plan to revitalize an ageing, but culturally highly significant, civic centre. Here the former Seattle Coliseum arena was reconstructed and renamed as the Key Arena as an integral part of the Seattle Center Entertainment District, resulting in a revamped city centre that retained much of its original heritage. In contrast, Portland chose to locate a new facility alongside an older, much smaller, arena and a relatively new convention centre in an out-of-town development that is now specifically marketed as a Sports Entertainment District. Finally, Vancouver, as Seattle, located the GM Palace within its city centre, but focused on a newly built sports arena with the aim of enhancing the city centre as a 'metropolitan core'. These cases illustrate three widely popular strategies for urban regeneration through sports and entertainment facilities likely to attract visitors, namely, reinvestment in existing facilities, development of new sports entertainment districts and investment in inner city revitalization and redevelopment. A key factor in the use of sport in urban regeneration, however, is that it is developed alongside other leisure, entertainment and tourism facilities (Rosentraub, 2000).

In Britain, the Sports Council identified, aside from any economic contribution, the potential for sport to give people a sense of purpose, improve people's health, reduce tensions within a community and generate community pride. 'In short sport can alleviate some of the effects of economic and social deprivation' (Sports Council, 1990: 1). In a similar vein, Standeven (1993) suggests that, unlike some more traditional forms of mass tourism, sports tourism, and event tourism in particular, can positively celebrate cultural differences and thus contribute to the reversal of the trend towards global cultural convergence. Events can be used as a celebration and assertion of the host culture, through opening and closing ceremonies, event locations and associated cultural programmes and promotions that can contribute to community identity and pride. Such cultural celebrations can also enhance the tourist experience, not only in such large events but also in smaller-scale sports tourism trips. The importance, for example, of the novel cultural ingredients experienced by Himalayan trekkers in adding appeal and giving meaning to their tour is discussed by Standeven in earlier work (Standeven, 1992).

Negative aspects of the sport-tourism link

The final area considered in this chapter is the negative aspects of the sport-tourism link. Many of these could be considered 'side effects' of the more positive outcomes mentioned above, but such effects will increase in significance if they are ignored or not properly addressed. Issues relating to the insensitive use of the countryside, the finite natural and individual resources required for sports tourism, the negative effects of sports tourism developments on local communities and visitor/host conflicts such as sports spectator disorder, all need to be addressed if sports tourism developments are to have the long-term positive effects described above.

In relation to the countryside, British policy documents from the Sports Council (1992) and the English Tourist Board (ETB/CC, 1993) have already been mentioned. Each of these seeks sustainable development of the countryside. However, the potential negative impacts of insensitive use of the countryside are never far away (Jackson and Glyptis, 1992) and Jackson and Weed (2003) identify a sustainable tourism approach and inter-agency collaboration as the way forward in avoiding these pitfalls. Some of the activities that have been seen as problematic, such as motorcycling, water-skiing and shooting, have, according to Sidaway (1991), resulted in erosion of the countryside and perceived noise pollution, and this has led to the terming of these sports as 'nuisance activities'. The problems are identified as lying not with the use of the countryside by clubs for these activities, but with the informal user who does not follow the land designations. Joint marketing campaigns are needed by sport and tourist agencies to inform users of the environmental dangers of unrestricted participation in 'nuisance activities'. Aligned to this is the problem of incompatible sports – particularly water sports. It is hardly possible, for example, for fishing and water-skiing to coexist in the same stretch of water, although Leung and Marion (1999) describe how spatial management strategies can address this problem. A further problem in Britain has been the relocation of soccer grounds to edge-of-town greenbelt sites where increasing sport and leisure developments have led to a great deal of concern about the loss of greenbelt land to development (CPRE, 1991). In addressing this problem the Department for the Environment, Food and Rural Affairs will now only allow development on greenbelt sites if it can be demonstrated that no other suitable locations exist. Furthermore, in line with priorities that use sports tourism as part of urban regeneration strategies, the British government is particularly keen on the redevelopment of 'brownfield' sites (derelict former industrial areas).

The growth in activity holidays across Europe, evidenced by some of the figures quoted earlier, has led to increasing concern over the safety standards and environmental impact of this sector. Activity tourism in Wales is served by an Activity Holidays Advisory Committee, established by the Wales Tourist Board, which supplements the work of the British Activity Holidays Association in maintaining standards and operating codes of practice. Sport England has also noted its concern over the impact of activity-based holidays on the rural environment, where most such holidays take place. However, Jackson and Glyptis (1992) noted that there is a great deal of scope for further collaboration on these issues.

Previous discussions have shown the value of sport and tourism in regenerating economies; however an overreliance on the leisure industry is not healthy. The town of Collingwood, Ontario, Canada (population 12 000) is almost completely dependent on the leisure industry. The town's economy is at the mercy of the leisure preferences of the 5 million inhabitants of economically prosperous Southern Ontario living within 250 kilometres of the town (Wilkinson and Murray, 1991). In addition, Keith, Fawson and Chang (1996) describe how those counties in Utah, USA, that are dependent on tourism and recreation to maintain economic viability have a much greater annual employment variability than those counties which have a wider portfolio of economic activities. In fact, in the literature focusing on tourism's potential to generate employment, much concern has been expressed about the part-time, seasonal and casual nature of the jobs that are created (Cooper et al., 1998; Shaw and Williams, 2002). Such dependency on recreation and tourism can result in a neglect of ecological and environmental concerns. For example, Weiss et al. (1998) studied reactions to ski tourism among ski tourists and ski resort residents in Austria and Belgium. They found that ski tourists and locals not financially dependent on tourism had a much higher ecological awareness than tourism dependent locals. This was clearly a result of the latter group's vested economic interest in the industry and was further highlighted by the fact that differences between these groups on general environmental issues were minimal, but environmental concerns in relation to ski tourism varied according to the extent of the personal sacrifice involved in addressing such issues. This raises an interesting debate regarding the extent to which environmental degradation is a result of inconsiderate visitors or tourist-dependent local interests.

Earlier in this chapter, work by Standeven (1993) was quoted as showing that sports tourism can have a role in celebrating cultural differences. However, Standeven (1992) also highlights the potential danger of sports tourism in fuelling the spread of a homogenizing global culture. She poses the question: does sports tourism lead to the celebration of cultural differences or is cultural identity homogenized? Furthermore, if it is concluded that sports tourism is a homogenizing force, creating a global cultural hegemony, is the phenomenon desirable, or should it be constrained. Standeven (1993) suggests that the potential of sports tourism to celebrate differences and assert identity outweighs any homogenizing forces, and the evidence earlier in this chapter certainly supports this view. However, various problems around the world relating to environmental damage have led to many governments implementing various controls that restrict individual experience and, in some cases, reduce the opportunities for innovation in celebrating and expressing cultural differences. Somewhat paradoxically, this can result in the protection of the natural environment contributing to the degradation of the cultural environment. In a similar vein, the packaging of sports tourism activities by commercial providers can lead to homogenized experiences. For example, Beedie (2003) describes the loss of some elements of the individual mountaineering experience as a result of the packaging of mountaineering holidays by commercial operators. The control of the experience is handed over to the commercial provider and individually meaningful experiences are curtailed. This is an important issue, because a trend towards a form of sports tourism similar to the mass package holiday would mean that the phenomenon would lose much of its uniqueness.

While the many positive elements of major games as economic and tourism generators have been highlighted earlier, many such games- and sports-related regenerative projects require the demolition of at least some low-income housing to make way for facilities, infrastructure or development. This can result in the traumatic break-up of entire communities. For example, in Edmonton for the Commonwealth Games of 1978 (Chivers, 1976) and in Calgary for the 1988 Olympics (Reasons, 1984) some working-class homes were relocated without consultation so that construction for the Games could take place. A similar displacement of indigenous communities took place in the development of Barcelona's waterfront for the 1992 Olympic Games and in Beijing's preparation for its bid for the 2008 Games. While many would see such redevelopment as a positive benefit that enhances the environment and image of the city, for those communities that are displaced the experience can be traumatic (Jackson and Weed, 2003). In many cases, although these communities are living in comparative poverty and are usually relocated to improved housing elsewhere, such relocation is often to distant and unfamiliar suburbs far away from other families with whom friendships have existed for generations, the result being the destruction of working and social networks and, in some cases, entire communities.

A final negative aspect of sports tourism is that relating to visitor/host conflict, an issue that is by no means specific to sports tourism as a review of the general tourism literature will confirm (Mathieson and Wall, 1989; Ryan, 1991; Shaw and Williams, 2002). Some of these conflicts can relate to the use of the environment by sports tourists, but perhaps the most high-profile conflict is the problem of spectator disorder at sports events. While research shows that this happens in a range of different sports around the world, it is the reputation of soccer hooligans as undesirable visitors that perhaps strikes the greatest fear into host communities. More effective policing of soccer stadia has resulted in the displacement of violence into the areas surrounding the grounds, while international tournaments such as the European Championship or World Cup can result in problems in the main squares of towns and cities (Williams, Dunning and Murphy, 1989). Even where the level of actual violence may be low, the disruption and anti-social behaviour of some soccer fans is a considerable 'side effect' of hosting a major football tournament (Weed, 2001c).

While the above may seem like a catalogue of disasters waiting to happen, none of these negativities are insurmountable if they are recognized and addressed by the relevant parties, which, in varying degrees, means all those involved in the sport-tourism link – participants, policy-makers and providers. Participants need to recognize the environmental and sociocultural problems they can cause; policy-makers need to balance the need for regulation with the nature of sports tourism as an activity that can celebrate cultural differences; and providers need to provide for the heterogeneous nature of sports tourism as an experience as much as an activity.

Conclusion: conceptualizing sports tourism

Together with the historical review provided in the previous chapter, the contemporary overview given in this chapter provides the context for a more detailed analysis of the sports tourism phenomenon. While these chapters have clearly established the sport-tourism link as being wide-ranging and multifaceted, and have shown that there are considerable social, economic and cultural advantages to be gained from its exploitation, they have not attempted to provide any insights into the motivations and behaviours of participants, the processes involved in formulating policy or the strategies of providers, for this is the role of the remainder of the book.

The introduction to this chapter described the broader concept of the sport-tourism link, which is particularly important in examining the benefits of linking the two areas and in considering the areas in which policy-makers should be collaborating. In fact, the analysis in this chapter contributes to the Policy Area Matrix for Sport and Tourism (adapted from Weed, 1999b; Weed and Bull, 1997a) discussed in Chapter 7. In addition to this, the prologue to this book discussed the use of terminology. Both the idea of the sport-tourism link and considerations relating to terminology are somewhat technical in simply trying to describe the areas included in the analyses. However, it is perhaps useful at this point, having gained a greater understanding of what sports tourism and the sport-tourism link involve, to attempt to understand what factors identify sports tourism as a unique phenomenon that is more than simply the amalgamation of sport and tourism. Some of the evidence cited in this chapter suggests that the sports tourism phenomenon is constructed as much around experiences as activities and, so, although activities are an important part of sports tourism, other factors also contribute to its uniqueness. One such further factor might be travel; however, in many cases, travel is perhaps merely an instrumental factor in arriving at a unique place. The interaction of activity and place is clearly important, as a comparison of cycling to work through the pollution of a major city with cycling through beautiful countryside in one of the National Parks throughout the world shows. Yet this does not fully complete the picture, as for many participants an important part of the leisure experience is the people with whom participation takes place. In relation to sports tourism this may range from people with whom you interact every day, but with whom you have travelled to a distinctive place to take part in sports activities, to like-minded people you may or may not have met before, who are travelling from a range of places to the same destination for sports activities. Drawing these strands together within the context provided in these first two chapters, it is possible to arrive at the following conceptualization of the sports tourism phenomenon:

> Sports tourism is a social, economic and cultural phenomenon arising
> from the unique interaction of activity, people and place.

While this conceptualization is not a definition as such, it is of great help in understanding the sports tourism phenomenon. Consequently, the analysis of sports tourism participants, policy-makers and providers that follows is framed not only by the parameters of the terms sports tourism and the sport-tourism link outlined in the prologue and the definitions discussed in the next chapter, but also by this conceptualization.

Part Two: Participants

Preface

The purpose of the first part of this book was to provide the context against which the sports tourism phenomenon could be examined. As such it provided a historical overview of the development of sports tourism prior to an in-depth examination of the effects of linking sport and tourism. This overview of the sport-tourism link focused on the impacts and consequences of sports tourism. The remainder of the book now seeks to examine how the motivations, behaviours and strategies of sports tourism participants, policy-makers and providers both generate and originate from the effects of the sport-tourism link.

The specific focus of the three chapters in this part of the book is to examine and understand the sports tourist, something that has been largely neglected in the sports tourism literature, which has tended to focus on impacts and supply-side considerations. The importance of identity and the sports tourism experience are examined, with particular emphasis on the nature of sports tourism as a social, economic and cultural phenomenon derived from the unique interaction of activity, people and place. The nature of this interaction, once developed in this part of the book, is a theme that will feature throughout the analysis of policy-makers and providers that follows in later chapters.

Much of the discussion in this part of the book is derived from a range of postgraduate, doctoral and post-doctoral studies carried out at the authors' institutions. These studies span more than ten years, and provide a unique insight into the development of sports tourism and, more specifically, the behaviours and motivations of the sports tourist. They are supplemented throughout by secondary research that develops the discussion beyond the largely British empirical material that these studies have developed.

Chapter 3 discusses the nature of sports tourism prior to attempting to conceptualize the sports tourist through a detailed discussion of their experiences of place and their motivations. This conceptual material is then used as the backdrop for the presentation of an illustrative range of profiles of sports tourists, largely derived from empirical research, in Chapter 4. Chapter 5 constructs a typology of sports tourists – a Sports Tourism Participation Model – that draws together the discussions in the previous two chapters into a dynamic model which, in addition to contributing to the understanding of sports tourists' behaviours, also provides a useful tool for understanding the behaviours and strategies of providers in later chapters.

3

Conceptualizing the sports tourist

In the prologue to this text some preliminary comment was offered on the use of the term 'sports tourism'. While this provided some guidance as to the focus of the book, the problems of defining 'tourism' and 'sport' in themselves, let alone 'sports tourism', meant that such discussion could only provide the briefest of understanding and the intention was always to explore the concept of sports tourism in far greater detail at a later stage. In many ways, the book as a whole is designed to provide this fuller understanding and this chapter will develop this task by looking at what makes the sports tourist unique. It will begin by outlining definitions of the sports tourist and will then turn to examine behavioural patterns that differentiate such a person from other tourists. The interaction of the participant with the activity and place will then be analysed as a significant factor in conceptualizing the sports tourist.

The concept of sports tourism is clearly problematic due to it resulting from a fusion of two separate terms, both of which are complex in their own right. Both sport and tourism defy simple definition and there is a great deal of debate about what each encompasses. Not only do official definitions vary and change through time, but the meanings which people derive from such concepts also vary. Given this complexity, it is clear that an understanding of sport and tourism as separate spheres must be provided before any conceptualization of sports tourism can be achieved.

Definitions of sport

Attempts to define sport have engaged the energies of many writers, both academics and those involved in sports administration. Given the difficulties of producing a precise and universally accepted definition, some have suggested that the pursuit of defining sport is fruitless as the concept defies definition (Haywood et al., 1995; Horne, Tomlinson and Whannel, 1999; Houlihan, 1994; Slusher, 1967). Nevertheless, an understanding of sports tourism requires some exploration of the meaning of sport. Part of the debate revolves round what activities should be classified as sport, linked to the idea that it may be defined on the basis of pursuits satisfying key characteristics such as vigorous physical activity and/or physical skill, competition and codified rules (Haywood et al., 1995; Standeven and De Knop, 1999). Yet, while a great many activities could clearly be identified as sport on this basis, there are many other physical activities that are not organized along formal competitive lines and which do not involve rules but which would still be regarded as sport, such as swimming (or at least the form in which most participants are involved), rambling and jogging. There are also many other situations where activities that can be pursued in a highly organized fashion are 'played' informally and thus the issue of 'context' may be important (Haywood et al., 1995). Here some would make a distinction between sport and physical recreation, whereas others would see both as sport.

Part of the definitional problem relates to sport's historical development. Many contemporary highly organized sports were at one time pursued in a very informal and unregulated manner, and it was the values of modern industrial society and the Victorian public schools that created many of the forms we see today. Pre-industrial sport also involved animal sports where cruelty to animals was a central characteristic, something that today would be regarded as completely at odds with the ideals of sport. Furthermore, there is a long tradition of field sports which, although not so important today, were once regarded as key sporting pursuits. As Horne, Tomlinson and Whannel (1999: xv) point out: 'Hunting and shooting are now seen as rather marginal sporting activities, yet in the eighteenth century they would have been at the heart of the meaning of the term, indeed the very notion of the sporting man referred to the hunting man.'

The term 'sport' has thus been socially constructed and has acquired different meanings at different times in its historical development as well as in different societies. Standeven and De Knop (1999) compare the different conceptions of sport across various continents comparing the much narrower definitions of sport in North America, where it is defined very much in terms of institutionalized, competitive activity, to those in Europe which are generally looser. For example, the Council of Europe (1992) defined sport as 'all forms of physical activity which, through casual or organized participation, aims at improving physical fitness and mental well-being, forming social relationships, or obtaining results in competition at all levels' (in Sports Council, 1994: 4).

Such a definition is wide-ranging and inclusive rather than exclusive, and embraces not only 'formal' activities (e.g. team games such as football), but also non-competitive recreational activities involving some form of active physical participation, such as walking and cycling in the countryside, which have considerable tourism potential. As such, and along with many other authors in the field (e.g. Horne, Tomlinson and Whanel, 1999; Houlihan, 2003; Standeven and

Tomlinson, 1994) it is this wide-ranging, inclusive definition that will be used here in attempting to understand the nature of sports tourism.

The discussion so far has focused on the nature of sport, but a related notion, and one that is central to the subject of this chapter, is a definition of the sports participant. Such a definition is generally accepted to involve those who actively take part in sport. However, a full examination of the nature of the sports participant must also include those who observe it. As outlined in Chapter 1, there is a long history of people watching live sport, and many sports such as football and cricket attract huge crowds. Such spectators make an important contribution to the social institution of sport, and many are equally motivated in their commitment to sport as the active participant (see Weed, 2003b). Furthermore, their presence has also had an important influence on the nature and development of sport itself. Those sports with significant numbers of spectators have developed to accommodate them and this has involved both the way the sport is played and the environment in which this occurs. In addition, spectators have provided much of the wealth that has enabled sport to develop. As such, not to include spectators in any consideration of sports participation would seriously reduce the scope of the analysis and, given the significant number of spectators who travel, would greatly underplay the nature of sports tourism.

Definitions of tourism

As with sport, there exists a variety of definitions of tourism. These all emphasize travel away from home and most also stipulate that travel is for leisure purposes, although some still include business trips. While the travel element is a necessary descriptor, the extent to which other characteristics and constraints are included is, in part, linked to different emphases (even motives) behind the varying definitions. For example, some would view tourism as an economic activity or industry and, according to Ryan (1991: 5), this might suggest tourism being defined as 'a study of the demand for and supply of accommodation and supportive services for those staying away from home, and the resultant patterns of expenditure, income creation and employment'. Similarly, Hay (1989) defines tourism as 'a process concerned with the redistribution of economic resources, from a home community to a host community which involves a trip for leisure purposes'.

Others highlight the psychological benefits and define tourism in terms of motivations (see Smith, 1989), while tourist organizations often suggest technical definitions which lay down minimum and maximum lengths of stay and strict 'purpose of visit categories' in an attempt to isolate tourism from other forms of travel for statistical purposes (Cooper et al., 1998).

The major distinction between most definitions is whether or not day trips are included. Whereas most earlier definitions of tourism included the requirement of one or more nights away from home (e.g. WTO, 1963; 1991), more recently there has been a willingness to extend the definition to include day trips as well. The problem with including day trips, of course, is that it introduces further definitional issues of what constitutes such a trip. Does it require a minimum length of time and minimum distance travelled away from home? Some definitions have attempted to include precise prescriptions in this respect.

The Scottish Tourist Board, for example, sees a leisure day trip as one involving more than three hours and focusing upon a specific activity (quoted in Standeven and Tomlinson, 1994). But essentially such prescriptions are arbitrary. Nevertheless, despite such problems, a number of authorities have suggested a wider, more inclusive approach. The British Tourist Authority (1981: 3), for example, has defined tourism in rather broader terms as 'the temporary short-term movement of people to destinations outside the places where they normally live and work, and their activities during the stay at these destinations; it includes movement for all purposes as well as day visits and excursions'. This is similar to the working definition adopted by Standeven and Tomlinson (1994) who see tourism as ranging from day trips within one's own locality to long-haul package holidays to the other side of the world – but, most importantly, always involving a sense of movement or visit. This perceptual definition is, like the sports definition earlier, inclusive rather than exclusive, encompassing all activities and trips that the tourist considers to be tourism.

Conceptualizing the sports tourist

Having reviewed a number of definitions of sport and tourism it is now necessary to consider how concepts from both can be fused together to provide a fuller understanding of sports tourism. Standeven and De Knop (1999: 12) briefly review the use of the term in recent literature and, having defined sport and tourism separately, proceed to define sport tourism as: 'All forms of active and passive involvement in sporting activity, participated in casually or in an organized way for noncommercial or business/commercial reasons, that necessitate travel away from home and work locality'. While on one level this all-embracing definition enables as wide an array of activity as possible to be covered by the term, essentially it involves no more than merely identifying tourist activity involving sport and is not particularly helpful in fostering a deeper understanding of the concept of sports tourism. In fact it begs the question as to whether sports tourism is a serious subject for study or whether it is merely a convenient descriptive term with little explanatory value. In this text it is maintained that there is something more substantial involved but, as a result, a different approach needs to be adopted. Instead of trying to combine two separate activities, one solution might be to define one in terms of the other. In other words, how can tourism, or rather specific segments of it, be defined by sport?

While a precise definition of tourism may be illusory, it is clear from the previous section that there are a number of core or primary characteristics of tourism that can readily be identified (Burkhart and Medlik, 1992; Cooper et al., 1998). These involve the temporary movement of people to destinations away from their home environment and workplace, the activities undertaken during their stay and the facilities created to cater for their needs (Mathieson and Wall, 1982). Thus, what can be said about the journeys, the destinations and the activities pursued from the perspective of sport? Furthermore, some definitions of tourism view it as an industry and define it in terms of 'firms, organizations and facilities which are intended to serve the specific needs and wants of tourists' (Leiper, 1990: 400). Consequently, how is the tourist industry, or at least parts of it, organized to serve the specific needs of sport? Finally, tourism is sometimes defined in terms of its motives as people seek psychological benefits (Ryan, 1991) or certain satisfactions (Kelly, 1985). So, how can the motives of tourists be combined with those of the sports person? These particular questions are clearly related to the framework outlined at the conclusion of the previous chapter, which suggested that sports tourism be viewed as a social, economic and cultural phenomenon arising from the unique interaction of activity, people and place. The destinations with their specific facilities and environments involve clear interactions between activity and place; the travel element, including the journeys and the way such travel is organized, is an interaction which links people with places; and the motives relate to the interaction between people and activities as well as places.

Sports tourism places

The essential characteristic of sport is that it involves some active pursuit and such activity requires specific resources. Such resources may involve particular environments or specific facilities but the essential point is that they are not ubiquitous; they are found at specific locations. Of course, some resources are more widespread than others. While there are a great many routeways along which people may run or cycle, facilities for activities such as skiing or rock-climbing are less widespread. However, even where resources are more readily available, the quality may be variable with high quality resources only to be found in a few locations. Football, played and observed in the local park, is a very different experience to that encountered at a Premier League stadium; and, as indicated earlier in the text, cycling through the scenically attractive landscapes of a national park contrasts markedly with cycling along the busy streets of towns and cities. Thus sports' participation will often require travel, some of which will clearly be travel to destinations away from the home environment, and it is the purpose of this section to examine the specific characteristics of these particular places by focusing on two particular perspectives. One concerns the physical characteristics and spatial patterns of sports places, and the second involves the way in which such places are perceived and culturally appraised.

Various writers have attempted to classify physical resources associated with recreation and leisure (Chubb and Chubb, 1981; Clawson, Held and Stoddard, 1960; Smith, 1983) although there have been few attempts to classify sports resources *per se* (Bale, 1989). Nevertheless, much of the general literature relating to recreation is also relevant to sport and, thus, this might be a useful starting point. Implicit in much of the discussion is the idea of some form of 'continuum ranging from biophysical resources to man-made facilities' (Kreutzwiser, 1989: 22), a concept with considerable relevance for sports resources as it accommodates outdoor pursuits at one end of the spectrum with those facilities, often urban based, that have been specifically designed for sport at the other. One of the earliest, and most frequently cited, examples of such a classification is that suggested by Clawson, Held and Stoddard (1960) who distinguished between recreation and opportunity on the basis of location and other characteristics such as size, major use and degree of artificial development. Under this system areas were arranged on a continuum of recreational opportunities from user orientated through intermediate to resource based. User-orientated areas were those located close to users with small space demands and often with artifi-cial features; they included such resources as urban parks, swimming pools, golf courses and playgrounds where the landscape elements are less important. Resource-based areas, at the other end of the continuum, involved an emphasis on the quality of the physical resource with large land units involved and remote-ness being a basic ingredient. National parks, forests and wilderness areas cater-ing for such activities as orienteering, canoeing, skiing and rock-climbing were typical of this group. Intermediate areas were located between the two extremes, both spatially and in terms of activity. Accessibility was relatively important with most sites within one or two hours' drive from potential users. Facilities for camping, picnicking, hiking, swimming, hunting and fishing were included in this category. This system and its subsequent application to England and Wales (Law, 1967) both 'confirm the importance of distance and the "zones of influence" of recreational resources according to whether they had a national, regional, sub-regional, intermediate or local zone' (Hall and Page, 2002: 97).

While the Clawson system has been criticized for its somewhat confusing terminology in that it involves a rather narrow interpretation of the term resources and seemingly ignores the fact that all recreation areas must be user orientated to some extent (Pigram, 1983), it still has some contemporary relevance for it can be modified to cover sport and it also begins to provide a solution to the distance problem relating to sports tourism. Under this system user-orientated places would not be included within sports tourism as they are specifically local, often being used after school or work, with no significant travel involved. Conversely, the other two areas would be involved in sports tourism as the resource-based areas are associated with vacations and the inter-mediate areas with day outings and weekend visits. Unfortunately, however, not all forms of sporting activity can be accommodated by such a scheme.

The essential problem with the Clawson model is that it does not accommo-date certain quality issues and quality is part of the cultural perspective of sports places.

As various writers have pointed out, sport is a cultural form (e.g. Bourdieu, 1978; Hargreaves, 1982) and so, too, is tourism (e.g. MacCannell, 1976). As Standeven and De Knop (1999) argue, sport is a cultural experience of physi-cal activity and tourism is a cultural experience of place. But, as well as defin-ing these two different cultural experiences as separate spheres, it must also be the case that the two are combined when the resources that people feel they need are not readily available in their immediate neighbourhood. A central tenet of sport is challenge. This challenge may be interpersonal, but more often than not some form of natural or human-made resource is part of that challenge (Haywood et al., 1995). It is also pursued at different levels: recreational, competitive and elite. As a result, a number of different environmental/ resource requirements are associated with sport. One relates to the necessary resource required to enable even the most basic activity to be undertaken. Local parks, for example, would provide open space for various types of recre-ational sport – 'jumpers for goalposts' being the epitome of this level of resource provision. However, where sport is pursued at a competitive or elite level, higher quality resources may be preferred, even required, and such resources are only found in certain locations. They may be specific natural or semi-natural resources such as mountains, rivers, lakes and forests, and thus located where they are as a result of physical geography. These resources, catering for such sports as skiing, climbing, canoeing and orienteering, would clearly be accommodated in the Clawson model both in terms of their environmental and locational characteristics. Other high-quality sports resources, however, may be found in very different places, located in key urban centres. These resources are characterized by their purpose-built features designed specifically for sport and their spatial distribution is conditioned by economic factors such as market thresholds (Bale, 1989), social and political considerations linked to social policy (Henry, 1993; 2001) or urban regeneration linked to tourism (Law, 1992; Page, 1990; Roche, 1992). For the people who live in such centres these sports places have a user-orientated location but from the perspective of those who lack such facilities in their home town and who have to travel to such centres to participate, the pattern is rather different. Thus a particular cultural perspective relating to the level of sport may require participants to travel.

Another aspect of resource quality and one that is also linked to cultural issues is the way people evaluate and perceive resources generally. It can be argued that all resources are in one way or other cultural appraisals (Everden, 1992; Short, 1991; Simmons, 1994), and nowhere is this more true than with various environments used for sport (Bale, 1994). While many people can quite easily pursue their sport close to home, they often choose to travel elsewhere to participate in what might be regarded as a preferred environment. This is not because the standard of the facility itself is better elsewhere but rather because of the ambience of the place: either the climate is better, the environment is less polluted or less crowded, it is more peaceful or the general landscape is more scenically attractive. An additional point is also provided by Urry (2002) concerning the carrying out of familiar activities in unusual visual environments. He cites swimming and other sports which 'all have particular significance if they take place against a distinctive visual backcloth. The visual gaze renders extraordinary activities that otherwise would be mundane' (ibid.: 12). The example of cyclists preferring to cycle through rural rather than urban areas has already been mentioned, but another example would be British golfers who might prefer to play golf in Southern Spain or the Algarve instead of, or in addition to, using courses at home. Of course, the distinctive backdrop does not have to be rural, it could have a different cultural significance, an example perhaps being the spectator who travels to watch sport at various sporting 'Meccas' such as Lords cricket ground in London or the Yankee baseball stadium in New York.

Places associated with sports tourism are many and varied but, if any attempt is to be made at identifying or classifying them, it is clear that such a scheme would have to take account of quality issues as well as locational factors. As will be clear in the later sections of this text, a number of specific sports tourism places can be identified on this basis which might include, for example, ski resorts, outdoor pursuits environments, major cities (associated with mega-sporting events) and sports camps.

The organization of sports tourism

A key part of the conceptual model of sports tourism outlined above is the interaction of people with places. Sports tourism involves an essential travel element and thus it is important to consider the type of journeys involved and the way such travel is organized to establish whether there are aspects which are essentially unique. While the complexity outlined in the previous section would indicate that there will be many different forms of travel involved, it is nevertheless possible to identify some specific forms of sport tourism travel and associated forms of organization. One of the best known is the winter sports holiday industry, especially skiing which can be pursued at different levels, by different age groups, and in different settings – at a ski school, a ski course, a ski club or privately (Standeven and De Knop, 1999). It is a well-organized industry, worth around £200 million to operators in the UK (Hudson, 2000) and involves the large-scale movement of people (in Europe it accounts for around 20 per cent of the total holiday market) from their various homes to a relatively small number of specific mountain locations, each possessing an instantly recognizable infrastructure of hotels, chalets, camp sites, chair lifts, ski runs and shops. Winter sports holidays are organized through the major travel companies but a number of smaller businesses specializing in winter sports holidays are also important (see Chapter 13 for a more detailed coverage of these aspects).

The model of the skiing holiday has recently been adopted by various other forms of sport. According to Standeven and De Knop (1999: 89) 'holiday concerns, holiday organizations, (cultural) societies, and private sport schools now provide holiday courses in sailing, gliding, riding, golf, diving, cycling, mountaineering, surfing, and so forth'. Furthermore, in addition to these single sport holidays, there is also a growing popularity with the multiple sports activity holiday where several sports are on offer at the one location. Sports camps and the more luxurious club-formula camps such as Club Med and Center Parcs are examples of this development. In addition, increasing numbers of hotels are promoting their sports facilities in travel brochures.

A further development is the emergence of specific sports travel companies. These companies tend to fall into one of two categories providing either tailor-made sports training or competition tours for sports teams, or all-inclusive packages for travelling sports spectators. Travel International Sports, for example, is an American company based in California that provides tailored sports tours in a range of sports including baseball, gymnastics, hockey, lacrosse, football and water polo. This company offers packages that include setting up fixtures with local teams, or tournament entry at inspected sites, travel and accommodation, travel orientation material and a tour leader. Providing a similar service for travelling sports spectators are companies such as Hospitality Worldwide. This company offers both 'off-the-peg' and tailor-made packages to a range of domestic and international sports events for individual travellers, with rugby union, cricket and Formula One motor racing comprising their main business. Finally, International Sports Tours, based in Australia, caters for both sports team tours and travelling sports spectators in football, rugby union, cricket, triathlon and netball, as well as 'golden oldie' events.

This brief overview of the organization of sports tourism shows that there are a growing number of companies emerging to provide for the specific travel needs of the sports tourist (see Chapters 8 and 9 for more detailed discussions). Notwithstanding the preferences of some sports tourists for independent travel, the types of sports tourism providers discussed here are an important part of the sports tourism phenomenon, linking people with places and, in some cases, providing for their activities at such places. Consequently, an understanding of the way in which such providers contribute to the organization of sports tourism provides an important link between the preceding discussion of place and the following discussion of sports tourists' motivations.

Motives of sports tourists

While the previous sections have been concerned primarily with the context of sports tourism, the following paragraphs will concentrate more on the sports tourists themselves and examine more closely how people interact with activity and place. What is it about those people who travel to participate in sport that makes them unique? One important question that needs to be examined in this respect is that of motivation. Both sport and tourism as separate activities involve a complex set of motivations and a considerable literature exists which reflects this. In his PhD thesis concerned with 'evidencing the sports tourism interrelationship', Reeves (2000) reviews the motivational literature relating to both sports participation and tourism and there is much evidence in this review that the motivations of both sports participants and tourists share a number of common traits which may offer some insights into the uniqueness of the sports tourist. According to Reeves (2000: 29) it is the socio-psychological rationales that dominate the sports motivation literature and it is this perspective that 'most closely mirrors that body of literature which attempts to explain reasons for individual engagement in tourism activity'. (General reviews of tourism motivation literature can be found in Ryan, 2002, and Shaw and Williams, 2002.)

People's motives for participating in sport are many and varied. Such activities may be shared (common) as well as unique to the individual, and they are dynamic in that they change over time. Such motivation embraces both psychological, social and philosophical perspectives. A significant amount of research on the motives behind sports participation involves the individual's characteristics – interests, needs, goals and personality (Weinberg and Gould, 1995) and is also linked to similar work on the social-psychology of leisure (e.g. Mannel and Kleiber, 1997; Neulinger, 1981). There are clearly motives which are more specifically identified with sport (rather than tourism) such as competitiveness, a desire to win, the testing of one's abilities and the development of skills and competencies, especially among more elite participants. However, many others might also be claimed by tourism.

This can be seen quite clearly in the classification system of the various travel motivators developed by McIntosh and Goeldner (1986) from a review of existing tourism motivation studies. Three of their four categories of tourist motivation – physical, interpersonal, and status and prestige motivators – also have immediate relevance to sport. The physical motivators include those concerned with refreshment of body and mind, health purposes and pleasure; interpersonal ones include a desire to meet people, visit friends or relatives, and to seek new and different experiences as well as the need to escape from routine experiences; and status and prestige motivators include personal development and ego enhancement. In attempting to consider these motivations in relation to the interaction of activity people and place, it seems quite clear that the physical motivators are related to activity and the interpersonal motivators to people. Status and prestige motivators appear to be related to the more holistic interaction of these three factors. As such, the discussion that follows will examine these three motivators in turn before discussing how a consideration of arousal theory and the concept of ritual inversion might both account for the importance of place, and link the areas together in understanding the unique attraction of the 'interactive experience' of sports tourism.

Several writers highlight the quest for health, fitness and general wellbeing (both psychological and physiological) as important motivations for sport (Astrand, 1978; 1987; Gratton and Taylor, 1985; Long, 1990). In sport these include such objectives as 'weight control, physical appearance and generally maintaining the body in a good physical state in order to maximize the life experience' (Reeves, 2000: 35). In tourism, the emphasis is more concerned with relaxation and recuperation, giving the 'batteries an opportunity to recharge' (Cohen, 1983; Crompton, 1979; Mathieson and Wall, 1982).

Such health benefits are also inevitably linked to the idea of enjoyment, pleasure satisfaction and excitement – positive affective experiences which some, dating back to the work of Sigmund Freud, collectively refer to as the 'pleasure principle', a feeling of wellbeing (Reeves, 2000) which has, in some cases, been related to physiological responses to exercise and excitement (Sonstroem, 1982; Sonstroem and Morgan, 1989; Williams, 1994). These have been claimed as important motives underpinning sports participation but they are equally relevant to tourism (Robinson, 1976; Urry, 2002). In addition to the associated physical and psychological benefits they provide, some writers have also offered philosophical rationales to explain people's desire for pleasure in terms of a desire for a 'good life' (Kretchmarr, 1994). Sport, for example, may be perceived as an important component within a particular lifestyle and, furthermore, may also mirror developments in contemporary society and be used by individuals as a means of escaping from the pressures of everyday life. Both these motives are equally important elements within the tourism motivation literature. Holidays are now regarded as an essential component of modern lifestyles, with people prepared to forego other items rather than their annual holiday (Ryan, 1991). In addition, the sense of escapism is also seen as an important influence on tourism behaviour (Leiper, 1984; Iso-Ahola, 1989). In fact, Urry (2002: 12) explicitly links the pleasure principle to escapism, suggesting that tourists 'must experience particularly distinct pleasures which involve different senses or are on a different scale from those typically encountered in everyday life'.

In relation to interpersonal motives, a particular strong motive for playing sport is a sense of affiliation, involving the need to belong to a team, group, club or society in general. Carron and Hausenblaus (1998) use theories of group cohesion to identify two main reasons to explain this need: involvement for predominantly social reasons and the subsequent satisfaction and pleasure derived from that social interaction and for task reasons, i.e. enjoyment of working with other members of the team in common pursuit of the task completion. While the latter motive may not have immediate resonance with tourism, although it would be applicable to various forms of special interest tourism such as conservation holidays, the social interaction motive involving meeting new people, visiting friends and relatives, and spiritual pilgrimage is clearly relevant and is identified in the literature on tourism motivation. Several studies in fact refer to tourists as modern-day pilgrims (Graburn, 1989; Hetherington, 1996; Urry, 2002) with most tourism involving people travelling in groups of one sort or another. As Reeves (2000: 34) points out the social interaction motive 'has clearly identifiable links with the travelling or "touring" of sports teams, at all levels of participation' and Green and Chalip (1998: 286) provide a useful illustration of this in their study of the Key West Women's Flag Football Tournament where their findings suggest 'that a pivotal motivation for these women's choice of travel and destination is the opportunity to come together to share revelry in the instantiation of their identity'.

Status and prestige motives are equally important for both sport and tourist activity. Goal achievement is often regarded as a key motive for sport, especially in relation to elite performance. As Reeves (2000: 35) points out, for some individuals winning provides the primary motive for participation which he suggests might be explained by Achievement Goal Theory. Here individuals who exhibit 'an ego-oriented outlook in life will tend to transfer this rationale to their participation in sport' and 'the goal or motive for such individuals is to maintain a favourable perception of their ability' (ibid.). This is closely linked to the pursuit of rewards, which may be tangible in the form of prizes, medals or trophies or intangible in the form of praise, encouragement, satisfaction and feelings of accomplishment. And, of course, all of this is related to the acquisition of status. Such motives are equally important for tourists. Several writers, borrowing from Maslow's (1954) hierarchy of needs, refer to the goal of self-fulfilment involving certain types of tourist achieving the ambition of 'collecting' places (Urry, 2002). Furthermore, there is the related motive of wish-fulfilment, with tourists seeking to achieve their dreams and fantasies, and this is also related to status, another ambition of the sports person. Just as the sports person can achieve status through winning and achieving high levels of performance, so too the tourist can acquire status through conspicuous consumption in the form of ever more exotic and expensive holidays.

In each of the areas discussed above, it is clear that the motives of the sports participant and the tourist can be remarkably similar. Given the ideographic nature of motivation, it is likely that some individuals motivated to achieve, for example, social goals through sport, may not be similarly motivated to experience those goals through tourism. However, for others the convergence of these goals in the activity of sports tourism may result in a very powerful motivating force. It is here that the concept of optimal arousal is useful.

The view that 'leisure should be optimally arousing for it to be psychologically rewarding' (Iso-Ahola and Wissingberger, 1990: 2) could be equally as applicable to sport as to tourism and could be particularly important for certain types of sports tourist. While much of the literature on arousal in sport relates to the issue of performance, arousal levels can still be achieved by participation at a less competitive level if competence motives such as skill development, or achievement motivations such as improved personal best performances are present. Furthermore, in sporting pursuits such as various outdoor and adventure activities, which are often necessarily sports tourism experiences, optimal

51

arousal levels may be achieved by the perceived level of risk involved (Carpenter and Priest, 1989; Ewart and Hollenhorst, 1994; Martin and Priest, 1986; Mortlock, 1984; Priest, 1992; Rossi and Cereatti, 1993; Vester, 1987). Important in determining arousal levels in these activities may be ideas associated with 'locus of control' (Rotter, 1966) and the perception of the extent to which the individual is able to exert control over the level of risk that exists – too little risk and the activity ceases to be stimulating and the participation is likely to cease due to boredom, too much risk and a need to withdraw from the activity through anxiety results.

In tourism, Iso-Ahola (1980; 1982) has emphasized 'the importance of understanding intrinsic motivation within the framework of the need for optimal arousal' (Pearce, 1993: 129), and subsequent work by Wahlers and Etzel (1985) has provided evidence that holiday preferences are influenced by 'the relative differences between optimum stimulation and actual lifestyle stimulation experiences' (ibid.: 285). Those who have a high level of stimulation in their working lives will therefore seek to 'escape' stimulation on holiday while, by contrast, those with low levels of stimulation at work have a tendency to seek greater novelty and stimulation on holiday (see also Iso-Ahola, 1984; Mannell and Iso-Ahola, 1987). This approach, which emphasizes the differences between 'home-life' and tourism experiences, might be considered alongside Graburn's (1983) concept of 'ritual inversion'.

One of the key motivations for tourism, according to a range of authors (Graburn, 1983; MacCannell, 1996; Reeves, 2000; Smith, 1977), is a desire to experience things that would not normally be experienced in everyday work or leisure lives. Reeves (2000: 45) describes tourism as 'a vehicle for escapism which frequently allows the individual to consume outside the "normal" pattern of everyday life', while Graburn (1983: 11) notes how: 'tourism involves for the participants a separation from normal "instrumental" life and the concerns of making a living, and offers entry into another kind of moral state in which mental, expressive and cultural needs come to the fore'.

In addition to tourism being motivated by the desire to consume outside the normal pattern of everyday life, the concept of ritual inversion on tourist trips is described by Graburn (1983: 21) as a situation where 'certain meanings and rules of "ordinary behaviour" are changed, held in abeyance, or even reversed'. Consequently, the concept of ritual inversion maintains that individuals on holiday feel released to behave in ways significantly different to those in which they are expected to behave at home. While for individuals who experience a high level of stimulation and arousal in their 'home-lives', this may simply relate to the freedom to relax and to not worry about tasks and activities that must be completed, for others the search for optimal arousal and the experience of ritual inversion can be a powerful motivating force for sports tourism activities.

The arousal levels felt during sports tourism participation can be significantly enhanced by the interaction of activity, people and place. Many sports tourists may also engage in the activities undertaken while on tourist trips in their home environment, and as such it is likely that these activities already provide some level of stimulation. However, arousal levels can be enhanced by the addition of the place experience to the activity. The desire to take part in activities in a range of interesting and unusual places is a result of a powerful combination of the various physical and status and prestige motivators described above.

When such combined place/activity experiences also take place in the company of like-minded people who share similar motives, then the experience is further enhanced by the achievement of social interpersonal goals. In a reflexive manner, the achievement of optimal arousal through these means is both likely to contribute to, and be enhanced by, the experience of ritual inversion, the 'other kind of moral state in which mental, expressive and cultural needs come to the fore' (Graburn, 1983: 11). Therefore, as this chapter has attempted to illustrate, the unique interaction of activity, people and place is a significant factor in understanding and conceptualizing the sports tourist.

Conclusion

This chapter has sought to examine the nature of sports tourism with a view to identifying whether it constitutes a distinct phenomenon. Given the problems of defining sport and tourism as separate activities, it is not surprising that a simple definition of sports tourism would not be possible. Similarly, an assessment of certain key components of sports tourism, namely, the places involved, the way it is organized and the possible motives of participants, demonstrates considerable complexity.

Nevertheless, while it may not be possible to identify a single specific place, there are certain types of places which can be clearly identified as sports tourism destinations, and distinct organizational structures exist to facilitate sports tourism activity. In addition, the section on motivation showed that sport and tourism share a number of motives in common and, while this does not provide a simple identification of a typical sports tourist, it may indicate the possibility of a number of types. It may well be that the most fruitful way forward in developing an understanding of sports tourism is through the concept of typologies. The development of such a typology is discussed in Chapter 5. However, in order to understand more fully the range of behaviours and motivations of particular sports tourist types, the next chapter examines a range of sports tourism participation profiles.

4

Participant profiles

While the largest proportion of sports tourism literature has focused on its economic, social and environmental impacts (see Chapter 2), very little has been written about the people who generate these impacts – the sports tourists themselves. Furthermore, where sports tourists are considered, they are usually presented as a homogeneous group (either event or activity based) generating a particular type of impact. Examples of this might be the economic impact generated by visitors to sports events, or the environmental impacts of various outdoor adventure activities. Only in very rare cases is there any detailed consideration of the behaviours and profiles of sports tourists. This is largely a result of the inherent problems in creating such a data set, which requires detailed investigations of individual preferences, decision-making processes and lifestyle profiles. However, the information generated by more detailed research represents a considerable advance in the field of sports tourism, because not only does it assist in developing a greater understanding of the sports tourist, but it can also deepen understanding of how sports tourism impacts are generated.

This chapter aims to develop the conceptual material on motivations and place experience discussed in Chapter 3 by presenting 'profiles' of a variety of sports tourists. The majority of these profiles are based on a number of studies over the last decade conducted at the authors' institutions

Table 4.1 Studies of sports tourists providing primary data sets

Sports tourists	Location	Source
Casual holiday sports participants	Butlins Holiday Worlds (UK)	McKoy (1991); Reeves (2000)
Athletics spectators	Europa Cup (Birmingham, UK); World Cup (Crystal Palace, UK)	Train (1994); Reeves (2000)
Active event participants and sports instruction	Malta	Bull and Weed (1999)
Outdoor adventure pursuits	Twr-Y-Felin (Wales)	Reeves (2000)
Cricket supporters	Test matches in England and following England abroad	Weed (2002a)
Football hooligans	England fans at Euro 2000 in Holland and Belgium	Weed (2001c)
Elite competition and training	Elite British track athletes around the world	Jackson and Reeves (1998); Reeves (2000)

(see Table 4.1), and as such they are based on primary data sets. However, because these studies are largely UK focused, other studies that have focused on sports tourist behaviours and preferences have also been used in order to give the chapter a broader relevance. The result is a wide-ranging discussion that presents a varied, although not exhaustive, picture of the profiles and behaviours of both active and passive participants in sports tourism.

As Table 4.1 shows, the studies contributing to the discussions in this chapter for which primary data sets were available represent a wide range of sports tourist 'types'. When these studies are supplemented by secondary data from other studies, the discussion potentially becomes unmanageable. Therefore, to allow a coherent analysis to take place the discussions in this chapter are structured under three headings. First, those sports tourists for whom sports tourism participation is the primary reason for travel (primary sports tourists) are discussed. Second, the discussion turns to sports tourists for whom sport is the primary reason for travel, but for whom factors other than the sport are the reason for their sports tourism participation (associated experience sports tourists). Finally, tourists for whom sport is not the primary trip purpose are discussed (tourists interested in sport).

Primary sports tourists

Primary sports tourists are the most straightforward group to address, and are the group that perhaps comprise the 'mainstream' sports tourism market. However, as with many tourism markets and submarkets, this group is not homogeneous and, as the discussion of six types of primary sports tourists that follows will show, it would be very difficult to assign any common characteristics across these sports tourists, except that sport is the primary motivation for their trip. The sports tourists discussed are: elite athletes; outdoor, adventure and alternative sports participants; athletics spectators; committed football and cricket fans; golf participants; and participants in mass-participation sports events.

Elite athletes

Elite athletes are an atypical group of sports tourists, but they are undoubtedly some of the most prolific travellers for the prime purpose of sport. Their travel is both domestic and international, and can be for either training or competition. Studies of elite British track athletes have shown that the number of days travelled per year can be significant, and ranges from sixty-nine days a year for a junior international, to 146 days for an established senior athlete (see Box 4.1).

Box 4.1 Travel patterns of elite British track athletes

Two illustrative examples of annual travel volumes for training and competition:

Andrew Young (20)
GB and Scotland Junior
International, 800m

Mark Richardson (23)
GB and England Senior
International, 400m

Days per year travelled for		Days per year travelled for	
Training in the UK	16	Training in the UK	40
Competition in the UK	29	Competition in the UK	20
Training overseas	14	Training overseas	38
Competition overseas	10	Competition overseas	48
Total	69	Total	146

Illustrative comments on training and competition overseas:

This year I went to Lanzarote for a week at the end of February. I then went to Jamaica for a week in March. I have also been to Portugal, America and Spain to train. (Mark Richardson, 23, GB and England Senior International, 400m)

I went to Portugal for one week, I have been to Gainsville, Florida for two weeks, I was also in France earlier this year for four or five days, to catch up on a bit of pre-season warm weather training. (Lesley Owusu, 17, GB and England Junior International, 200m)

I have been to Portugal for two weeks, I have been to New Zealand for a month, I have been to America for a week and I have been to Spain for a week on numerous occasions. (Paul Hibbert, 30, England Senior International, 400m hurdles)

I've been to Uruguay, Holland, California, Tenerife, Spain, South Africa and most other European countries. (Jackie Agyepong, 26, GB and England Senior International, 100m hurdles)

Source: Jackson and Reeves (1998); Reeves (2000).

The group is, however, atypical on a number of levels. First, while for the vast majority of sports tourists the unique interaction of activity, people and place is central to the sports tourism experience, for elite athletes, the place experience is often unimportant except in the sense that it provides quality facilities, expertise or a warm climate. For most elite athletes, whether supported by commercial sponsors or government funding, their sports participation is essentially their job. As such, elite athletes might be considered as business tourists, for whom travelling expenses are paid, and for whom the destination is chosen by others, be this a venue for a training camp or location of a competition. Consequently, in the majority of cases, travel is incidental to the motivation of elite athletes; it is a necessary part of their participation, but not a central part of the experience. In this respect, elite athletes are almost the exact opposite of the 'tourists interested in sport' group, for whom sport is an incidental part of the sports tourist trip, in that travel is an incidental part of the sports tourist trip. In fact, the research among British track athletes (Jackson and Reeves, 1998; Reeves, 2000) showed that many athletes consider the travel element an inconvenience.

Box 4.2 Potential injury as a barrier to recreational sports tourism participation

Illustrative comments of elite British track athletes on fear of injury:

We go swimming. Quite often we use it as a session. We play a bit of basketball, but I tend not to play too many other sports because your muscles are not used to it and there is a greater chance of sustaining an injury. (Mark Richardson, 23, GB and England Senior International, 400m)

I tend not to play other sports as I'm usually too tired after my athletics training. There is also the risk of injury. I do a bit of swimming, but really when I am away I believe that I'm specifically there to train. I try not to do too many active things so that I can conserve my energy and put it into my training. I cannot risk getting injured. (Angela Davies, 28, GB and England Senior International, 1500m)

A couple of years ago when I was in Lanzarote, I went in early December so you are not too close to competition time. So that time I got involved in surfing, cycling and played tennis. When I went in March time just before competition, I would not do anything for fear of injury. I did swim recreationally, but nothing dangerous. (Sonya Bowyer, 23, GB and England Intermediate International, 100m)

I do fancy skiing holidays, but the risk of injuries is so high that I would be worried about breaking a leg and missing a season. (Spencer Newport, 29, England Senior International, 3000m steeplechase)

Source: Jackson and Reeves (1998); Reeves (2000).

While most other sports tourists will show some 'tourist-type' behaviours in terms of shopping, sightseeing, eating out, etc., in many cases elite athletes do not exhibit such behaviours. Time not spent training or competing is spent resting for the next training session or event. Some sightseeing may take place, but as dietary considerations are often essential, eating out is not possible. Furthermore, recreational participation in other sports, while often welcome as a diversion from training, can be problematic due to the fear of injury (see Box 4.2).

Clearly the motivation for this group is advancement and achievement in elite sport, and as such the 'status and prestige' motivations discussed in Chapter 3 will be the primary motivators, with the place element of the sports tourism experience being less important. However, there may be exceptions to this. In some team sports, such as rugby and football, the social element of the trip may be more important. Interpersonal motivations, such as being part of a team of people who are the best in their country at their sport, may be an important part of the experience. Similarly, both anecdotal (e.g. Times, 2003) and academic (e.g., Bale, 2003) sources have described how some places can be an inspiration to top-quality performances in sport, heightening the experience of 'optimal arousal' (Iso-Ahola and Wissingberger, 1990) discussed in Chapter 3. The backdrop of the Barcelona skyline during the diving competition at the 1992 Olympics must surely fall into this category, as would competing at 'sporting Mecca's' such as the Yankee stadium in New York or Lords cricket ground in London. In fact, in the latter case, it has often been said that visiting teams draw more inspiration from this ground than do England, hence England's dismal record at Lords. Although others might argue that England's poor run of results at Lords is simply a function of the poor quality of the team!

Outdoor, adventure and 'alternative' sports tourists

The outdoor, adventure and 'alternative' sports tourists are an interesting group because the nature of many of these sports is such that participants cannot take part in them at home. This is because, as discussed in Chapter 3, they are usually dependent on natural resources that cannot be found in the home area. Thus, in a similar way to the elite athlete described above, travel is a necessary part of their sports participation. However, where these groups differ from the elite athletes is that the place experience is a central part of the sports tourism experience.

Notwithstanding the availability of 'synthetic' or human-made facilities for some of these activities (e.g. indoor climbing walls), the dependence on natural resources means that the interaction of activity and place plays a big part in the experience of this group of sports tourists. Furthermore, facilities such as indoor climbing walls have been shunned by many 'purist' mountaineers as an aberration and not part of the sport as they see it (Morgan, 1998). This group of participants encompasses those taking part in traditional outdoor activity tourism, such as kayaking, sailing, mountaineering, potholing and hiking, and those involved in what have become termed 'alternative' sports. Participants in such alternative sports are usually characterized by a 'counter-cultural', post-American model lifestyle, where a structured competitive approach to sport is shunned in favour of a more aesthetic experiential approach (Donnelly, 1993; Lentell, 1997). Sports generally recognized as falling under this 'alternative' label would include surfing, windsurfing, snowboarding and skateboarding which, with the exception of the latter, all require specific natural resources, access to which will usually involve travel.

A defining characteristic of this group, therefore, and one which differentiates them from many other sports tourists, is that they do not take part in the sports activity at home. Consequently, some favourite destinations may become perceived as their 'home' places, even though they may be many miles from where they live and work. Such 'home' places may be a beach, a particular river or lake, or a favourite activity centre. Quantitative evidence from Reeves (2000) study of activity tourism participants at Twy-Y-Felin in Wales suggests that a significant minority see the area as a 'home' place, with 30 per cent of visitors having visited previously within the last six months, and a further 15 per cent within the last month. Furthermore, 44 per cent stated their intention to 'definitely return' to the centre.

As a result of the lack of opportunities at home, these sports tourists are often very regular participants who will take any opportunity to get away to pursue their chosen activity. Again, quantitative evidence from the study at Twr-Y-Felin (Reeves, 2000) suggests that this is the case, with a very significant 85 per cent of visitors on the centre's mailing list indicating that they take these types of activity holidays between monthly and four times per year. For many (although having a favourite 'home' place) the collection of places referred to in Chapter 3 (Urry, 2002) can be an important characteristic of their behaviour, and in some cases potential or planned visits to 'mythical' places – such as Oahu's North Shore in Hawaii for surfers – can become a defining moment in the 'careers' of such sports tourists. This relates to the status and prestige motivators described in Chapter 3, with the addition of a diverse range of sports tourism places being a significant element of status within some sports tourists groups, particularly 'alternative' groups given their subcultural flavour.

There is increasing literature surrounding surfing, windsurfing and snowboarding discussing the subcultural nature of these activities. Furthermore, there is some evidence that suggests that many participants take part in more than one of these activities (National Ski Areas Association, 2000, quoted in Hudson, 2003b), perhaps because the subcultural flavour is similar. These activities have been variously characterized as encompassing a 'culture of commitment' (Wheaton, 1998), a 'subculture' (Butts, 2001; Wheaton, 2000), a 'distinct cultural community' (Johnson and Edwards, 1994), and a 'fraternity' (Weed, 2000) or 'scene' (Farmer, 1992). Within such subcultures the place experience is clearly valued, with many surfers describing the 'serenity of the ocean' and the importance of the condition of the ocean and the environment (Butts, 2001). However, the very nature of subcultures as providing the 'structure of an alternative value system' (Longhurst, 1995) which is constructed by members of the subculture, means that clearly interpersonal motivators are important, and the interaction of not only the activity and the place, but also the people is important. As such, what might be termed 'alternative' sports tourists perhaps most obviously exemplify the nature of the sports tourism experience as being derived from the unique interaction of activity, people and place.

59

However, it is not just 'alternative' activities that can lay claim to the subcultural label. While some authors have argued that the term subculture relates to a group with norms and values that are in opposition to the 'dominant' culture (see discussions in Crosset and Beal, 1997), others have argued that subcultures do not have to be in opposition to dominant culture; they are simply characterized by their own, unique value system and norms of expected behaviour (Albert, 1991; Donnelly, 1993). As such, many groups of sports participants might be considered as subcultures. Mountaineers have certainly been described in this way by Johnson and Edwards (1994), while Beedie's (2003) discussion of a range of adventure sports tourists can be viewed through a subcultural lens. This view is perhaps further strengthened by studies that have examined 'career trajectories' among such sports tourists (e.g. Bartram, 2001). Drawing on Stebbin's (1992) work on serious leisure, it is possible to examine the ways in which participants in such activities develop and become accepted into the wider 'fraternity' of participants as their knowledge, experience and ability increases. Consequently, in a similar manner to 'alternative' sports tourists, the experience of outdoor adventure sports tourists is also derived from the interaction of activity, people and place.

A final note is required on the pursuit of some activities, climbing perhaps being an obvious example, in a solitary environment. In this case, the solitary nature of the activity, in relation to the often imposing nature of the place can be important. However, even in such a solitary environment, participants symbolically demonstrate their membership of a subculture – both to themselves and to others – by their adherence to the norms and values of that subculture in the way the activity is carried out (Williams and Donnelly, 1985). Consequently, and particularly in relation to the participant's 'identity' as a particular type of sports tourist, the symbolic presence of the subculture through adherence to its norms and values, means that people are still an important part of the sports tourism interaction, even when participation takes place alone.

Athletics spectators

With the exception of studies of their economic contribution (e.g. Gratton, Dobson and Shibli, 2000; Shibli and Gratton, 2001), research on sports spectators has largely focused on deviant behaviour (see next section). While there has been some work conducted on various elements of spectator behaviour and identity by Daniel Wann and his colleagues in the USA (see Wann et al., 2001), it is generally fair to say there is little known about the behaviour patterns and motivations of non-violent sports spectators. This is particularly the case when such spectatorship is not related to some specific long-term commitment to a particular team (such spectators are discussed in the next section). Consequently, the discussions in this section draw largely on two studies of athletics spectators in the UK in the 1990s (Reeves, 2000; Train, 1994). While this might appear to result in a limited and somewhat specific discussion, the issues raised are likely to be illustrative of behaviours of similar types of spectators in other contexts.

The studies in question were of the Europa Cup athletics event, held in Birmingham in 1994, and the Athletics World Cup, held at Crystal Palace,

London, in 1994. The results from these two surveys were very similar, and as such the studies verify and validate each other. The attendance profile of the vast majority of spectators did not include an overnight stay (see Figure 4.1), and as such most were only attending one day of the two-day event. Nevertheless, in all but the smallest minority of cases, sport was the prime purpose of the trip (see Figure 4.2).

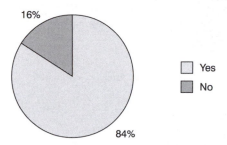

Figure 4.1 Did your visit to the Athletics World Cup involve an overnight stay?

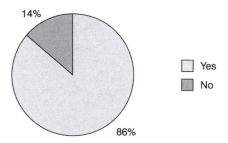

Figure 4.2 Was the Athletics World Cup the main reason for visiting London?

The largest number of spectators were attending with family members, while a significant number attended with friendship groups (see Figure 4.3), and the vast majority were not regular attenders at sports events (see Figure 4.4). A significant minority (25 per cent) were regular athletics participants themselves, while a further minority (19 per cent) had attended because a family member had wanted to come. For many of the spectators, the novel experience was an important motivation for attending, as they had not travelled to spectate at an athletics event before. This is illustrated by the 60 per cent of respondents who stated that they were spectating in London for the first time.

What observations, then, can be made about the features of these athletics spectators that might be generalizable to similar types of spectators in other contexts? First, there was a significant group, mostly families with children, that attended because the event provided a unique day out. It is likely that this type of spectator will be common at many large 'one-off' events, such as the Olympic, Pan-American and Commonwealth Games, but also at smaller scale events such as those described here. Furthermore, such 'curiosity' spectators are also a feature at many league matches in sports such as ice hockey and baseball (subject, of course, to the availability of tickets). Similarly, there was

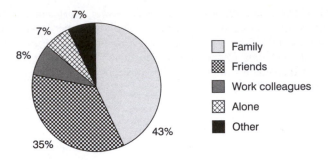

Figure 4.3 With whom did you travel to the Athletics World Cup?

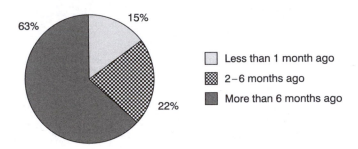

Figure 4.4 Prior to your visit to the Athletics World Cup, when did you last watch an athletics event?

a significant minority for whom interest in the event was derived from their own participation, and it is likely that 'championship' events in a whole range of less popular sports will attract this type of spectator. Finally, the type of spectator that has attended because a family member wanted to attend is likely to feature in crowds for the vast majority of sports events.

It would appear, however, that it is possible to build a profile of a particular type of 'irregular' sports spectator, for whom sports spectating is the prime trip purpose, who attends with family members or friends, for whom the experience is a relatively unique one, who does not stay overnight and who may or may not be a participant in the sport him or herself. In all but the smallest minority of cases, such irregular attendance is unlikely to be converted into a long-term career as a sports spectator.

Committed football and cricket fans

As mentioned in the previous section, much of the work on football fans has focused on violent or deviant fans (Armstrong, 1998; Dunning, Murphy and Williams 1988; Kerr, 1994), with one study focusing specifically on the way in which football hooligans might be conceptualized as undesirable sports tourists (Weed, 2002b). However, there has been some work that has examined the behaviours of non-violent fans (e.g. Giulianotti, 2002; Jones, 2000). Taken together, what these studies highlight as a common element among both violent and non-violent fans is the level of commitment that exists among those who regularly travel to watch 'their' team play and, as such, violence aside, many of their behaviours and motivations are remarkably similar. The same might be said of the 'Barmy Army' group of England cricket fans who spend vast amounts of time and money travelling the globe to watch what has been in recent years a less than successful team. While there have been those among cricket's 'traditional' support who do not approve of their vocal 'carnivalesque' behaviour (Weed, 2002a), what is not in doubt is their commitment to following the team, and consequently it would seem reasonable to consider them alongside committed football fans.

It could be argued that these fans should be considered 'associated experience' sports tourists, because a significant motivating factor for these fans on trips to support their team away from home is the 'whole package' involving the trip itself, associated social activities and, in some cases, the stay away from home. However, where these fans differ from 'associated experience' sports tourists is that their interest in the sport and their team is deep-rooted and genuine. The sport is the central event around which the rest of the experience is organized, rather than simply providing a convenient 'excuse' for socializing.

For many committed football and cricket fans, an identity as a sports fan is a central element in their lifestyle. Like the outdoor, adventure and alternative sports tourists discussed above, there is a distinct subculture that surrounds their sports spectating, and this has been noted by Marsh, Rosser and Harre (1978), Weed (2001c; 2002b) and Jones (2000). The desire to be with like minded people, an 'in-group' (Jones, 2000) towards which an elevated positive attitude exists, and within which a 'career' as a sports spectator develops (Marsh, Rosser and Harre, 1978; Stebbins, 1992), provides a powerful mix of 'interpersonal' and 'status and prestige' (related to spectator 'career development') motives for this type of sports spectating. Furthermore, the importance for these fans of the wider experience associated with travelling sports spectating means that the place experience is a broad one, with memories of particular matches being related not only to the experience of the stadium, but also of the place in which the fans stayed and socialized (cf. Bale, 2003; King, 1996). Consequently, the interaction of activity, people and place is seen, once again, as contributing significantly to the sports tourism experience.

Not surprisingly, the profile of these sports fans is largely male, although cricket fans are less exclusively so, with travelling companions being friendship rather than family groups. The subcultural nature of the groups means that newcomers need to demonstrate their commitment before being fully accepted (hence the concept of 'career development'), although the cricket fans studied (Weed, 2002a) appeared to be generally more welcoming and inclusive of newcomers than the football groups, as the following extract from the Barmy Army website illustrates:

> The Barmy Army is a style of support started by a large group of
> dedicated cricket fans that follow England's team around the world
> giving highly vocal and visual support. Its core aim is 'To make watching
> cricket more fun and much more popular'. It is free to join because

there isn't any membership scheme, the groups that you see on television evolve spontaneously because what we are is a style of support and the group will be made up of whoever wants to join in with the fun on the day. (Barmy Army website, quoted in Weed, 2002a)

While trips are often made on a budget, and thus accommodation is usually in cheap hotels or youth hostels, the sheer volume or length of trips taken means that over the course of a year spend per person is relatively high. Due to the commitment levels required to retain a 'status' position in the subculture, many people will eventually move on from the type of committed participation profile described here. This may be due to growing family or work commitments, lack of time and money, or simply moving on through the life course. It is unlikely that sports spectating participation will cease, but the nature of the participation as an all-consuming, committed, subcultural experience will change. This 'post-career' stage is likely to involve fewer away trips, or may involve family groups with children being taken to matches. In such cases, the broader social experience of the trips will obviously change.

Golf and skiing tourists

As described elsewhere in this book, golf and ski tourists, despite the very different nature of the activities, are very similar in many ways in terms of their behaviours and motivations. Some golf and ski tourists, for whom the 'nineteenth hole' and the 'après-ski' experience may be more important than the sport itself, will fall into the 'associated experience' sports tourist category, and as such are discussed in a later section. However, if the market for school skiing trips is left to one side, many adult golf and ski tourists exhibit very similar characteristics.

Two types of golf/ski tourist can be identified: those who are experienced participants and those who are using the trip to learn to ski or play golf (see Hudson, 2003b, and Readman, 2003, respectively). For both types of participant, an important reason for the trip is the need for the resources to take part. This may simply be the physical resource, but may also include the 'expertise' resource of an instructor. As discussed in Chapter 3, for many sports tourists resource quality is an important issue. For golf and ski tourists resources to participate in these activities may exist in the home area, perhaps a dry-ski slope or a municipal golf course or driving range, but the desire for a higher quality resource, along with associated facilities in terms of relatively luxurious accommodation (Weed, 2001a), is a central motivator for these sports tourists. As ever, the company of like-minded people is a further enhancement to the experience, highlighting again the importance of the interaction of activity, people and place.

The concept of 'novelty' is likely to play a significant part in the consideration of golf and ski tourists (Petrick, 2002). For some participants on their first golf or ski trip, the novelty of a different type of vacation is likely to have been a significant element in the trip decision-making process. For other, more experienced, participants the novelty of taking part in a new destination, of 'collecting places' (Urry, 2002), may be an important motivating factor. In the latter case, golf or skiing is likely to be a defining part of the participants' lifestyle, while for the former it is simply a novelty trip. However, many new participants take golf or ski instruction on holiday with a view to developing a longer-term interest (Mintel, 2002b). For golf, the reason for developing such an interest may be linked to work interest, given the acknowledged links between golf and business trips. Generally, the profile for golf tourists is less likely to involve family groups than is skiing, although in both cases, given the often luxurious nature of the attendant accommodation and facilities, spend per trip is usually high (Weed, 2001a; Mintel, 2002b; 2003a). Such attendant facilities often include the opportunity to try other activities and, notwithstanding a primary interest in skiing or golf, such trips often include incidental participation in other sports.

Mass-participation events

The range of events considered here might vary from some major events, such as the New York Marathon, which may be the highlight of the sporting year for some participants, to more regularized events, such as local 10-kilometre races or half-marathons, that stimulate relatively brief day-trip tourism. In fact, it might be argued that many of the latter events should not be considered sports tourism at all. However, as for the purposes of this book a definition of tourism is being used that relates to travel for activities that are 'out of the ordinary' and that are perceived to fall outside the rhythm of everyday life, it is reasonable to consider such smaller events that are likely to involve other family members, either as spectators or as participants, as being, in the majority of cases, sports tourism trips.

Research in Malta (Bull and Weed, 1999) revealed that some mass-participation events, such as the Malta Marathon and some Masters swimming events, were attracting participants who were extending their stay for a week or more after the event for a family holiday. Thus, a pattern of sports tourism exists among some participants that comprises a specific sports tourism event as part of a more traditional family holiday. In such cases the event has been the deciding factor in choosing the holiday destination, but after the event sports tourism is not a significant element of the trip. This is a rather specific but very interesting pattern of participation about which very little is known.

In many cases, mass-participation events involve trips with family groups, who often attend as spectators supporting their partners, parents or, in some cases, children. With the exception of the types of trips described in the previous paragraph, this type of sports tourism tends to be a day trip or to involve only one overnight stay. While spend per person may be fairly low, the size of some events – the London Marathon accepted 45 500 entrants in 2002 (London Marathon Ltd, 2003) – means that the cumulative economic impact of this type of sports tourist can be significant.

For many of these participants, sport may be a significant part of their lifestyle – considerable time is known to be spent by non-elite athletes training for and competing in such events (Smith, 1998). However, sports tourism may not be perceived to be equally as important. Such participants are interested in the activity, and the interaction with other participants but, with the exception of major events such as the big city marathons, the place may not be so important.

65

The concept of subculture is important in relation to this group. However, in many cases the interaction with the subculture is likely to be through conspicuous consumption of the symbols associated with it, such as magazines and a particular type of dress (Smith, 1998). At events interaction with other participants is on the level of 'familiar strangers' (Nixon, 1986, detailed in Nixon and Frey, 1995), where people may know who others are and may have raced against and spoke to them many times, but will know very little else about any other aspect of their lives. There are, however, some patterns of participation that involve a different type of subcultural interaction. Here, the stay away from home is longer than the short day trip or overnight stay, often being around four or five nights, with the event either being a tournament or gala spread over a number of days (Dobson, Gratton and Holliday, 1997), or a one-day event with a programme of associated activities over a number of days. The participation pattern in such cases is often with friendship groups, with the event being seen as an opportunity to meet up with old friends to 'celebrate' their involvement in the subculture. Green and Chalip (1998) describe a womens flag football tournament in these terms, with other examples being events such as the World and European Masters Swimming Championships, that occur in alternate years, and provide an annual opportunity (for Europeans at least) to meet up with old friends in new and interesting places.

Associated experience sports tourists

The 'associated experience' sports tourist is a somewhat difficult category to delineate. As some of the discussions above have suggested, some types of sports tourist may fall into this category if their primary motivation for participation relates to some aspect of the experience other than the activity itself. Mass-participation sports tourists may be more interested in meeting up with old friends than in participating in the activity, while golf and ski tourists may be more interested in the post-activity experience. Consequently, the 'après' experience associated with golf and skiing trips is discussed in this section, but first perhaps the best example of 'associated experience' sports tourists is discussed – horse-racing spectators.

Horse-racing spectators

Fox's (1999) anthropological study, *The Racing Tribe*, was not limited to spectators, but covered all members of the racing fraternity, including jockeys, trainers, owners and bookmakers. However, it is possible to use her data to comment on the participation profiles of 'race-goers'. Fox identified two distinct groups of horse-racing spectators, which she named 'socials' and 'enthusiasts'. As might be expected, the socials were spectators who knew little about horse racing, and who were in attendance for the associated social experience. However, some of the enthusiasts might also be described as 'associated experience' sports tourists because, although they have some knowledge of and interest in horse racing, other aspects of the experience were more important to them than the horse racing itself. Fox (1999) estimated that 'socials' could comprise between 30 per cent and 70 per cent of the horse-racing crowd, depending on the weather, the day of the week (Sunday being most popular) and the importance in the social calendar of the event. Fox recognized that the structure of the sport lent itself to such 'associated experience' participants. The following, somewhat lengthy, quotation notes this point, and also gives a useful flavour of the social aspect of horse-racing spectating:

> I had to recognize that racing is qualitatively different from any other spectator sport, in that all of the actual sport takes place in just a few minutes of the afternoon, interspersed with half hour periods in which there is no 'action' at all. This promotes a much higher than usual degree of social interaction among spectators. At almost any other spectator event, socializing means missing the action; at the races, social contact is an integral part of the action. This factor is instrumental in transforming an amorphous crowd into a distinctive and complex society. Out of the half-hour gaps between races an entire culture has developed, with its own language, religion, traditions, customs, rituals and etiquette. (Fox, 1999: 13)

Notwithstanding the above, the 'associated experience' horse-racing spectator is by no means a homogeneous group. A number of distinct 'types' were identified (Fox, 1999). For three of these – 'pair-bonders', 'family day-outers' and 'lads' and girls' day-outers' – the races simply provide an unusual day out spent with partners, family or friendship groups. The 'suits' are those occupying the hospitality boxes, and are corporate race-goers who are either trying to forge business relationships, or for whom a trip to the races is part of an incentive package paid for by their company. The final 'social' category are the 'be-seens' who are concerned with conspicuous consumption, and are most in evidence at the 'big occasions' such as Royal Ascot.

The features that link these various groups are their lack of interest in or knowledge about horse racing, their 'interpersonal' or 'status and prestige' motives for attendance (see Chapter 3) and the experience of some level of 'ritual inversion' (Graburn, 1983) in their behaviours when they become part of what Fox (1999: 21) describes as a 'liminal world' segregated from everyday life. Given the range of 'types' outlined in the previous paragraph, it is very difficult to 'profile' these sports tourists in the way that profiles have been presented for other groups. However, their unusual nature, and their almost complete ignorance about the sport that has provided, at least nominally, the reason for their trip, makes them a particularly interesting group to include in these discussions.

Skiing and golf

The discussion of 'primary' skiing and golf tourists above noted the existence of a group for whom the 'après-ski' experience and the 'nineteenth hole' could be more important than the skiing or the golf itself. Little is known about these groups of sports tourists, but it is possible to speculate on the trends in such participation.

Hudson (2000: 164) believes that resorts need to concentrate more on the après-ski experience, noting that the trend is toward skiers spending less and less time on the slopes, the average now being three hours per day. Williams and Dossa (1990) estimated that between 20 per cent and 30 per cent of visitors to ski centres in Canada did not ski at all, with Cockerell (1994) noting that the estimate for non-skiing French ski resort visitors is around 40 per cent. Hudson (2000; 2003b) suggests that there is now a trend towards the development of 'mountain theme parks' rather than ski resorts, offering a whole range of activities, some of which (e.g. swimming, tennis and indoor golf) have no association whatsoever with traditional snowsports. In fact, in Zermatt, one of Switzerland's top ski resorts, where one in eight visitors is a non-skier (Wickers, 1994), visitors can even take language courses. Aspects of conspicuous consumption associated with ski resorts cannot be ignored, and 'social and prestige' motivators will interact with the more obvious 'physical' and 'interpersonal' motivators among many ski resort visitors.

A similar trend is to be found among many golf tourists, aided by the increasing development of golf tourist venues as country-house hotels offering a range of activities associated with sport and health. The 'nineteenth hole' may be a particularly attractive part of the golfing-trip experience for the business traveller who is not too keen on the activity itself, but for whom attendance on such trips makes an important contribution to developing business relationships. Of course, the lifestyle image associated with golfing holidays may be part of the attraction for many 'associated experience' golf tourists. The image of a luxurious country-house hotel, bathed in sunshine, with a view over a picturesque golf course can provide powerful 'status and prestige' motivations for many participants, but also provides an easy way to 'buy into' a particularly desirable lifestyle, even if for only a few days in the year.

Both skiing and golf tourists whose primary trip purpose is the 'associated experience' tend to be high spenders because of the importance of conspicuous consumption. This is described by MacCannell (1996), who believes that 'returning' is an important part of the tourist experience, to the extent that the 'status and prestige' conferred on people as a result of their tourist experiences can be, as described in Chapter 3, a prime motivator for travel in the first place.

Generally, 'associated experience' sports tourists are only nominally attracted to a particular location by sports opportunities. Consequently, although sport appears to provide the prime purpose for the trip, the activity element of the activity, people and place interaction is far less important than the experience provided by the interaction of people and place. The people and place combination is often seen by this type of sports tourist as being associated with a lifestyle image that the participant finds particularly desirable. That this lifestyle image is also dependent on association with a sports activity is, in the majority of cases, purely incidental.

Tourists interested in sport

Tourists interested in sport are the incidental sports tourists for whom sport is not the prime purpose of the tourist trip. However, that is not to say that sport is always irrelevant in the holiday decision-making process. For many tourists interested in sport, particularly families, sports opportunities will be one of the factors considered in choosing a holiday destination. For others sports participation on non-sports holidays may be an entirely spontaneous decision that was not considered in the pre-trip period. The 'tourists interested in sport' category is potentially huge, and might comprise any number of different types of holiday or types of tourists. Consequently, the discussion here is limited to two types of 'tourists interested in sport' that have attracted attention in the literature – first, nostalgia sports tourists and, second, holiday camp and traditional beach tourists.

Nostalgia sports tourists

In two relatively recent reviews of the sports tourism field, Gibson (1998; 2002) identifies three categories of sports tourism (which she refers to as 'sport tourism' – see discussion in the Prologue to this book) derived from the following definition of sports tourism as: 'Leisure-based travel that takes individuals temporarily outside of their home communities to participate in physical activities, to watch physical activities, or to venerate attractions associated with physical activities' (Gibson, 1998: 49).

Thus, the three categories of sports tourism identified are 'active sports tourism', 'event sports tourism' and 'nostalgia sports tourism'. The use of these three categories is in contrast with the approach of many other authors that simply delineate between 'participating' and 'watching' sport. The approach of this text is not to use such polarized categorizations but, particularly in relation to participants, to focus on behaviours. However, Chapter 8, in the providers section, does propose a Model of Sports Tourism Types, derived from Glyptis's (1982) classification, that identifies the features that might characterize different types (see Figure 8.1). The five types identified, which are not necessarily mutually exclusive, are 'sports participation tourism', 'sports training', 'sports events', 'luxury sports tourism' and 'tourism with sports content'. It is suggested here that in the majority of cases nostalgia sports tourism, rather than meriting a category in its own right, will fall within the 'tourism with sports content' type, and thus nostalgia sports tourists are being considered here as 'tourists interested in sport'.

Gammon (2002: 65) describes two journeys that take place during nostalgia sports tourism, 'the journey made to the attraction or event and the imagined journey that takes place once there'. He includes visits to sports museums, such as the Wimbledon Tennis Museum, visits to sports halls of fame, such as the National Baseball Hall of Fame, and participation in 'sports fantasy camps', where sports tourists are coached by former sports heroes or take part in sport in famous venues. The approach to nostalgia sports tourism in this text is that it is one of many motivations for sports tourism participation. The visiting of sports halls of fame or sports venues may, for some, be similar to pilgrimage, and involve a certain amount of wish fulfilment or 'place collecting' (Urry, 2002). However, there are many other types of sports tourists for whom the collection of places is a motivating factor (see above discussions and those in Chapter 3), and to allocate 'nostalgia' a special and elevated place among such motivations does not seem to be a useful way to proceed. As such, the paragraphs that follow will highlight the nature of most nostalgia sports tourists as 'tourists interested in sport', and also comment on those nostalgia sports tourists who may not fall into this category.

With the exception of day-trippers, who are considered below, for the majority of nostalgia sports tourists, sport will not be the prime purpose of their trip. It may be part of their decision-making process, and many sports museums or halls of fame will be 'must-see' attractions for many tourists interested in sport when visiting a particular destination. However, in only the smallest minority of cases will a visit to a sports museum or hall of fame be the prime purpose of a trip involving an overnight stay. Such 'sports tourism pilgrims' (Gammon, 2002) do exist, but are far outnumbered in relation to tourism involving an overnight stay, by those visiting the area for other reasons.

Nostalgia sports tourism day-trippers do, of course, exhibit a different participation profile, and for many of these a visit to a sports hall of fame or museum will be the prime purpose of their trip. Such sports tourists might be considered alongside other prime purpose sports tourists described above and might be seen to exhibit similar types of behaviours and participation profiles as the type of 'irregular' sports spectator described in the section on athletics supporters. This would not, however, apply to participants in 'sports fantasy camps', who either gain instruction from a high-profile former player, or play in a famous venue. These sports tourists would fall within the sports participation tourism category of the model described in Chapter 8 and, depending on the cost and attendant facilities and accommodation, may exhibit similar characteristics to either prime purpose or associated experience golf tourists.

Nostalgia sports tourists are difficult to profile because little is known about them (Gibson, 2002). However, it does seem safe to surmise that many will fall into the 'tourists interested in sport' category, will often attend with family groups, particularly children, and are likely to spend significantly on merchandising and souvenirs. Although no specific data is available, it would seem unlikely that nostalgia motives will generate a 'regular' pattern of sports tourism, with participation more likely to be irregular and in many cases opportunistic. This profile is likely to differ in terms of participants in 'fantasy camps', about which very little is known.

Holiday camp and traditional beach tourists

The final sports tourist profile to be examined in this chapter is that with which the majority of people are probably most familiar – sports participation on traditional beach or holiday camp holidays. The holiday camp is perhaps a peculiarly British phenomenon, but it is useful to consider it alongside traditional 'mass' beach tourism for two reasons. First, the holiday camp concept evolved from demand for traditional British seaside tourism, with the original camps being situated in popular resorts such as Skegness and Bognor Regis. Second, for a time, the 'mass' tourism market among the working classes in Britain was the market for holiday camps, which provided accommodation, meals, entertainment and activities for an all-inclusive price. As such, there are many similarities between mass beach tourism and the British holiday camp market.

The participant profiles for these holidays tend to be either families with children, or young friendship groups. In both cases, the provision of sports facilities has become an important feature. For many of these incidental participants, the availability of sports opportunities, particularly water sports on beach holidays and activities for children on holiday camp tourism, can be an important factor in destination choice. Reeves's (2000) study of sport at Butlins (a British holiday camp) illustrates this, with 73 per cent of respondents being on holiday with their children. Many respondents were repeat visitors (85 per cent had been to Butlins in the previous three years), and for 69 per cent the availability of sports opportunities and facilities had played a part to some extent in the choice of Butlins as their holiday destination, with some specific comments including:

> When we were thinking about a holiday this year, we knew that Butlins holiday camps had loads of sports, particularly for the kids, so we actually spent most of our time discussing which camp to come to.

> We weren't really bothered about the sports and recreation facilities for ourselves, but we have two young children and they get bored very easily, so this was an easy choice to keep them out of trouble and in one place.

> To be frank the wife booked it and the kids were really happy about it. They looked at the brochures and were excited about the swimming pool and the go-karting.

However, a further feature of the participation profiles of these 'tourists interested in sport' is that take up tends to be much lower than intention. Tokarski (1993), in a relatively dated study of sports participation on beach holidays in Corfu, compared the sports participation of British and German tourists and discovered that, excluding walking and swimming, only 30 per cent of Britons and 20 per cent of Germans took part in any sport at all on such holidays. More recent evidence from the UK (Keynote, 2001) suggests that sports facilities (particularly those in hotels), while playing an important role in the marketing mix, are actually used by surprisingly few guests. The Butlins studies (McKoy, 1991; Reeves, 2000) further substantiate these findings, with the comments of tourists including:

> I must admit, I had all these great ideas of taking advantage of the facilities both indoors and outdoors, and in ten days all I've managed is a couple of games of snooker with a guy I met on the first day.

> It all looked great in the brochure, and . . . [the sport] . . . was one of the reasons we chose Butlins, but I've got to admit I've found it hard to motivate myself to actually do anything, particularly after a night in the bar.

The simple fact in relation to this type of incidental sports participation by tourists is that there are often many other, more immediately attractive, activities that tourists would prefer to take part in. In fact, for some, participation in sport on holiday is something that is to be avoided, although participation does sometimes take place to please partners or other family members, as noted by some tourists in the Butlins studies (McKoy, 1991; Reeves, 2000):

> I do more than I probably realize, to be honest I prefer to relax. But I'm always having to play with the kids or I'm in the pool with them, but none of that is my own time and not really organized. It just happens when you have to look after the young ones.

> Having the sports going on adds to the atmosphere of the place, but it's not really my idea of what to do on holiday, although my wife has got me playing badminton a couple of times.

Due to the incidental nature of participation in sport on these types of tourist trip, spending is relatively low, with some participation opportunities, particularly those in holiday camps, being included in the price of the holiday. There has been some suggestion that this type of participation could be used as a way to introduce people to sports participation that might be continued upon returning home. However, while this seems a perfectly reasonable proposition, the evidence to support it is sketchy (see Weed, 2001b, for an overview) and there have been few, if any, studies dedicated to investigating the potential of sports tourism to contribute to sports development in this way.

Conclusion

The discussions in this chapter have served to provide specific illustrations, largely based on empirical research, of the nature of sports tourists' motivations and experiences of activities, people and places discussed in Chapter 3. The three groups of sports tourists – 'prime purpose', 'associated experience' and 'tourists interested in sport' – vary in the extent to which sport is important in the sports tourism experience, and thus in the importance of the interaction of activity, people and place. The examples of sports tourists discussed under each of these headings illustrate the wide range of sports tourism behaviours within the broader group, and serve to further highlight the heterogeneous nature of both the sports tourist and the sports tourism phenomenon. Given this heterogeneity it is all but impossible to establish a workable definition or profile of the sports tourist that is of any use in anything but a technical sense. However, following the preceding discussions, it becomes apparent that there are similarities in motivations and behaviours between sports tourists involved in a range of different activities that might lend themselves to the construction of a 'typology' of sports tourist types. Such a typology – a Sports Tourism Participation Model – is developed in the next chapter.

5

A typology of sports
tourists

Chapter 3, the first chapter in this participants
section, opened with a discussion of possible
definitions of sport, of tourism and of sports
tourism, and found the establishment of such
definitions to be problematic. This is because, as
Houlihan (1994: 4) states: 'the more one attempts
to capture the essence of meaning of a human
activity, the more one becomes aware of the
ambiguities and the compromises necessary to
arrive at a plausible definition'.

Furthermore, as demonstrated by Chapter 4,
both sports tourism and the sports tourist are
heterogeneous concepts and therefore no single
definition is adequate. Consequently, much of the
discussion in Chapter 3 focused on conceptualizing the sports tourist, attempting to go beyond a
simple definition and moving towards a deeper
understanding of the nature and motivations of
the sports tourist, which was subsequently
evidenced by the profiles discussed in Chapter 4.

The previous two chapters have demonstrated
that, although sports tourists are a heterogeneous
group, there may be similarities in motivations
and behaviour profiles that allow a number of
sports tourist 'types' to be conceived, and consequently allow a typology to be constructed. This
chapter presents such a typology, derived from the
discussions in the previous two chapters and, in
particular, from the empirical studies that shaped
the discussions in Chapter 4. The typology – a

'Sports Tourism Participation Mode' – is a dynamic model that is not only useful in developing an understanding of the behaviours of sports tourists, but also of how impacts are generated and how providers might operate to develop a successful sports tourism product.

Previous typologies of sports tourism

There have been a number of attempts at developing a typology of sports tourism or of sports tourists. Perhaps the first attempt was that proposed by Glyptis (1982) following her investigation of the relationship between sport and tourism in five European countries. She suggested five 'demand types', namely, sports training, 'up-market' sports holidays, activity holidays, sports opportunities on general holidays and sports spectating. While these categories were proposed as demand types, they essentially amount to a supply-side categorization of sports holidays. However, the Glyptis categorization has been taken up by a number of other authors with, for example, Weed and Bull (1997a) using it to demarcate sports holidays within their Policy Area Matrix for Sport and Tourism. Two key concepts that Glyptis's early work highlights are that sports tourism may be either active or passive (i.e. include involvement in activities themselves or as a spectator), and that sports may be the primary purpose of the trip or be 'incidental' to holidays that have other prime purposes.

The active/passive distinction is one that has been used subsequently by other authors. Hall (1992a), for example, in his conceptual framework for adventure, health and sports tourism, plots the level of activity against the level of competitiveness to derive a nine-category matrix (see Figure 5.1). The use of competitiveness as a dimension is a useful one, and Hall's model is helpful in that it illustrates the range of activities from those in the top left-hand corner that are

	Less active ———————————————— More active		
Non-competitive	**Health tourism** (e.g. spa tourism, health travel)	**Health tourism** (e.g. fitness retreats)	**Health tourism** (e.g. whitewater rafting, SCUBA diving, hiking)
	Adventure travel (e.g. yacht chartering)	**Tourism activities** ... which contain elements of health, sport and adventure (e.g. cycling, sea-kayaking)	**Adventure travel** (e.g. climbing)
Competitive	**Sport tourism** (e.g. spectating)	**Sport tourism** (e.g. lawn bowls)	**Sport tourism** (e.g. ocean racing)

Figure 5.1 Hall's (1992a) Model of Adventure, Health and Sports Tourism

recreationally based, to those in the bottom right-hand corner that fall clearly into the competitive sport category.

In plotting out 'forms' of sports tourism, Stendeven and De Knop (1999) also use the active/passive distinction, alongside a number of other subdivisions. 'Tourism relevant to sport' is split into holiday and non-holiday trips, each of which is subdivided into active and passive trips before further subdivisions are made (see Figure 5.2). A useful concept introduced in this categorization is the distinction made under passive sport between the casual observer and the connoisseur. While in some senses this may be analogous to the primary/incidental distinction made by Glyptis (1982), it also implies that the level of importance attached to the sports tourism trip is a key factor. This is a slightly different distinction, therefore, to the trip purpose division proposed by Glyptis, and while it is not accorded any great significance within this categorization, it is something that has not been raised in other models. Strangely, however, Standeven and De Knop do not make a similar distinction for active sports tourism.

			Passive sport		
		Non-holiday			
			Active sport		
TOURISM	Relevant to sport		Passive sport	Casual observer	
				Connoisseur	
		Holiday			
			Active sport	Holiday sport activities	Organized
					Independent
				Sport activity holiday	Multi-sport
					Single sport

Figure 5.2 Standeven and De Knop's (1999) 'forms of sports tourism'

Later in their book, Standeven and De Knop (1999) propose a 'conceptual classification of sport tourism' which they describe as a 'theoretical framework to support the concept of sport tourism as a cultural experience on two dimensions: sport and tourism' (ibid.: 49). In this model, the sport experience (based on Haywood's, 1994, classification of sport as environmental or interpersonal challenge) is plotted against the touristic experience (based on Burton's, 1995, description of tourism environments as natural or manmade). While this may seem a useful conflagration of two established models, the further subdivisions made make the model overcomplicated. Furthermore, plotting sport against tourism results in a model, like those already described above, that is activity based. While this may be useful in illustrating the range of sports tourism types, it is of little use in analysing or examining the sports tourist or, in fact, the sports tourism phenomenon. In fact, it provides little information beyond that which would be provided by an extensive list of sports tourism activities.

Developing a Sports Tourism Participation Model

In developing a model that might be used as an analytical tool, both to appreciate the complex nature of the sports tourist, and to develop a greater understanding of the sport tourism phenomenon, a focus is required, as has been the case in the previous two chapters, on the sports tourist him or herself. Previous work at Loughborough University, some of which has been described in the previous two chapters, has contributed to the development of a 'Sports Tourism Demand Continuum', early versions of which were described by Reeves (2000) and Collins and Jackson (2001), before it was presented in its final iteration by Jackson and Weed (2003). As well as focusing on the nature of the sports tourist, rather than sports tourism activities, this model is derived from empirical research. The model takes its basic concept from the English Sports Council's 'Sports Development Continuum' that plots the movement of sports participants from the introductory Foundation level, through Participation and Performance, to the elite Excellence level. The Sports Tourism Demand Continuum, similarly, begins with Incidental sports participation on general holidays and moves through various levels of commitment – Sporadic, Occasional, Regular and Committed – ending with the Driven sports tourist involved in year-round travel for elite competition and training (see Figure 5.3).

This model, however, while undoubtedly the strongest and most useful yet proposed, still has a number of implicit weaknesses. First, there is an implication that in moving along the continuum from Incidental to Driven participation there is an increase in sports ability. This is particularly highlighted by the conceptualization of the Driven group profile as 'elite groups or individuals'. This also calls into question the applicability of the model to 'passive' sports tourists or spectators. In every other sense it appears that the continuum would apply to spectators, but the implication that levels of ability increase with movement along the continuum is difficult to reconcile with the concept of sports spectating. How would one's ability as a sports spectator be defined? The dual concept of sports tourists as both active participants and passive spectators has been one that authors have struggled with in developing models of sports tourism, as there are often significant differences in behaviour patterns and motivations between active and passive sports tourists. In fact, this might be said of sports tourism as a whole because the range of activities often included as sports tourism makes it a heterogeneous rather than a homogeneous phenomenon. This heterogeneity is what makes activity-based models problematic, as it becomes increasingly difficult to include the full range of issues within a model that is simple enough to be useful.

Perhaps the most significant weakness in the Sports Tourism Demand Continuum is the assumption that for participants towards the Incidental end of the scale, sport is insignificant and, consequently, sports tourism is unimportant. While this may be the case for a significant number of people towards this end of the continuum, it fails to recognize the importance of sports tourism trips to individuals' perceived self-identity, the result being that, even where levels of participation are low, the importance placed on that participation can be significant. In seeking to address this weakness, this chapter is proposing a 'Sports Tourism Participation Model' which uses the Sports Tourism Demand Continuum within a model that plots sports tourism participation against the importance placed on sports tourism activities and trips (see Figure 5.4).

Summary characteristics	Incidental →	Sporadic →	Occasional →	Regular →	Committed →	Driven →
Decision making factors	Impromptu	Unimportant	Can be determining factor	Important	Very important	Essential
Participation factors	Fun or duty to others	If convenient	Welcome addition to tourism experience	Significant part of experience	Central to experience	Often sole reason for travel
Non-participation factors	Prefer relaxation non-activity	Easily constrained or put off. Not essential to life profile	Many commitment preferences	Money or time constraints	Only unforeseen or significant constraints	Injury, illness or fear of illness
Typical group profile	Family groups	Family and friendship groups	Often friendship or business groups	Group or individuals	Invariably groups of like-minded people	Elite groups or individuals with support
Lifestyle	Sport is insignificant	Sport is non-essential. Like but not a priority	Sport is not essential but significant	Sport is important	Sport is a defining part of life	Sport is professionally significant
Sports expenditure	Minimal	Minimal except sporadic	High on occasions	Considerable	Extremely high and consistent	Extremely significant. Funding

Figure 5.3 Sports Tourism Demand Continuum

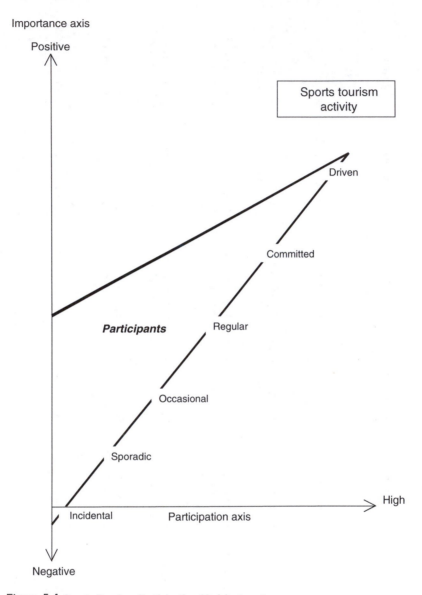

Figure 5.4 Sports Tourism Participation Model: stage 1

Figure 5.4 illustrates the first stage towards developing a Sports Tourism Participation Model. Levels of participation increase along the horizontal axis, and it is here that the Demand Continuum illustrated earlier is included. However, an important additional dimension is the inclusion of the vertical scale for the amount of importance attached to the sports tourism trip by individuals. The model illustrates that towards the Incidental end of the scale the level of importance attached to a trip may vary from a relatively high level, to little importance, or even negative importance. At the Driven end of the scale, however, both importance and participation are high. This creates a 'triangle' of participation, the size of which corresponds to the number of sports tourists at each particular level. Consequently, the model shows that there is a much greater number of Incidental sports tourists than there is Driven sports tourists. This, however, refers to numbers of participants rather than levels of activity, as those towards the Driven end of the scale will generate a much higher level of activity per participant than those at the Incidental end of the scale.

Reeves (2000), using empirical data from his study of sports participation at Butlins Holiday Worlds in the UK, describes reluctant participation in sport on holiday that accounts for the existence of participants who attach a negative importance to sports tourism. For such people it is actually important *not* to take part in sport on holiday. Such participation is usually a result of a sense of duty to others, particularly family members such as children or partners. Participation takes place although there may be an antipathy towards it. At the other end of the importance axis at the Incidental end of the scale is participation that individuals feel is important to their sense of self or identity even though actual levels of participation may be low. Such participation is important as it affects the identity that participants wish to portray to their peers on return from the sports tourism trip. The importance of 'returning' as a significant part of the tourism experience is described by MacCannell (1996: 4) who explains that 'returning home is an essential part of being a tourist – one goes only to return'. MacCannell believes that tourists are people who leave home in the expectation that they will have some kind of experience of 'otherness' that will set them apart from their peers on their return. Here the experience of otherness is the participation in sport while on holiday, with the importance being attached to the perceived kudos that the telling and retelling of the experience, often based on only sporadic or incidental participation, gives the participant on returning home.

An example of this level of importance may be someone who takes a beach holiday abroad and spends most of the time soaking up the sun on the beach. However, this person may be goaded by his or her family into participating in a thirty-minute water-skiing session. This may be the sum total of this individual's sports participation on this holiday, but the impression that may be conveyed to his or her peers on return, through exaggerated retelling of the experience, would be of a holiday full of water-sports activities – an impression that may accord the individual a certain level of esteem among his or her peers. A perceived identity is constructed that means that the sports tourism element of his or her trip has a relatively high importance despite the very low level of actual participation. Of course, in this example, the level of importance is a result of extrinsic factors – the identity which is portrayed to others. For other participants towards the incidental end of the scale, and perhaps having more significance for the sporadic and occasional groups, sports holiday participation may be important for more intrinsic factors. Holiday sports participation may be an opportunity to take part in lapsed activities for which the time or opportunity for participation does not exist at home. Here significant importance may be attached to such participation because holiday sports participation, no matter how low, may be the only link that such individuals have with past sports participation and, consequently, with a continued conception of themselves as a 'sportsperson'. This is something that may be of major importance to someone who has previously been a very active sports participant, but for whom other responsibilities now restrict participation. In both these examples, the contribution which sports tourism can make to individuals' perceived and self identities, means that sports tourism can be important to individuals for whom actual levels of participation are low.

As levels of participation, and broad levels of importance, increase with a move along the triangle, the quality of the sports tourism experience becomes more important. As Figure 5.3 highlights, once the continuum moves beyond the sporadic participant, sport becomes a significant factor in tourism destination choices. For such participants sport is the prime purpose of the trip, and as such a shift has taken place in the nature of sports tourism from 'sports participation on holidays' to 'sports holidays'. Consequently, the quality of the sports tourism experience becomes an important factor in choosing and planning a sports tourism trip. As discussed in Chapter 3, the nature of the place can contribute considerably to the quality of such experiences. This may be through the standard of facilities available at the destination, but also as a result of the general environment, the place ambience, the scenic attractiveness, and the presence of other like-minded people.

The significance of the unique interaction of activity, people and place would appear to increase with the move along the participation triangle. However, for some at the Driven end of the scale, the place experience may be less important than technical requirements related to the quality of facilities. Such participants are the elite athletes described by Jackson and Reeves (1998) and Reeves (2000). For these participants, factors related to place environment – with the exception of climate which is, of course, important for 'warm-weather training' – are relatively insignificant. This, along with their elite sports ability, sets such participants apart from other sports tourists, and is a further argument for, as suggested earlier, discounting the implication that levels of sports ability increase with a move along the Sports Tourism Demand Continuum. With the exception of the elite athlete, high levels of sports ability and performance are not a prerequisite for even the most committed of sports tourists. Furthermore, participants at this extreme of the scale may be taking part in non-competitive activities such as potholing, in which case the concept of an elite athlete is difficult to apply, or may simply have very high levels of commitment to the sports tourism experience, with all its associated environmental attractions, rather than to the technical requirements of elite sport. It is perhaps useful, therefore, to think of elite athletes as a specific group within the Driven category of participants, rather than as defining that category.

Removing the implication that elite performance is a defining characteristic of the Driven category also assists in making the model applicable to sports spectators. As mentioned above, the idea of an 'elite' sports spectator is difficult to conceptualize. However, it is certainly possible to conceive of spectators in a number of sports for whom both participation and importance are high, and for whom sports spectating is a defining part of their self-identity. An example from this end of the scale might be the 'Barmy Army' group of England cricket fans who, since their emergence in the mid-1990s, have demonstrated a very high level of commitment to following a less than successful

England cricket team around the globe. Football fans are also a good example of the committed sports spectator, and much of the work on football hooliganism (see Carnibella et al., 1996; Dunning, Murphy and Williams, 1988; Weed, 2001c) certainly suggests that many are Driven participants for whom their identity as a hooligan is of central importance. That is not to suggest that football supporting is not important to non-violent football fans – in fact, the level of commitment shown by some fans has been compared to religion (Bale, 2003) – but is merely an indication of the area in which the majority of research on sports fans has been concentrated.

The example of football fans is a useful one with which to continue, to illustrate how the Sports Tourism Participation Model is equally applicable to sports spectators at the Incidental end of the triangle. Here there will be a vast number of people for whom identity as a football fan is of great importance, but for whom participation in live football spectating as a sports tourism experience is minimal. Similarly, there will be those who have spectated at football, but for whom it is not an important part of their identity. In fact, as with participants in active sports tourism, it is likely that, for some, such participation has a negative importance as it has taken place out of a sense of duty to others such as partners or children.

A discussion of sports spectators provides a useful avenue through which to introduce another concept into the model – that of the 'Intender'. Intenders were described in relation to arts audiences by Hill, O'Sullivan and O'Sullivan (1995: 43) as 'those who think the arts are a "good thing" and like the idea of attending, but never seem to get around to it'. Such a concept would also seem to be useful in relation to sports tourism, and perhaps sports spectators provide the most useful illustration. The growth in televised coverage of sport has created a vast number of sports spectators who are highly committed, and for whom watching sport is important, but who rarely travel to a live event. Many such spectators often express a desire to go to a live event, but like Hill, O'Sullivan and O'Sullivan's (1995) arts Intenders, 'never seem to get around to it'. Of course, some Intenders will attend the odd match, and so the boundary with incidental participation is fluid. However, this group is largely made up of those for whom watching sport is important, but for whom attending a live event never becomes more than a whimsical intention.

The Intenders categorization is, of course, equally significant in relation to active sports tourism. In the same research in which he identified holiday sports participation that takes place as a duty to others, Reeves (2000) also describes those who go on holiday with the intention of taking up some of the sports opportunities available, but never actually get round to it. The promotion of the range of sports opportunities available in hotel and resort brochures can create the intention to participate in sport on holiday, but in many cases such intention is not converted into actual participation. Even where such incidental sports opportunities may play a part in resort or hotel choice, and the intention may be described to peers pre-trip (in the same way as low levels of participation may be exaggerated post-trip as discussed earlier) as a way of boosting perceived identity, there is no guarantee that such intention will be converted into actual participation. Thus, while importance may be high, participation is very low or non-existent, and such people never become actual participants. The Intenders group is shown in the full Sports Tourism Participation Model illustrated in Figure 5.5.

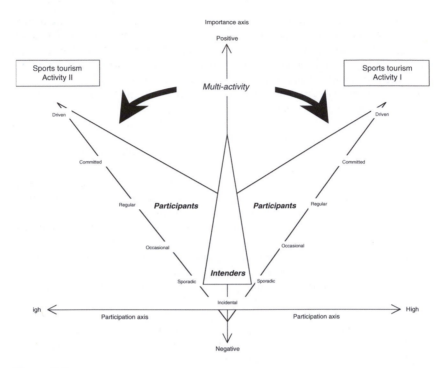

Figure 5.5 Sports Tourism Participation Model

The full model also shows that sports tourism participants are likely to take part in multiple activities, and although Figure 5.5 only illustrates two activities, the model can be envisaged as three dimensional with a potentially infinite number of activities 'growing out' around a central Intenders 'cone' to create a 'bowl' shape. Adding this multi-activity dimension allows for the different characteristics of individual sports tourists to be plotted in relation to their full-participation profile. Take, as an example, the elite athlete within the Driven category of sports tourist. During warm-weather training for their main sport, such athletes are likely, within the constraints of avoiding injury (Jackson and Reeves, 1998), to take part as Incidental or Sporadic participants in other activities for relaxation purposes whereas, in relation to some activities, they may never move beyond the Intender category. Conversely, participants in outdoor activity holidays (such as those described in the Wales case study in Chapter 12), are often Committed participants across a range of activities. The range of activities may, of course, involve active participation or spectating, or a mixture of the two, and many profiles are likely to include some classification within the Intenders group for some activities.

The inclusion of this multi-activity dimension also allows a comparison between the profiles of participants who are genuinely 'multilingual' in relation to sports tourism activities, and those for whom one or two activities dominate with others occurring only in an Incidental manner. Each of these types of participant is likely to have a high participation rate in sports tourism, and is likely to fall towards the Committed/Driven end of the scale, but their behaviours and needs are likely to be very different.

Conclusion: the utility of the model

The 'Sports Tourism Participation Model' described in this chapter allows for the profiling of a range of characteristics of sports tourists and can assist in the analysis of sports tourist behaviour. However, it can also be of practical use to both policy-makers and providers in sports tourism, as it provides a fairly comprehensive illustration of a range of sports tourist types.

Providers, for example, are likely to be interested in the 'Intenders' group, and the extent to which they will be able to develop strategies to convert such intention into participation, thus boosting their customer base. Policy-makers may also be interested in the Intenders group and the development of strategies that might stimulate sports tourism participation that can contribute to healthy lifestyles. At another level, policy-makers might be interested in the development of a 'sports tourism' identity for a particular area as part of a regeneration or diversification strategy. Such development and promotion is likely to be aimed at both Intenders and Incidental and Sporadic participants, but also at the genuinely 'multilingual' sports tourist who may be a committed participant in a range of activities. At the Driven end of the scale, some providers, such as Club La Santa in Lanzarote, have developed a reputation of providing quality facilities for the elite athlete on warm-weather training, but also for Regular, Committed and even Driven sports tourists who want to take part in a sports training holiday at a non-elite level while also sampling some of the other sports on offer.

The conceptualization of sports tourism as being the result of the unique interaction of activity, people and place is a theme that has run throughout these participation chapters. Chapter 3 examined how this interaction might motivate sports tourism behaviour, while Chapter 4 discussed the interaction in relation to a range of sports tourist profiles. In modelling sports tourism participation, this chapter has sought to illustrate how a range of sports tourist types might interact with activities, people and places. In the remainder of the book, and particularly in the study of providers, both the model described here and the underpinning idea of the interaction of activity, people and place, will be important concepts in examining, analysing and understanding the behaviour and strategy of those involved in sports tourism provision.

Part Three: Policy

Preface

The first part of this book, comprising Chapters 1 and 2, which sets the 'context' for the study of sports tourism, established that there are a significant range of mutually beneficial advantages to be gained from a link between the sport and tourism sectors. However, as the two chapters that comprise this policy section will show, agencies responsible for policy for sport and for tourism around the world have shown a distinct reluctance to work together. Consequently, while in an ideal world these chapters would focus on the most effective ways in which sport-tourism policy might be developed to cater for the unique interaction of activity, people and place outlined so far in this book, the focus is necessarily on the paucity of meaningful policy partnerships that cater for the sport-tourism link. As such, the clear links that are made between related issues in other areas of this book are not as prevalent in this section. This is because the discussions here draw on perspectives from policy studies to focus on how the lack of liaison between sport and tourism agencies might be explained and understood, rather than on how sport-tourism policy should be developed in the light of knowledge about the behaviours and motivations of participants and providers.

There are some examples of sports tourism activity by policy-makers around the world, and a number of these are referred to in the following chapters. However, as Weed and Bull's (1997a) review of regional policy in England showed, many policy initiatives related to sports tourism are implemented unilaterally by agencies from the sport or the tourism sector. Consequently, Weed and Bull (1997a: 146) concluded that:

> while there exists an increasing level of sport-tourism activity, this has not been matched by an increase in liaison amongst the agencies responsible for sport and tourism policy . . . It may be that these bodies are generally reticent to collaborate with any agency outside their area of interest . . . as they may feel their interests would be threatened.

While this comment is based on UK research, it does appear that similar situations exist in other countries around the world and, as such, it is the role of the following two chapters to explore the full extent of this reticence and its effect on sport-tourism policy development. Chapter 6 uses the concept of the policy community, and the related ideas of policy universe and policy network, to establish a theoretical framework for the study of sport-tourism policy. This is followed by a consideration of the potential for the future development of collaborative sport-tourism policy in Chapter 7.

6

The policy context

An examination of policy responses to the sport-tourism link suffers from a 'double dearth' in terms of supporting literature. While the previous chapters of this book have provided an overview of sports tourism and analysed in detail the motivations and profiles of sports tourists, in comparison to other areas of study the area of sports tourism, while growing, is not particularly well served by a significant body of literature. Similarly, although leisure studies is now a relatively established field of academic analysis, there is still surprisingly little literature relating to the dynamics of the leisure policy process. With the exception of work such as that by Henry (1993; 2001) on the politics of leisure policy, which focuses more on ideological concerns than the dynamics of the policy process, examples of the limited work in this area are those by Houlihan (1991; 1994; 1997) on sport, and Hall (1994) and Hall and Jenkins (1995) on tourism. Furthermore, while the work of these authors is useful in informing an examination of sport-tourism policy, they do not extend their analysis beyond sport and tourism respectively, nor do they look in any detail at cross-sectoral liaison.

Across the globe there are few examples where agencies responsible for sport and tourism have developed links or worked together. Furthermore, in the very few areas where links have emerged, they have done so in a very piecemeal and ad hoc manner. This is evidenced by perhaps one of the highest profile areas of the sport-tourism link, major events. In many countries the potential of major events to attract visitors to an area is recognized, however, the partnerships that emerge are often short term or uncoordinated and, in some cases, virtually non-existent. In the UK, for example, the national sports agency, UK Sport, has a Major Events Group, which works to attract events to the country. Similarly, the British Tourist Authority has established a Sports Tourism Department to promote sport in Britain to overseas visitors. However, to date, there are very few significant examples of any partnerships between these agencies in this area, and certainly no longer-term strategic collaborations. Yet there are some examples of how such long-term policies for the promotion of sport event based tourism can be developed, one of which is illustrated by the case study of Sheffield in Chapter 11.

Notwithstanding any reluctance among sport and tourism agencies to work together, developing policy to support the diverse nature of sports tourism, evidenced by the discussions of participants in the previous three chapters, is no simple task. The heterogeneous nature of sports tourism, based on the interaction of activity, people and place, makes the task of policy development in this area a complicated one. That the development of such policy takes place against a general backdrop of indifference from many of the policy agencies that might reasonably be expected to be involved only serves to make the task more complicated. A number of factors can be initially identified that contribute to such indifference. In many countries around the world the agencies and structures that exist for developing sport and tourism respectively have been established and have developed entirely separately. This separate development is often compounded by a significantly different 'culture' or 'ethos' in the two sectors. There is often a tradition of public sector support, subsidy and/or intervention in the sports sector (the exception, perhaps, being the USA, where the US Olympic Committee, although granted a role via legislation, receives no public sector funding), while the tourist sector is largely seen as a private sector concern, and agencies are often limited to a marketing or business support role. These factors are further complicated by the different levels at which responsibility for policy development lies. Organizations may exist at national, regional and/or local level, and in countries such as the USA or Australia, which have federal systems of government, the significant role of state governments also needs to be considered. The respective responsibilities of these agencies can mean that in some instances liaison would need to take place not only across sectors, but also between levels. In England, for example, the business support role of the English Tourism Council often means that the Regional Tourist Boards are the more appropriate bodies for the nationally focused Sport England to liaise with. The relative scarcity of such liaison is a testament to the range of problems that exist.

However, before the detail of policy liaison is addressed, a framework within which sport-tourism policy might be analysed is required. This book draws on literature on policy communities, both general and in relation to sport-tourism policy, to provide such an analytical framework. This chapter initially discusses the origin of the policy community concept, before developing a descriptive Model of Cross-Sectoral Policy Development. It then draws on empirical work, largely based in the UK (although also highlighting examples from other countries), to examine how sport and tourism policy communities might be structured before discussing how such structures affect the emergence of sport-tourism policy networks. This analysis provides the context against which the potential for integration of sport and tourism policy is assessed in Chapter 7.

The origins of the policy community concept

The theory of the policy community stems from several different areas of research many of which are longstanding concepts which have, nevertheless, survived considerable academic scrutiny. Organizational sociologists comment on the concern of organizations with the requirements of organizational mainte-nance and enhancement (Wilson, 1973) and their occupancy of 'policy space' (Downs, 1967) which Jordan and Richardson (1987) likened to the concept of 'territory'. Group theorists see public policy as the product of the interaction of clusters of interest groups identified with particular policy areas which reflect the balance of influence at that time, but which also exhibit a degree of stabil-ity over time (Richardson and Jordan, 1979).

Combining these two areas of research, it is possible to view policy-making as taking place inside a sectorized arena where the policy process tends to fragment into relatively autonomous sectors. It is in conceptualizing these sectors that the idea of the policy community has emerged.

The concept of the policy community is a descendant, albeit a distant one, of the general pluralist theory of the state. Political pluralism developed as a rejection of absolute, unified and uncontrolled state power as exemplified by the absolutist monarchies of Western Europe in the eighteenth century (Skinner, 1978). The rationale for institutionalized pluralism – the separation of powers and federalism – was set out during the writing of the American Constitution by James Madison, in Federalist Paper No. 10 (1787). Madison argued that a number of institutional checks and balances were required to prevent the abuse of power. First, that the powers of the executive (the Presi-dent), the legislature (Congress) and the judiciary are vertically separated and, second, that sovereignty is horizontally divided through federalism and the provision of vetoes. In addition, Madison suggests the cultivation of an extended republic of heterogeneous social groups and territorial areas in order that political factions are numerous and diverse. Dahl (1956) argues that social pluralism – non-institutionalized checks and balances on authority such as the extended republic suggested above – is as important as institutionalized plural-ism. It is this idea of social pluralism that contributes to the policy community model.

However, while pluralist ideas provide a context for the development of policy community models, other strands of research, such as the American sub-government literature, have had a more recent and more direct influence. Unlike pluralism, sub-government theory is applicable at the level of the partic-ular policy process rather than the general level. Freeman (1955) is identified by Jordan (1990) as an important figure in the development of the sub-govern-ment literature. He emphasizes the need for the study of policy-making to be disaggregated to subsystems in which bureaucrats, Congressmen and interest groups interact. Freeman (1955: 11) describes such a subsystem as:

the pattern of interactions of participants or actors involved in making decisions in a special area of public policy . . . although there are obviously other types of sub-systems, the type which concerns us here is found in an immediate setting formed by an executive bureau and congressional committees, with special interest groups immediately attached.

Sub-governments are viewed as being concerned in the main with routine areas of policy. However, the sum of these 'routine' policies represents a significant influence on public policy as a whole (Marsh, 1983). Furthermore, sub-governments will attempt to deal with as many items of policy as it is possible to reach agreement on. Failure to reach agreement will result in the drawing together of a wider audience which may impinge on the activities of the sub-government. The deliberations of such a wider audience may result in basic policy realignments that may reduce the power of, or work against the interests of members of the sub-government (Ripley and Franklin, 1980). Therefore, there is a strong incentive for sub-governments to compromise and reach agreements.

Although the influence of the sub-government literature on the concept of the policy community is indisputable, Rhodes (1986) emphasizes that this literature owes a lot to non-American sources, particularly European work on interorganizational theory and work by Heclo and Wildavsky (1974) on decision-making in the British Treasury. Regardless of its origin, the policy community/network literature is related to the American sub-government work in that it focuses on the integration of interest groups into the policy-making process. There are a number of reasons why governments involve interest groups in policy-making, three perhaps being particularly influential. First, most groups have political connections with the media and thus, if they are not involved, have the potential to make 'noise and nuisance' (Jordan and Richardson, 1987). As a result it is better for governments to pre-empt such 'noise and nuisance' through co-option. Second, in some cases governments lack experience in particular policy areas, and it is therefore sensible to draw on the knowledge of interest groups. Finally, it is now accepted that implementation is an important factor in the policy-making process, and thus co-operation at the implementation stage is essential.

Models of the policy community

The most interesting developments in the policy community literature took place when, in the early 1980s, the Economic and Social Research Council in the UK funded two initiatives using the concepts of policy community and policy networks: the intergovernmental relations (IGR) initiative focused on central–local government relations, while the second initiative focused on government–industry relations (GIR). Between them these initiatives generated thirty research projects with a number of important theoretical developments (IGR, see Goldsmith and Rhodes, 1986; GIR, see Wilks, 1989). However, these initiatives developed in distinctive ways, and while the GIR initiative was designed to build on the IGR studies, the GIR study produced a recognizably different model.

The IGR studies used the Rhodes model (Rhodes, 1981) while the GIR studies developed a different model (Wilks and Wright, 1987). One of the major problems in comparing these two models is the different definitions used for the concepts of policy community and policy network, something which is a source of considerable confusion in subsequent literature with a number of authors confusing the models and definitions used.

Rhodes initially uses Benson's (1982: 148) definition of a policy network as a 'cluster or complex of organizations connected to each other by resource dependencies and distinguished from other clusters or complexes by breaks in the structure of resource dependencies'. However, he subsequently elaborates on this, identifying five types of networks along a continuum from highly integrated policy communities to loosely integrated issue networks. The term 'policy network' is used as the generic term encompassing all types (see Figure 6.1).

Type of network	Characteristics of network
Policy community	Stability, highly restricted membership, vertical interdependence, limited horizontal articulation
Professional network	Stability, highly restricted membership, vertical interdependence, limited horizontal articulation, serves interests of profession
Inter-governmental netwoek	Limited membership, limited vertical interdependence, extensive horizontal articulation
Producer network	Fluctuating membership, limited vertical interdependence, serves interests of producer
Issue network	Unstable, large number of members, limited vertical interdependence

Figure 6.1 The Rhodes model

A problem with the Rhodes model, later recognized by Rhodes himself (Rhodes and Marsh, 1992) is that while it is easy to see the policy community and issue network as opposite ends of a continuum, it is difficult to see the other three models as progressive points on that continuum. It was partly in order to address this problem that Marsh and Rhodes (1992) revised and updated the Rhodes model. The updated model continues to conceptualize the policy network as existing on a continuum, with at one end the tightly formed policy community and at the other the loosely structured issue network. However, the new model does not, as previously, include other types through the continuum, but describes five dimensions along which communities may vary, these being membership, interdependence, insulation, resource distribution and members interests. The first four of these will change incrementally along the continuum, while members' interests may be governmental, economic or professional at any point on the continuum (see Figure 6.2).

Both the updated and original versions of the Rhodes model emphasize structural relationships between institutions at the sectoral level. However, it

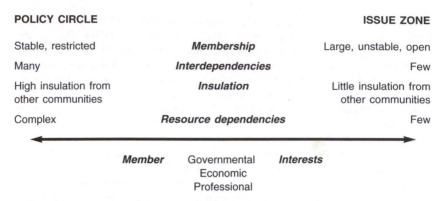

POLICY CIRCLE		ISSUE ZONE
Stable, restricted	*Membership*	Large, unstable, open
Many	*Interdependencies*	Few
High insulation from other communities	*Insulation*	Little insulation from other communities
Complex	*Resource dependencies*	Few

Member   Governmental   *Interests*
Economic
Professional

Figure 6.2 Features of the policy community continuum

might be argued that a significant shortfall of these models is their failure to include any analysis of relationships at the disaggregated subsectoral level.

The GIR model, outlined by Wilks and Wright (1987), stresses the disaggregated nature of policy networks, using the term 'policy community' to describe interaction at the aggregate or sectoral level. A policy community is seen as having three characteristics: differentiation, specialized organizations and policy-making institutions, and interaction (Grant, Patterson and Whitson, 1989). Beyond this level, subsectoral policy networks can be identified. Grant, Patterson and Whitson (1989: 74) conclude that the policy community is 'a useful conceptual tool for ordering the material . . . [but] . . . any analysis which ignored the sub-sectoral level would be incomplete'.

The GIR model thus uses the term 'policy community' as a generic at the aggregated sectoral level in the same way the Rhodes model uses the term 'policy network'. However, 'policy network' in the GIR model is reserved for the disaggregated subsectoral level. In addition, the term 'policy universe' is used to refer to the general policy area within which activity takes place (see Figure 6.3).

The groupings of these policy actors can be defined (based on Wright, 1988: 606) as:

> *Policy Universe* . . . the large population of actors and potential actors who share a common interest in a policy area (e.g. leisure) and may contribute to the policy process on a regular basis.

	Policy level	*Policy actors*
Policy area	education, health, leisure, etc.	Policy universe
Policy sector	sport, tourism, arts, etc.	Policy community
Policy sub-sector	sports tourism, countryside sports, elite sport, etc.	Policy network

Figure 6.3 Levels in the GIR model

Policy Community . . . those actors who share an interest in a particular
policy sector (e.g. sport or tourism) and who interact with one another
in order to balance and optimize their mutual relationships.
Policy Network . . . a linking process, the outcome of those exchanges
within a policy community or between a number of policy communities.

Wilks and Wright (1987) argue that a major advantage of the GIR distinction
between community and network is that it allows for the possibility that
members of a policy network may be derived from different policy communities. This is of major significance here where the specific focus is on the cross-
sectoral policy liaison required in sport-tourism policy development. A simple
Venn diagram (Figure 6.4) illustrates the location of sport and tourism policy
communities within a leisure policy universe, where the area of overlap is where
a sport-tourism policy network should emerge.

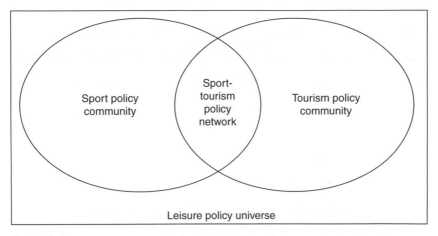

Figure 6.4 The sport-tourism policy network (GIR model)

There is, however, a third dimension to this diagram, because the membership of a particular network need not come exclusively from within the policy
universe (Wright, 1988). Thus it is conceivable that an interest in the sport-
tourism policy network may come from, for example, the economic development or foreign affairs policy communities.

It would appear that the GIR model provides the most useful framework for
analysing sport-tourism relations as it focuses on relations at the subsectoral
level. However, the updated Rhodes model (Figure 6.2) would also seem
capable of offering useful insights. This is particularly the case in this examination of cross-sectoral liaison where the nature of communities at the sectoral
level influence the formation of cross-sectoral networks at the subsectoral level.
In fact, Dowding (1995), in his critique of the Rhodes model, identifies its
failure to address the subsectoral or micro-level as a significant omission.
Therefore, in addressing this criticism, and given the cross-sectoral nature of
sport-tourism policy, the most productive way to proceed is to combine the two

models. In doing so, the three policy levels of the GIR model are maintained
– policy universe, policy community (sectoral level) and policy network (subsectoral level) – but the continuum outlined in the updated Rhodes model is
included at the sectoral level, thus allowing for an analysis of the influence on
the subsectoral level of the structure and organization at the sectoral level.
Combining the models in this way creates problems with terminology, with the
terms 'community' and 'network' meaning different things in each model. As
the overall framework is provided by the GIR model, the conceptions of 'policy
communities' as occurring at the sectoral level and 'policy networks' as referring to the subsectoral level are maintained. To avoid confusion, the updated
Rhodes policy community continuum (although the updated Rhodes model still
uses the term 'policy network' as a generic term at the sectoral level) will be
characterized as having a tightly structured policy circle (Rhodes's policy
community) at one end and a loosely structured issue zone (Rhodes's issue
network) at the other. The combined Model of Cross-Sectoral Policy Development is illustrated in Figure 6.5.

POLICY UNIVERSE	
POLICY COMMUNITY	
Policy circle	**Issue zone**
Stable, restricted membership	Unstable, open membership
Many interdependencies	Few interdependencies
Highly insulated from other policy sectors	Little insulation from other policy sectors
Complex patterns of resource dependencies	Few resource dependencies
Governmental, economic or professional member interests	
POLICY NETWORK	

Figure 6.5 A model of cross-sectoral policy development

This model can now be used to examine and compare the respective structures of sport and tourism policy communities. The following discussion is
based on empirical research conducted by the authors in the UK, but it refers
to structures and problems in other countries by way of further illustrative
examples. The focus of the analysis is on the extent to which the structures of
sport and tourism policy communities might affect the emergence of a sport-
tourism policy network.

The structure of policy communities for sport and tourism

Policy community membership varies from being fairly stable and restricted to
being relatively unstable and open to a wide range of groups. Smith (1993)
claims that a tightly formed policy circle will usually involve one government
agency or section within that agency which Rhodes (1986) believes will usually

give a lead to the community. However, leadership in both sport and tourism policy communities is often not clear cut. In the UK the lead government department would be expected to be the Department for Culture, Media and Sport; however, historically policy issues for sport and tourism have been devolved to partially autonomous, 'arms-length' government agencies, namely the Sports Council (restructured into Sport England and UK Sport in 1997) and the English Tourist Board (replaced by the English Tourism Council in 1999) respectively. In 1997 the Department for Culture, Media and Sport established a Tourism Advisory Forum, made up of prominent figures from the tourism industry, to advise it on tourism matters, which is the exact role the ETB was set up to fulfil in 1969. The establishment of the Tourism Forum was a clear first step in the replacement of the ETB with the English Tourism Council, the central role of which is to act as a business support and advice organization. The Department for Culture, Media and Sport also increasingly restricted the autonomy of the Sports Council, to the point where its drawn out restructure into UK and English Sports Councils has resulted in the new Sport England spending much of its time focusing on distributing Lottery Sports Fund grants in accordance with principles established at government department level. The Department for Culture, Media and Sport now exerts a much greater level of control over Sport England direction and, consequently, the organization has become an agent rather than an instigator of national sports policy. In both sport and tourism policy communities this situation creates tensions between governments, which ultimately control the purse strings, and national agencies where, in theory, expertise is invested.

In other countries around the world the situation is often less complex because tensions are not created by any formal 'arms-length' principle. Consequently, while tensions may exist between government departments and national agencies, these tensions are often resolved by the power or resource superiority of the government, or the status of national agencies as a branch of the government. In France, for example, there is no national agency for sport, and sports policy is developed directly by the Ministry of Youth and Fitness. As to tourism, the Loi Mouly (a new law for tourism administration passed in 1992) made provision for regional contributions to tourism policy, albeit under strict central control by the federal government who, as might be expected given France's formal economic planning system (Jeffries, 2001), maintain tight control over the registering and classification of resorts, and the subsectors of accommodation and catering. In Canada, both Sport Canada and the Canadian Tourism Commission (CTC) are branches of the federal government, which obviously prevents any tensions between government and national agency. The Australian system is perhaps most similar to that of the UK, with the Australian Sports Commission (ASC) and the Australian Tourism Commission (ATC) reporting to separate departments of the federal government. However, a significant difference exists in that both the ASC and the ATC accept that they are subject to direction over policy by the government, and thus while tensions may emerge, there is little question as to where the power of veto lies. The one major country where government control over both sport and tourism is slight is the USA. The general ideological commitment in many areas of life in the USA to the supremacy of the free market means that the majority of sport and of tourism provision is dictated by market forces. This obviously leaves little room for government agencies and, in line with such thinking, the country's national tourism organization, the United States Travel and Tourism Association (USTTA), was abolished in 1996, leaving the operation of the industry to the private sector. Similarly, the United States Olympic Committee (USOC), although having a legislative base, receives no government funding but funds its activities through the significant share of monies it receives from the International Olympic Committee's television contracts.

Laumann and Knoke (1987) believe that policy communities have primary and secondary communities. The primary core contains the key actors who set the rules of the game and determine membership and the main policy direction of the community, while the secondary community contains the groups that, although abiding by the rules of the game, do not have the resources or influence to greatly affect policy. It would appear that this distinction of a primary and secondary community is useful in examining the differences between structures of sport and tourism policy sectors. In the UK, although neither community could be said generally to have stable restricted membership, as is the case in a policy circle, the nature of the primary and secondary communities does vary. The sports policy community has a fairly stable primary community which includes the Department for Culture, Media and Sport, Sport England and the other national Sports Councils, and UK Sport. The secondary community, the membership of which is fairly open, contains a wide range of interest groups, sports organizations and clubs, and local authorities. It might be argued that local authorities, or at least their representative organizations, form part of the primary community, although evidence suggests (Weed, 1999a) that they have little input into the development of national policy. Similar situations can be found in other countries. In Australia, for example, a fairly tight group of organizations exists around the ASC, although the primary focus of Australian sports policy tends to be elite sport (Green, 2002). The Australian government, the ASC, the Australian Institute of Sport (AIS) and, to a certain extent, the Australian Olympic Committee (AOC) constitute a fairly closed primary community for elite sport in Australia. The position of the AOC in this primary group has been boosted by the recent hosting of the Olympics in Sydney. Although Australia has a federal system of government, sport, particularly elite sport, is seen as something that is too important to be managed by the states, who are expected to follow the lead given by the federal government and the ASC (Houlihan, 2002).

The situation in tourism policy communities is often different, and it may not be possible to define clearly primary and secondary communities. This is often due to the nature of tourism as a primarily commercial concern. In England, as in many other countries, there is a government-sponsored tourism agency, but the change from the developmental role of the former ETB to the business advice role fulfilled by the English Tourism Council, means that there are no key group of organizations to comprise a primary core. This tends to be the case in many other countries around the world – for example, as mentioned above, the USA abolished their government-funded national tourism organization in 1996, and now the commercial sector, under the auspices of the entirely privately funded Travel Industry Association of America (TIAA), conducts any overseas marketing that takes place (Jeffries, 2001). In some countries, such as France, there is a greater public sector involvement due to a tradition of providing for *social tourism* (subsidized development for the benefit of low-income groups). However, this does not mean that there is an identifiable group of agencies which comprises a primary core across the full range of issues (which in tourism sectors around the world are particularly diverse) and, consequently, tourism policy communities tend to lack the division between primary and secondary communities. This leads to the conclusion that tourism policy communities tend to show more of the characteristics of an issue zone, where membership is unstable and groups join or leave the community according to the issues being discussed. This often contrasts with sports policy communities which, while having fairly open secondary communities, appear to have primary communities of which membership is fairly stable and restricted, and thus, at least in comparison to the tourism sector, show some of the characteristics of a policy circle.

These differences in the basic structures of the communities clearly cause problems for sport-tourism liaison. In the UK, the lack of an identifiable lead agency in the tourism policy community means that there is no organization with which sports agencies can liaise on strategic matters. Although, arguably, the Regional Tourist Boards may fulfil this lead role at subnational level, their regional nature means that they cannot provide a lead for the tourism policy community at national level. This situation has resulted in some liaison taking place at regional level (Weed and Bull, 1997a), but a dearth of initiatives nationally. In countries with federal systems of government, such as France, Canada, the USA and Australia, it might be expected that there would be a greater focus on this regional level. In Australia, as discussed above, while the states are expected to follow the lead of the federal government in relation to elite sport, they do have a freer reign in relation to recreational participation. Furthermore, in many states there are specific government departments and statutory agencies with a tourism promotion remit. This may mean that, as in the UK, the regional level is likely to be where most productive sport-tourism partnerships are established. The exception is in relation to what has become known as 'leveraging' major events, which refers to a range of strategies employed to maximize the economic effects of events such as the Sydney Olympic Games. Here a national lead has been taken by the federal government.

In the USA, given the independence of the USOC and the entirely commercial operation of the TIAA, and the variation in the ideological commitment to state involvement among the fifty-two states, it is not surprising that it is difficult to provide any sort of general characterization of structures for sport and for tourism in the USA. However, while at national and state level this may be the case, it should be noted that over 100 'sports commissions' have been established, often under a Convention and Visitor Bureau umbrella, in cities and regions across the USA (Standeven and De Knop, 1999). The range of studies of the use of sport in 'city marketing' in the USA (see, for example, a number of papers in Gratton and Henry, 2001), further highlight that the city level is perhaps the most important for sport-tourism partnerships in this country.

In Canada, the states and municipalities are often quite fierce about their independence. It might be argued that this has affected Canadian sports policy over the last thirty years. During this time there has generally been an overt or underlying emphasis on 'National Unity' in sports policy at the federal level (Green, 2002) and as such, particularly in relation to elite sport, the federal government and Sport Canada have taken a controlling lead role, based on historical precedence, legislation and funding. There has been a fairly overt split in responsibility for sports policy in Canada, with the states/municipalities being asked to take responsibility for recreational sport, while the federal government takes responsibility for elite sport. However, the more militant states, such as Quebec, have developed their own elite programmes, based on developing state identity. In relation to tourism, the CTC has been promoting 'product clubs' that are based on tourism niches rather than particular regions or destinations. It would appear, therefore, that the adoption of 'product clubs' based on sports tourist niches would appear to be a significant opportunity for the promotion of state identity, and serves to make the regional state level an important level for sport-tourism liaison in Canada.

One of the major issues facing both sport and tourism policy communities in many countries is the extent to which they can insulate themselves from other policy areas. Houlihan (1991) highlights the inability of the sports policy community in the UK to insulate itself from other more powerful policy areas. An example of this is the response to the problem of football hooliganism in the 1980s, where the sports policy community was overridden by the law and order policy community in defining responses to that problem. Another example would be the inner city policy area, which in the UK and in many other countries often impinges on the work of sports policy communities. While the 'city marketing' emphasis was identified above as being important in the USA, there may still be a worry about the extent to which initiatives are for the benefit of sport, or for marketing purposes. Of course, the market-orien-tated ideology of many US states means that often no distinction is made between the two.

The changing priorities of the inner cities also impinge considerably on the work of tourism policy communities. In the UK, often the funds that are offered to Regional Tourist Boards by the government on a competitive bidding basis are for urban regeneration purposes through the Single Regeneration Budget. In this way the government is able to direct the Regional Tourist Boards' activ-ities towards their regeneration priorities by offering them funds with condi-tions attached that direct the focus of initiatives towards the economic and social regeneration of communities. Of course, regeneration is not always focused on urban areas. The programme for the regeneration of the Langue-doc Roussillon region of France focused on an area of coast running 180 kilometres from the south of Montpellier to the Spanish border. This programme, initiated in 1963, had the personal and powerful backing of the then French President, General de Gaulle. While this initiative was largely successful in developing a tourism product, it was undoubtedly driven by the need to restructure the regional economy and provide employment opportuni-ties for an area where income was significantly lower than the national average (Jeffries, 2001). The French emphasis on social tourism was also incorporated into this development, as it also aimed to provide subsidized recreational outlets for the French population (Ferras, Picheral and Vielzeuf, 1979). The conclusion to be drawn in the instances of both sport and tourism policy communities is that they cannot insulate themselves from other, more powerful and politically important, policy communities and thus, in this respect, they both display the characteristics of an issue zone. Perhaps the reason for this is that, in all but the smallest minority of cases, political ideologies for both sport and tourism are often linked to other policy areas rather than seeing the provision of sport and tourism as an end in itself. The extent to which this occurs can perhaps be best illustrated by a consideration of the effect the European Union (EU) has had on tourism. Jeffries (2001) suggests that a superficial examination would suggest that the EU's involvement has been virtually negligible if the focus is on the work of the Tourism Directorate within Directorate Generale for Enterprise (DGE). The part played by the DGE is slight because the EU has no formal competence in tourism. However, the EU has considerable powers to decide policies and allocate funding to shape development in areas, which are also bound to shape tourism. The European Commission's (1995) paper, *Tourism and the European Union*, lists over twenty such areas, which include regional and social development, competition policy, transport policy, environmental protection, economic and monetary union (single currency), and employment and social policy. Thus tourism policy at European level is clearly and overtly derived from other policy areas. Furthermore, the situation for sport is little different (Henry and Matthews, 1998), and this European example reflects, although perhaps to a more extreme degree, the situation in many countries throughout the world. Deriving policies from other policy areas clearly makes long-term strategic planning difficult because political objectives for sport and tourism are liable to change in the short to medium term. This obviously does not assist in the creation of links between the sport and tourism agencies as each are dealing with more specific aims and objectives laid down by the political thinking of the time.

The level of interdependency in a policy community is often linked to resources. Resources come in a range of forms, most obvious are financial resources, but also important are knowledge, information, legitimacy and the goodwill of other groups (Smith, 1993). A policy circle has many interdependencies, and the relationships between groups are often exchange relationships. In the more loosely constituted issue zone, the relationship changes from being one of exchange to one of transmission or consultation. Tourist agencies, as discussed above, may often have to forgo their independently established strategic plans in order to tap into funds offered by governments on a competitive bidding basis – control over direction is exchanged for financial resources. To a certain extent this has also occurred in the sports policy community in the UK, where Sport England has sacrificed much of its independence (although not necessarily willingly) in exchange for a central role in the distribution of Lottery funds. There does, however, appear to be more significant interdependencies in sports policy communities than is the case with the tourism sector.

Although a complex pattern of resource dependencies often exist in tourism policy communities between commercial sector organizations, and between the commercial sector and semi-public sector bodies, governments tend to retain a privileged position due to their greater economic resources (Rhodes, 1988). This means that governments are often able to wield considerable influence in the areas they consider to be important. However, the open and unrestricted nature of tourism communities' membership means that, with the exception of that with government, there are no major resource relationships upon which such communities are dependent. The relationships are complex, but they are small, and the loss of any one of them would not greatly affect the operation of the community as a whole.

In contrast, sports policy communities do tend to have a range of resource relationships upon which the community is dependent. In the primary community the resource relationship between government and national agencies are important because such national agencies could not survive without government grant aid. In the UK, this relationship helps ensure that Sport England accepts the lead of the Department for Culture, Media and Sport over general policy direction. However, the government in general does not wish to involve itself with the detail of all aspects of sports policy, and thus Sports England's expertise is required to convert general policy direction into implementable specifics. It is this exchange relationship that ensures these agencies comprise the primary core of the sports policy community. Their relationship with the secondary community is as a result of the dependence of much of that secondary community on Sports England grant aid and Lottery Sports Fund money. The actors in the secondary community do not have anything to exchange for these resources and, as a result, have to accept the general policy directions and terms and conditions under which they are offered. The primary cores of the sports policy communities in the Canadian and Australian cases described earlier are similar to the UK situation, with the distinction between primary and secondary communities being largely, although not exclusively, based on the resource dependence of much of the secondary community on the primary actors. In addition, in the USA, the USOC, apart from its legislative base in the 1978 Amateur Sports Act, is able to wield a powerful influence over the rest of the sports policy community due to its significant resource base derived from the large proportion of the television rights money it receives from the International Olympic Committee.

In summarizing the nature and features of sport and tourism policy communities it is possible to characterize tourism policy communities as showing many of the characteristics of an issue zone. Membership is often unstable and open with no clear leadership and few major interdependencies. Furthermore, there is often virtually no insulation from other policy sectors and member interests are mainly economic, although governments often retain a privileged position as a result of their resource position. By contrast, while sports policy communities are often not strong enough to be labelled so (Houlihan, 1997), they do show some of the characteristics of a policy circle, certainly in relation to the tourism community. The membership of the primary core tends to be stable and restricted, although the secondary community is fairly open; there are a number of major interdependencies, both in terms of finance and expertise, that dictate the structure of, and relationships in, sports communities; and member interests, particularly in the primary community, are mainly governmental, supplemented by professional connections. The one factor that prevents sports policy communities being characterized as a policy circle are their historical lack of insulation from other, more powerful, policy areas such as education and thus, at times, their inability to define their own agenda, something that Laffin (1986) sees as a significantly important variable.

However, while neither the sport or tourism communities are able to exclude more powerful policy sectors from impinging on their respective work, they are able to define their agenda within the leisure policy universe. In fact, within the leisure area the communities are able to establish a greater degree of insulation as neither tourism or sport sectors are seen as more politically important than each other. It is perhaps the case that, due to their greater correspondence with the features of a policy circle, sport policy communities are more able to exclude tourism interests than tourism communities are able to exclude sport. This may have a significant effect on the extent to which such communities can generate a sport-tourism policy network, particularly as they are often more concerned with defining their own agenda within the leisure policy universe rather than seeking connections.

Conclusion

The discussions above would seem to indicate that the structures of both sport and of tourism policy communities have the potential to cause problems for liaison between sports and tourism agencies, and may affect the development of sport-tourism policy networks. Problems such as these lead Houlihan (1991: 161) to state: 'while every policy sector will generate a policy community this is no guarantee that a policy network will emerge to deal with particular issues. Some communities may lack the necessary value consensus or strength of mutual interests to provide the basis for the formation of a network'. Research in the UK suggests (Weed and Bull, 1997a) that sport and tourism agencies and communities act independently, due to a lack of value consensus or perceived mutual interest across the two policy communities, and thus, at least at national level, no sport-tourism policy network emerges.

It is perhaps useful to return at this point to the conceptualization of sports tourism as a unique interaction of activity, people and place, and to consider how this might dovetail with the work of policy agencies for sport and for tourism. A useful way of approaching this might be to consider the work of sports policy makers as focusing on the interaction of activity and people, while policy-makers in the tourism industry focus on the interaction of people and place. Clearly, when sports agencies consider, for example, policy for supporting voluntary sports clubs, there is little overlap with tourism policy. However, in relation to sports tourism, the activities of these agencies should overlap because they are considering policy for the same people – sports tourists. While these ideas might provide a useful framework for considering the areas of policy on which sports and tourism agencies should liaise, the reality is that an understanding of policy for sports tourism is necessarily concerned with identifying how policy-makers for sport and for tourism can be encouraged to work in together in the first place.

The discussions in this chapter have set out the context and suggested a theoretical framework against which the potential for development of collaborative sport-tourism policy might be explored. The next chapter develops the policy discussion further, highlighting in particular the importance of specific regional contexts, histories, geographies, administrations and perceptions, alongside the commitment and background of key individuals, as key factors determining the extent to which sustainable sport-tourism policy networks might emerge.

7

Prospects for integration

The previous chapter has set out the policy context within which the sport and tourism sectors operate, outlining in the process the usefulness of ideas associated with policy communities and developing a Model of Cross-Sectoral Policy Development as a theoretical framework with which to understand this context. Examining sport-tourism policy using the policy community concept is useful because the model developed is a fluid one, which can be adapted in order to be a useful explanatory tool in a range of countries where the nature of the policy process differs. The model allows, for example, for dominant member interests to be professional, governmental or economic (i.e. commercial), thus the model is useful in describing both the sports policy community in the USA, where commercial interests dominate, and in Canada, where governmental interests are more prominent. Such flexibility allows disparate policy processes to be understood in a consistent way and, consequently, provides a very useful backdrop for the discussions in this chapter which seek to further develop an understanding of the sport-tourism policy process and to focus particularly on the prospects for greater integration between sport and tourism policy communities throughout the world

This chapter examines the potential for sport-tourism policy networks to develop in a range of countries around the world. However, initially it is useful to review those areas in which it might reasonably be expected that mutual benefits would accrue to members of sport and of tourism policy communities in working together in a sport-tourism policy network. A 'Policy Area Matrix' is presented which illustrates such areas, and the issues associated with them. Following this a number of tensions within and across policy communities which might affect the potential for sport-tourism policy networks to develop are discussed. Finally, the ways in which sport-tourism policy networks might operate are discussed.

Areas for policy integration

Standeven and De Knop (1999), in their introductory text, describe their belief that: 'the international trend toward market-led economies has brought about a growing emphasis on a market-oriented entrepreneurial approach to sport tourism . . . [Furthermore] we identify an inexorable global shift toward efficiency and income maximization and away from public involvement' (ibid.: 294).

While undoubtedly the trend towards market-led economies is internationally identifiable, the claim that there is an 'inexorable' shift away from public involvement is doubtful for two reasons. First, there are very few examples around the world of public policy partnerships in relation to the sport-tourism link, therefore it is hardly possible that there can be a move away from public involvement. Furthermore, there are distinctly different trends in the sport and tourism policy communities. While there are exceptions in some countries, generally there seems to be an increase in government interest in sport, and a move away from government involvement in tourism, which in itself creates tensions for policy development. Second, there are undoubtedly strategic and developmental issues, leading to a range of mutual benefits, that can only be addressed by some form of public sector policy partnerships. Perhaps the best illustration of this is the range of issues identified by Weed and Bull (1997a) in their Policy Area Matrix for Sport and Tourism.

Previous attempts have been made to identify the different areas of sport-tourism linkage that require attention or guidance by policy-makers. Glyptis (1991a: 169), for example, identified 'potential roles that governments may choose to adopt in relation to sport and tourism'. She sought to *suggest* roles that governments could *choose* to adopt, depending on the administrative arrangements in their particular country. However, while this gave a broad overview of the issues, it did not identify detailed areas for policy attention.

In 1997, Weed and Bull (1997a) conducted a review of regional policies for sport and tourism in England. A framework was required for this review, and so the Policy Area Matrix for Sport and Tourism was compiled (Figure 7.1). The matrix identifies six broad areas for policy attention, these being; Sports holidays (taken from Glyptis, 1982), Facility issues, Environmental countryside and water issues, Resources and funding, Policy and planning, and Information and promotion. These areas are further subdivided into twenty-one subgroups. Of course, many links can be identified across the groups and subgroups. For example 'marina development' under 'Environmental, countryside and water issues' is linked to 'spectator events' under 'Sports holidays' due to the potential of many marina areas to stage large events (an example would be the World

Sports holidays

Sports training	Activity holidays	'Up-market' sports holidays	General holidays with sports opportunity	Spectator events
Specialist facilities	Nuisance activities	Conference market	Water sports	Economic contribution
Major arenas	Out-of-season tourism	Nuisance activities	Leisure centres	Regional identity
Off-peak use	Water sports		Conference market	Specialist facilities
Sports development	Cycling/walking		Sports development	Conference market
	Sports development			Major arenas
	Social goals			

Facility issues

Dual use of tourist facilities	Hotel leisure facilities	Use of tourism to sustain local facilities
Differential pricing	Out-of-season tourism	Major arenas
Off-peak use	Conference market	Specialist facilities
Major arenas	Off-peak use	Differential pricing
Specialist facilities		Leisure centres
Social goals		Social goals

Environmental, countryside and water issues

Farm diversification	Countryside access and integration	Marina development
Nuisance activities	Water sports	Conference market
EU funding	Cycling/walking	Out-of-season tourism
	Nuisance activities	Major arenas
	Social goals	Specialist facilities
		Water sports
		Nuisance activities
		Regional identity
		Leisure centres
		EU finding

Resources and funding

Supplementary funding	Joint bids for funding	Economic and social regeneration
Major arenas	Major arenas	Conference market
Specialist facilities	Specialist facilities	Out-of-season tourism
Economic distribution	Economic contribution	Major arenas
Regional identity	Regional identity	Economic contribution
	EU funding	Regional identity
	Social goals	EU funding
		Social goals

Policy and planning

Regional forums	Marketing activity	Resolving conflicts	Codes of practice
Regional identity	Economic contribution	Water sports	Major arenas
Social goals	Tourist information centres	Nuisance sports	Specialist facilities
	Leisure centres		Water sports
	EU funding		Nuisance sports
			Social goals

Information and promotion

Joint lobbying	Information distribution channels	Research and advice
Major arenas	Regional identity	Specialist facilities
Specialist facilities	Leisure centres	Major arenas
Water sports	Tourist information centres	Nuisance activities
Cycling/walking		Conference market
Nuisance activities		Economic distribution
Regional identity		EU funding
EU funding		
Social goals		

Figure 7.1 Policy Area Matrix for Sport and Tourism

Powerboat Championships held at Hartlepool Marina in the North East of England in 1994).

There are many issues and considerations that will affect policy development in these areas, and these are also illustrated in the Policy Area Matrix (Figure 7.1). Sixteen considerations have been identified, these being:

1 The conference market.
2 Out-of-season tourism.
3 Provision of major arenas.
4 Provision of specialist facilities.
5 Differential pricing for the tourist and the local community.
6 Off-peak use of facilities.
7 Provision for water sports.
8 Promotion of cycling/walking.
9 Provision for and regulation of perceived nuisance activities.
10 The contribution of sport and tourism to the economy.
11 Developing a regional identity.
12 Use of leisure centres.
13 Use of tourist information centres.
14 Funding from the European Union.
15 Sports development.
16 Social goals.

Obviously, all of these issues do not affect all of the policy areas, thus the matrix illustrates which issues are relevant to which areas. The matrix aims to summarize those areas in which it might reasonably be assumed that agencies responsible for developing policy for sport and tourism might collaborate, and there are examples from around the world of such collaboration. Such examples might usefully be considered in the context of the nature of sports tourism as being derived from the interaction of activity, people and place, with many policy initiatives focusing on the place element. Perhaps the most obvious examples are in relation to major events under Sports Holidays. While the focus is usually on maximizing the economic contribution of such events, a further consideration relates to the post-event use of major arenas and specialist facilities constructed for such events. The athletics stadia used for the Atlanta Olympics (1996) and the Manchester Commonwealth Games (2002) incorporated temporary stands which allowed for the adaptation of the facilities for the long-term use of the Atlanta Braves Baseball team and Manchester City Football Club respectively. In each of these cases the experience of place generated by and associated with athletics is different to that required for both baseball and football. Consequently, modifications to these stadia were made to ensure their long-term use, where a different group of people would expect a different place experience in watching a different type of activity. An example from the 'Facility issues' section of the matrix is provided by the City of Sheffield, who were keen to ensure that the facilities constructed for the 1991 World Student Games were suitable for dual use for both spectator events and general casual community sport. Here the requirement was for a place that would be capable of adaptation to produce different place experiences for different people participating in or watching a range of different activities. Consequently, the Ponds Forge swimming pool is one of the most flexible facilities in the world, and is continuously adaptable for use by Sheffield local residents, and as part of the city's ongoing sports events strategy.

One of the areas that has received little attention in the literature under the 'Environmental, countryside and water issues' section of the matrix is that of farm diversification into tourism. Sports tourism can comprise a significant element of this with Busby and Rendle (2000) listing horse-riding, fishing, shooting and boating as part of this product. Farm tourism has become particularly important in some economically depressed areas of Europe, with the EU offering funds to develop this type of recreational sports tourism product. Here the experience of the place is changed, not by wholesale physical changes, but by its interaction with a new group of people participating in new activities.

Securing and using 'Resources and funding' to promote and develop sports tourism is a key area of the matrix where collaboration between sport and tourism interests could develop much further than is presently the case. While the channelling of resources into projects that use high profile sport to regenerate communities has been a feature of city marketing in the USA for some time, there are also some less high profile examples of the use of resources for sports tourism as part of the marketing of rural areas. For example, the Adirondack North Country Region of New York State has developed a regional marketing plan based on cycle tourism with the aim of supporting the rural economy and sustaining local tourism services. In such cases the emphasis is on attracting new people to an area through the packaging and promotion of a range of new and existing activities. The aim is that new people and activities will serve to revitalize the place and consequently improve both the sports tourism experience and the lives of local residents. Related to such initiatives are areas of 'Policy and planning' such as the development of codes of practice. In Wales, where activity tourism is an important market, the Wales Tourist Board established an Activity Holidays Advisory Committee to supplement the work of the British Activity Holidays Association, through which it liaises with the Sports Council for Wales to develop and maintain codes of practice to ensure the safety of activity holidays. The final section of the matrix relates to 'Information and promotion', and Gunn (1990) describes a collaborative initiative in South Africa relating to research and advice. The South African Tourism Agency and the Recreational Planning Agency collaborated on a joint research programme to identify tourism strengths in relation to sports and recreation facilities and resources. These examples highlight the ways in which the sports tourism experience might be enhanced by collaborative accreditation and research initiatives that ensure that people use the most appropriate places in the most effective and safest ways for the most appropriate activities.

Of course, the collaborations described above do not necessarily indicate the existence of sustained strategic sport-tourism policy development. In fact, although the research on which the matrix is based (Weed and Bull, 1997a) revealed an increasing amount of sports tourism activity among policy agencies in England, such activity was not matched by any significant liaison between them. The vast majority of sports tourism activity that the agencies were involved in was promoted unilaterally, with no involvement of agencies in the other sector. Genuine examples of multilateral sport-tourism initiatives were few and far between, and there were very few signs that a sport-tourism policy network might emerge.

However, there are some examples around the world of piecemeal liaison between sport and tourism policy communities, but there are few places where sustained strategic collaboration leading to the emergence of a sport-tourism policy network takes place. The reasons for the lack of any longer-term strategic liaison are perhaps explained by examining the various tensions that exist within and between sport and tourism policy communities

A note is perhaps useful at this point on the nature of policy research in the sports tourism field. It might be expected that the study of sport-tourism policy should relate to the ways in which, as described above, policy-makers might respond to various issues associated with the interaction of activity, people and place that make the sports tourism experience unique. However, as touched upon at the end of Chapter 6, until sports agencies and tourism agencies around the world begin to work consistently and strategically together in supporting sports tourism, the focus will necessarily be on the factors that inhibit liaison, and the ways in which such factors might be addressed and overcome.

Tensions in the sport-tourism policy process

The previous chapter, in developing and using a Model of Cross-Sectoral Policy Development, outlined the way in which the sport-tourism policy process is structured and operates. Now that the areas in which sport and tourism policy communities might be expected to collaborate have been established, it is useful to outline some of the tensions within sport-tourism policy processes that might affect long-term integration. Such tensions might be within or between national government and the respective national agencies, or between national, regional and local tiers of administration, or between any combination of these organizations. However, they all have the potential to affect relationships within and between sport and tourism policy communities and are summarized in Figure 7.2.

Figure 7.2 lists five main tensions (derived from research in the UK by Weed, 1999a; 2001d) within sport and tourism policy communities. Also listed are a number of subsidiary tensions related to each of the five main tensions. Of

Income generation	V.	Strategic direction
Resources	*v.*	*Knowledge*
Top-down policy	V.	Bottom-up policy
National	*v.*	*Regional*
Imposed initiatives	*v.*	*Ownership of initiatives*
Change	*v.*	*Evolution*
Organization	V.	Individuals
Professionalism	*v.*	*Adhocracy*
Framework	*v.*	*Flexibility*
Internal focus	V.	External focus
Organizational survival	*v.*	*Future development*
Project-based liaison	V.	Ongoing liaison
Initiatives	*v.*	*Advocacy*

Figure 7.2 Tensions in the sport and tourism policy communities

course, these tensions are by no means mutually exclusive, in fact they are inextricably interlinked, and are important because their causes are the factors that can affect the development of sport-tourism policy networks.

The way in which non-statutory agencies such as the Regional Tourist Boards (RTBs) in England and the Regional Tourism Organizations in New Zealand (which are similar in structure to the English RTBs) can sustain a central role in policy communities is through the development of a strategic function. However, there is often pressure to focus on income generation. Such tension between income generation and strategic direction is the first major tension highlighted in Figure 7.2. Agencies can often virtually be forced into bidding for funds for projects of minor relevance to their strategic priorities because they need to generate income, the result being that strategic developments are increasingly secondary to the generation of funds. This change is highlighted by Hall (2000: 152), who believes that strategy is becoming increasingly secondary to more commercial interests in national tourism agencies 'in countries as geographically dispersed as Australia, Austria, Canada, New Zealand and the UK'. This means, therefore, that unless central funding mechanisms are promoting sport-tourism relationships (which has been the case in only a very few examples), this tension is likely to work against sport-tourism links because agencies will not have the strategic capacity to develop such links. The subsidiary tension also works in this way because governments often use their control of national agency funding to dictate policy direction. The tension here is between the specialist knowledge that resides with national agencies and the resource control exercised by governments (Gouldner, 1954). Even where agencies are part of the federal government, as is the case in Canada, there is still the potential for tension between those with specialist knowledge and those who control the purse strings. However, there are two ways in which governments could alleviate some of the problems associated with this tension. Governments could take a more holistic view of the leisure sector and, as suggested above, allocate funding to projects that might encourage the development of relationships between sport and tourism agencies. For example, funding opportunities offered by governments could include sport-tourism partnership criteria. Alternatively, if governments were to respect the independence of national agencies for sport and for tourism then it may be likely that they would move towards greater collaboration as they identify their own strategic priorities. That it is difficult to find any examples of this around the world is testament to the continued interference of governments in national agency activities rather than an indication of the potential for collaboration to develop in such circumstances.

The second tension highlighted in Figure 7.2 is between top-down and bottom-up policy development. This obviously is related to the previous tension as in many countries there is clearly a significant element of top-down influence from government. The previous chapter describes how often both sport and tourism policy communities are unable to insulate themselves from the imposition of initiatives or priorities from other, often more important or influential, policy areas (Houlihan, 1991). For example, many funding opportunities offered by governments for tourism focus on economic and social regeneration. In addition, research has shown (Weed 2002c) the importance of staff and organizations feeling they have ownership of initiatives. In this respect, initiatives or directions suggested or developed internally by organizations were shown to have a much greater chance of success than those imposed externally. Analogous to these ideas is the differentiation that can be made between evolution and change. Evolution can be seen as a development of the organization that usually would be internally instigated, whereas change is often seen as disruptive and as being externally imposed. Consequently, it is often the case that externally imposed change causes organizational instability and can lead to an internal focus on organizational maintenance. This was certainly the case with the drawn-out restructure of the Sports Councils in the UK, the objectives of which changed considerably over a seven-year period in the 1990s (Weed, 1999a). Similar problems occurred in Canada, with Green (2002: 10) pointing out that: 'because of the emphasis put on elite sport development by the federal government, the period dating from the early 1990s and into the 21st century can be characterized as one of confusion, turmoil and introspection for the Canadian sports community'.

The consequences of these tensions are twofold. First, that while governments continue to take a segregational view of leisure, imposed or top-down initiatives are unlikely to assist in developing sport-tourism partnerships. Second, even if governments were to attempt to impose sport-tourism initiatives on sport and tourism policy communities, it is unlikely that they would meet with much success. Strategic sport-tourism relationships, and consequently a sustainable sport-tourism policy network, are only likely to emerge if organizations are encouraged to draw up their own agenda for liaison of which they feel they have ownership.

A central tension, not only in the sport-tourism policy process, but in the policy process more generally, is the tension between the organization and the individual (Crozier, 1964; Dalton, 1959). The extent to which this tension manifests itself will depend on the structure and culture of the organization (Morgan, 1986; 1997). In fact, given the nature of much of the work in sport and tourism agencies throughout the world, which often allows staff some autonomy, the tension between individual and organization can be magnified because staff have the opportunity to divert from organizational goals and priorities. Research in the UK has shown that the sports agencies there tend to work with a 'professionalized' structure that allows employees autonomy within a framework, while the tourist agencies, particularly at regional level work to a more 'adhocratic' structure that gives employees greater flexibility (Weed, 1999a). Because, in many cases, relationships between sport and tourism bodies are new and therefore outside of the parameters of many organizations' structures, flexibility is a key element in developing such relationships. In fact, where sport-tourism relationships have developed in the UK, key staff have been given the flexibility to pursue such relationships. However, this UK research also highlights that it is possible for key individuals within organizations to work outside the framework laid down by their organization if they have the seniority and inclination to do so (Weed, 1999a). Nevertheless, examples also exist of situations where staff have attempted to work outside the framework laid down by their organization which have resulted in tensions that have caused the staff members concerned to leave the organization.

Tensions between internal and external foci of organizations have already been touched upon above. In many cases such tensions are explicitly related to the tension between income generation and strategic direction. The emerging commercial culture that Standeven and De Knop (1999) claim exists within sports tourism, certainly exists throughout most of the world in tourism policy communities. Such a culture can lead to a more internal focus on organizational maintenance and 'fire-fighting', dealing with the day-to-day survival of the organization rather than focusing externally on future development. In some cases, such as the Thames and Chilterns Regional Tourist Board in England, and the United States Travel and Tourism Administration, the fight for organizational survival has been lost, and this can do little to reassure other such agencies that this will not happen to them. As already noted, non-statutory agencies must continue to operate strategically if they are to sustain a central position in policy communities, and a requirement in doing so is an external focus and a concern for future development.

At the sectoral level, the tension between an internal and external focus exists in both sport and tourism policy communities. Discussions have already taken place on the inability of both policy communities to insulate themselves from other policy areas (Houlihan, 1991), and this may lead communities to focus on establishing a clearly identifiable policy heartland (Jordan and Richardson, 1987), rather than on working on areas in their policy periphery – which is where the majority of sport-tourism issues lie. Added to this is perhaps an ideology in some quarters of many sport and tourism policy communities that sport-tourism issues are not a legitimate concern of either the sport or tourism policy communities, or of their organization, or in their geographical area. The sum of these factors is an internal focus for both sport and tourism communities, whereas what is required for successful sport-tourism liaison is an external focus and a culture of developing partnerships outside immediate policy heartlands.

The final tension highlighted in Figure 7.2 is that between project based and ongoing liaison. Notwithstanding the discussion in the previous paragraph, there is usually a general acknowledgement within sport and tourism policy communities that some liaison between them is desirable (although in many cases both organizations and individuals believe the responsibility for developing such liaison does not lie with them). However, opinions often vary as to whether ongoing strategic liaison is required, or whether liaison should take place in an ad hoc manner as and when projects arise. Quite patently, those who favour a more commercial culture within their organization are likely to believe that liaison should take place in an adhocratic, project based way, while those who believe the focus should be strategic would prefer to see ongoing liaison. It would appear that a focus on advocacy and developing an agreed agenda for responding to projects proposed by other organizations might be the best way forward. Such an approach represents a compromise between the project-based and ongoing approaches and has been successful in some areas. A useful example of this approach is provided by France, where partnerships have been established as a result of a general understanding and acceptance of the relationship between sport and tourism at national government level. One example of such a partnership would be the programme for the regeneration of the Languedoc Roussillon region discussed in the previous chapter, while another would be the interministerial group established to administer land planning on the Aquitaine coast, which included a number of sports tourism projects.

Having identified tensions within the sport-tourism policy process, it is important to focus on those factors which are the root causes of such tensions. Weed (1999a; 2003c) has attempted to do this, suggesting six factors that might affect relationships within and between sport and tourism policy communities, namely, ideology, definitions, government policy, regional contexts, organizational structure/culture and individuals.

First, ideology causes tensions at all levels of the policy process. At one level ideology can be identified as important in the policy context, contributing to the environment within which policy is made. However, it is also clear that tensions between income generation and strategy, change and evolution, organization and individuals, and organizational survival and future development are caused in some instances by conflicting ideological stances. Such ideologies may be the result of political beliefs, professional frameworks, or they may be more personal ideologies that are not necessarily professional or political.

Linked to ideology in some respects is the influence wielded by individual and organizational definitions and conceptions of sport, tourism and sports tourism. Government definitions of sport and tourism are often imposed on national agencies, causing conflicts related to the tension between resources and knowledge. Definitions and conceptions can also cause tensions between organization and individual and between internal and external foci. A more narrow definition of either sport or tourism leads to a more sharply defined policy heartland and less willingness to work in an organization's or community's periphery (see later discussion), and this is one area which varies considerably around the world. In Australia and Canada, for example, the focus of the national sports agencies is on elite sport, which consequently narrows the focus for collaboration with tourism agencies at national level largely to issues related to major events. However, this is not the case at regional/state level, where examples of sport-tourism collaboration are more common, because the sports agencies have a wider focus which encompasses recreational sport.

Perhaps one of the most significant influences is 'regional contexts'. In this respect, historic, geographic, administrative, economic, structural and a whole range of other factors that vary between regions can cause tensions in different ways in different regions. For example, the extent of the tension between project based and ongoing liaison is affected by regional contexts such as geographical resources for sports tourism, historical liaison (or non-liaison) between regional bodies, and the strength and structure of the regional economy. To a certain extent individuals may be seen as regional contexts as they can cause specific tensions in their region. However, the influence of individuals is also prevalent at national level and within government and therefore still merits separate consideration. While 'regional contexts' may appear a slightly eclectic label, it is nevertheless a useful one in helping to understand the variations between regional approaches to the sport-tourism link.

Government policy is perhaps the most straightforward cause of tensions within the sport-tourism policy process. As earlier discussions show, government policy, in a range of forms and both intentionally and non-intentionally, causes tensions between income generation and strategy and between top-down and bottom-up policy development in a number of ways. Organizational structure and organizational culture clearly contribute to many of the tensions identified in Figure 7.2, and it might be expected that they should be considered separately, as originally proposed by Weed and Bull (1998). However, subsequent work (Weed, 1999a; 2002c; 2003c) has shown that it is almost impossible to separate out their influence in practice. In fact, it appears that, in many cases, culture and structure evolved together and are inextricably interlinked. Consequently, it is perhaps more useful to combine these factors and consider them as one.

Individuals have already been mentioned briefly in the discussion of regional contexts. However, initial work on this influence on sport-tourism policy (Weed and Bull, 1998) referred to 'key staff' rather than 'individuals'. It is perhaps more useful to use the term 'individuals' as this would also allow for the influence of, for example, significant political figures. In this respect, John Major as British Prime Minister has had a significant influence on sport-tourism relationships because the sports policy statement, 'Sport: Raising the Game' (DNH, 1995), that contained proposals for the English Sports Council to withdraw from the promotion of recreational activities in order to focus more on competitive sport, is widely seen as bearing the personal stamp of the Prime Minister (Collins, 1995). Consequently, John Major was responsible for a number of tensions related to top-down policy development and organizational change and instability. However, it should perhaps be pointed out that individuals are not always aware of the wider implications and repercussions of their actions. It is unlikely that John Major gave any thought to the effect his proposals would have on sport-tourism relationships and, as such, the consequences for sport-tourism links were unintended.

These causes of tension within the sport-tourism policy process can now be viewed within the Model of Cross-Sectoral Policy Development outlined in the previous chapter. This model allowed for an analysis of the way in which the structure of policy communities at the sectoral level might affect the development of policy networks at the subsectoral level. As such, the structure of the communities themselves might be causes of some tensions within the policy process. Generally, sports policy communities were identified as having a closed primary core but a more open secondary community, while tourism policy communities were altogether more open. Although in relation to tourism policy communities, sports policy communities tend to show more of the features of a policy circle, both communities are often unable to insulate themselves from other, more politically important policy areas. Consequently, tensions surrounding the imposition of initiatives and the ability to define strategic direction may be related to the structure of the two policy communities. Specifically, that both policy communities are susceptible to the imposition of initiatives from other, non-leisure, communities.

Locating the causes of the tensions discussed here within the Model of Cross-Sectoral Policy Development results in a general model where a leisure policy universe will contain a sports policy community with a tightly defined primary core, but a more open secondary community, and a generally open tourism policy community. Six influences can be identified as affecting relationships between these communities and, as per the above discussion:

1 Ideologies.
2 Definitions.
3 Regional contexts.

4 Government policy.
5 Organizational culture and structure.
6 Individuals.

The next stage of the analysis is to assess the extent to which the influences discussed above affect the abilities of sport and tourism policy communities around the world to generate sustainable sport-tourism policy networks. This assessment also includes an evaluation of the prospects for more strategic integration between sport and tourism through a discussion of the potential operation of sport-tourism policy networks.

The potential operation of sport-tourism policy networks

This final section of the chapter attempts to link the previous discussion of factors affecting the development of sport-tourism policy networks with an evaluation of the potential for the development of long-term strategic sport-tourism collaboration through a consideration of those issues pertinent to sport-tourism that concern the effective operation of policy networks. Wright (1988: 609–10) identifies a number of 'rules of the game' that act as an 'unwritten constitution', guiding the behaviour of actors within policy networks. The first of these rules is mutuality. Members of a network accept and expect that mutual advantages and benefits will result from their participation in the network. It is therefore necessary that both sports and tourist agencies believe that there is a positive link between sport and tourism and that they both stand to benefit from it. Earlier chapters, and indeed the very existence of this book, are testament to the wide range of benefits to be gained from linking sport and tourism. However, it often appears to be the case that sport and tourist agencies and their employees are not aware of the full extent of these benefits and thus they believe that mutuality does not exist within a sport-tourism policy network. That is not to say that such agencies and employees dismiss that any link between sport and tourism exists, rather that a belief exists that the benefits of such a link are minimal, or exist in only one or two areas, most often perceived to be related to major events. This is the case at national level in Australia (as highlighted earlier) and increasingly in the UK, where the establishment of a Major Events Group within UK Sport and a Sports Tourism Department within the British Tourist Authority has focused work on this area. There remains, however, little ongoing strategic liaison (as opposed to ad hoc collaborations) between the UK agencies, even in relation to this high-profile area of the sport-tourism link. Therefore, in many countries around the world often liaison is considered either to be required only on an ad hoc basis or in relation to specific events (as with the UK and Australian examples), or to yield so few benefits that it would be unproductive. It still appears, therefore, that one of the most significant factors in the future development of sustainable sport-tourism policy networks is the education of policy-makers about the full range of mutual benefits that could be gained from greater integration. However, a broadening of focus is also needed among the academic community in its discussion of sports tourism. There are many areas of the sport-tourism link that receive very little attention from both academics and policy-makers.

A second rule relates to consultation, both the willingness of an agency to consult within the network and the expectation by agencies that they will be consulted. In the case of sport-tourism, where the policy network draws its membership from two different policy communities, it may be that some issues are seen by the sports policy community as falling exclusively within their 'territory', while the tourism policy community will feel that certain issues fall exclusively within their territory. This obviously creates problems for consultation within the policy network. However, Jordan and Richardson's (1987: 55) discussion of the extent of organizations' territory is helpful in addressing this issue:

> each organization has a notion of its own 'territory', rather as an animal or bird in the wild has its own territory, and it will resist invasion of this territory by other agencies. There is not a precise definition of exactly where the territory ends. For example, there is territory which is at the periphery of the bureau influence and where it has some, but not great influence and there is territory which is quite 'alien' to the bureau and where it has no influence. On the other hand, it has its heartland which is quite alien to any other bureau and which it will defend with great vigour and determination.

It is perhaps useful to modify Figure 6.4 in Chapter 6 to show the areas of policy heartland and policy periphery of the sport and tourism policy communities. Figure 7.3 shows that much of the policy deliberations of a sport-tourism policy network will fall within the policy periphery of both the sport and tourism policy communities. In these cases there should be no problem with consultation. However, in order to deal with those areas falling within one or other communities' policy heartland it is necessary to consider the issue of leadership. Neither a sports agency nor a tourist agency could provide a permanent lead to a sport-tourism policy network as they would be invading the other's policy space, and consequently some sort of joint or floating leadership initiative would be necessary. It is certainly the case that in order for a sport-tourism policy network to consider the full range of issues, one of the sports agencies must be allowed to lead the network on issues falling within their policy heartland while one of the tourist agencies must lead on predominantly tourism issues. Major conflict is avoided because the policy heartlands of the two communities do not overlap and thus a flexible, floating network leadership allows the full range of issues pertaining to sport-tourism to be addressed. Of course, the perceived and actual policy heartlands of the agencies concerned will vary between countries according to the roles such agencies have been assigned. The difference, for example, between the tourism policy heartland in the UK, where social tourism is not a key policy issue, and in France, where social tourism is a major concern, will be marked, and while this may lead to greater mutual ground with sports organizations, it may also create greater conflict. Similarly, problems can also occur if the sports and tourism communities have differing perceptions of their individual policy heartlands and the issues which they feel they own exclusively. Paradoxically, a further problem for the development of a sport-tourism policy network occurs where almost all sports tourism issues fall in the periphery of both agencies. This might be considered to be the case in the USA where the TIAA focuses on overseas

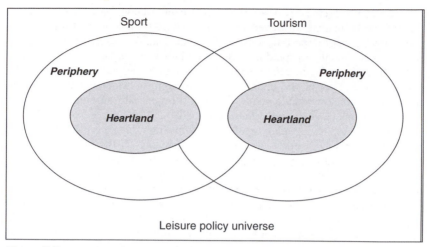

Figure 7.3 Sport and tourism policy communities: heartland and periphery

marketing, while the USOC largely concerns itself with the administration and organization of representative sport at all levels. Situations such as this can result in the neglect of sports tourism as a policy area because each community perceives that it is on the margins of their work and, as discussed above, mutuality is not considered to exist. Clearly the extent of mutuality will vary around the world according to the definitions of, and policy traditions in sport, tourism and sports tourism.

The third 'rule' identified by Wright (1988) emphasizes informality within the network. In a sport-tourism policy network it would be expected that the officers of sports and tourism agencies would feel able to communicate with each other on an informal basis. Evidence from the UK (Weed and Bull, 1998) suggests that informal contacts can be vital to the development of a sport-tourism policy network. In one example from the English regions, the departure of one member of staff led to the cessation of informal contacts and the failure of an emergent sports tourism initiative to move beyond an initial joint policy statement. Other examples describe the contribution of informal networks, often sustained outside of the work context, to the success of initiatives. While these examples are from UK research, the observations are clearly applicable to other countries.

In many cases, informality can be assisted by a fourth rule: that policy issues are discussed in a commonly accepted language. However, this may be problematic in a sport-tourism policy network, where the actors in the network may come from distinctly different backgrounds and cultures which use different modes of communication and specific technical languages. On a more basic level, as suggested above, there may be different perceptions of definitions of sport, tourism and sports tourism which, if communication is already minimal, can lead to a lack of liaison through misunderstanding or misconception. Of course, this is an area where differences will occur around the world. In Australia, where the work of the sports bodies is almost entirely focused on elite sport, and a relatively tight primary core of organizations exists supporting this goal, room for discussions in a commonly accepted language with the tourism sector may be limited. However, in France, where both sport and tourism are considered, at least in part, to contain elements of social-welfarist policy, discussions in a commonly accepted language are likely to be easier.

The final network rule relates to the recourse to higher authority, be that the courts or the state, or the opening up of an issue to wider debate involving those outside the immediate policy network. It is generally accepted that, as far as possible, policy networks will resolve issues within the network. This is generally because the opening up of an issue to wider debate outside the policy network will result in other organizations impinging on the network's 'territory'. Consequently, as far as is possible, policy networks attempt to resolve issues within the network. It is unclear how this rule might work within a sport-tourism policy network as there are relatively few examples of long-term or strategic sport-tourism policy partnerships. However, it may be the case that were an issue to become contentious, the sport and tourism agencies would retreat to their policy heartlands and take up fairly entrenched positions. This may result in the issue going unresolved, or in it being left either to the sport or the tourism agencies to resolve unilaterally or, if the issue is important enough, in decisions being made without either sport or tourism policy communities being consulted. In short, rather than recourse to higher authority, the inability of a sport-tourism policy network to resolve problematic issues is likely to lead to the withdrawal of one or more agencies from the network.

Conclusion

The discussions in this and the previous chapter have served to highlight the relatively undeveloped nature of sport-tourism policy partnerships around the world. Few countries have any long-term strategic sport-tourism policy collaborations at national level and, given the significant influence of regional contexts and individuals discussed above, it is perhaps unrealistic to expect such collaborations to develop. However, it would appear that the potential for collaboration is greater at regional or state level, where partnerships can focus more clearly on the particular needs of the region or state and where individuals who believe that mutual benefits are derived from the sport-tourism link may wield greater influence. As discussed above, a major factor in the success of such networks will be their ability to determine their own agenda according to the resources, people and attitudes that exist in their area. Consequently, it would seem reasonable to conclude that the most effective antecedent of greater sport-tourism links would be the raising of awareness of the benefits of the links among key policy-makers and organizations who may then work up their own agenda for greater collaboration.

These policy chapters have necessarily focused on the reasons for the limited liaison that exists between sport and tourism agencies around the world. However, some brief final comment is perhaps useful on the links between policy and both participants and providers. The conceptualization of sports tourism as an interaction of activity, people and place may, again, be useful in this regard. Tourism policy tends to focus largely on the development of place, while much sports policy focuses on the activity element (although also on the development of appropriate facilities and places in which activities can take place). The link between these two areas is a common need to consider people, and it is here that the discussions in Chapters 3, 4 and 5 can feed into policy development, highlighting particularly those areas where sports people and tourists are one and the same. Consequently, policy-makers might be encouraged to consider how policy for activities and places might be developed to maximize the benefits for both the tourist and the sports participant and more specifically, for the sports tourist.

The relationship between policy and providers is a complex one because, particularly at destination level, policy-makers can effectively also be providers. The most obvious examples of this are in relation to events, where cities, states/regions, and, in the case of the largest events, nations, become both policy-makers and providers. In other areas, policy-makers can assist in promoting confidence in providers, through various safety and accreditation schemes, particularly for outdoor adventure and activity tourism. Policy-makers may also play a role in policing developments ensuring, through planning regulations, strategies, legislation and advice, that sports tourism provision is both appropriate to the area, and is co-ordinated with other related developments to ensure an efficient overall pattern of provision. The relationships between providers and policy-makers, and the occasional blurring of the roles of the latter with the former, will become clearer as providers are discussed in the next two chapters.

Part Four: Providers

Preface

The previous policy part has highlighted the various problems associated with developing sports tourism policy partnerships. However, sport and tourism have long been linked in the minds of commercial providers, from large multinational tour operators such as Thomsons to small independent single-site outdoor activity providers. Public sector providers which, as the previous part highlighted, are also often policy-makers, have been less quick to link provision for sport and tourism, although in some cases (e.g. sports events) and in some locations (e.g. urban areas) the public sector has been more involved (see Sheffield case study in Chapter 11). In fact, it is perhaps in the area of sports events which, as Gammon and Kurtzman (2002) note, are mistakenly viewed by some as the only significant area of sports tourism, that the most extensive provision partnerships exist. Furthermore, much that has been written about sports tourism provision has, as with much other work in the field, focused on impacts, and even then the subject of this work has largely been sports events or outdoor activity sports tourism. Consequently, a significant proportion of this part of the book is taken up with establishing the full extent of provision for sports tourism.

The first chapter in this section examines the supply side of the market for sports tourism, developing in the process a categorization of types of sports tourism modified from Glyptis's (1982) work. This categorization is used to examine the nature and extent of sports tourism provision and the range of sports tourism providers. A number of potential features of sports tourism are derived from this discussion and developed into a Model of Sports Tourism Types in the conclusion to Chapter 8. As both the second providers chapter and the final substantive chapter before the case studies in Part Five, Chapter 9 draws together material from the participants and policy parts, in conjunction with the Model of Sports Tourism Types developed in Chapter 8, to examine a number of provision strategies that might be employed by sports tourism providers. Consequently, this chapter provides not only an overview of provision, but is also useful in demonstrating the inherent links between issues associated with sports tourism participants, policy and providers.

8

The market for sports tourism

It may seem a little strange, eight chapters into this book, only now to be considering the market for sports tourism. In fact, some authors would argue that it has been providers, particularly commercial providers, who have led the growth in sports tourism. However, while this might very well be the case, and acknowledging that the relationship between participants, policy-makers and providers is cyclical, the need for providers to understand the motivations and behaviour of participants and the problems of developing a coherent policy for sports tourism means that providers are most profitably considered after participants and policy-makers have been examined.

As the title suggests, it is the role of this chapter to consider the range of sports tourism provision and types of sports tourism providers. In doing so it is also useful to consider the aims and objectives of such providers, which might range from creating an image for an area to simply running a profitable business. The ways in which providers attempt to fulfil their aims and objectives are the subject of Chapter 9, which considers provision strategies.

The tradition within leisure and sports studies is to consider providers under the categories of commercial, public and voluntary sector provision, and it is worthwhile considering the extent to which such a structure would be useful here. Clearly much sports tourism provision is by the commercial sector, ranging from large-scale conglomerates such as Thomsons Holidays, through sports holiday village providers such as Club Med or Center Parcs, to very small-scale independent companies that provide a specific activity or set of activities at one particular destination. The public sector is involved in provision through financial support for sports events at national level, promotion of destinations at regional level and sports facility provision at local level. Other aspects of public provision might include supporting or providing 'social tourism' and contributing to the attraction or maintenance of sports franchises. While it might be argued that much of this provision is not primarily aimed at sports tourists, it does make a significant contribution to sports tourism provision. Such provision also shows that policy-makers can often also be providers.

It might be expected that the voluntary sector would contribute little to sports tourism provision. Yet, if this sector is conceptualized as a broader 'not-for-profit' sector, then it does make a contribution. A number of membership organizations, such as motoring organizations, cycle touring and camping clubs, and youth hostel associations, make up a significant minority of sports tourism provision.

It is, however, doubtful whether examining sports tourism providers under commercial, public and not-for-profit categories would allow for a particularly sophisticated analysis given that the vast majority of provision occurs by the commercial sector. The nature of providers as commercial, public or not-for-profit is clearly important in understanding motivations and objectives, but it does not allow for the required level of detail in analysing the full range of providers. In addition, some providers, such as outdoor activity education centres do not fall easily within such a categorization.

Another option in examining providers might be to consider provision that is made to cater for the particular types of sports tourists detailed in the Sports Tourism Participation Model described in Chapter 5. Clearly, provision made for Incidental sports tourists is very different to that needed to cater for the Driven sports tourist. However, examining providers in this way would define provision in terms of participation patterns, which would not be particularly useful in understanding the nature, aims and objectives of providers. Furthermore, the ways in which providers cater for different types of sports tourists is more relevant to the examination of provision strategies in Chapter 9, which uses the Sports Tourism Participation Model to help illustrate and understand such strategies.

It appears, therefore, that neither 'types of provider' nor 'types of sports tourist' provide a fruitful categorization for analysing sports tourism providers. However, an analysis based on 'types of sports tourism' would seem to be possible. In Chapter 5, a number of previous 'typologies' of sports tourism activities were briefly reviewed. Standeven and De Knop (1999) suggested a categorization (see Chapter 5, Figure 5.2) based on a number of polarized dimensions, namely: holiday/business, active/passive, casual/connoisseur, incidental/prime purpose, multi-/single sport, and organized/independent. While some of these dimensions are useful in understanding sports tourism types, the categorization is of little use in analysing provision as the number of dimensions results in a proliferation of categories that would make any analysis too fragmented. Hall's (1992a) model of adventure, health and sports tourism (see Chapter 5, Figure 5.1) would also not be appropriate to use as it does not illustrate the full range of provision as it is based on only two dimensions. However, the five 'demand types', suggested by Glyptis (1982), may provide a useful framework for analysis if they are reviewed and updated according to the contemporary nature of sports tourism

In one of the pioneering works in the field, Glyptis (1982) investigated the links between sport and tourism in five European countries and made some comparisons with Britain. She identified five 'demand types' – namely, general holidays with sports opportunities, activity holidays, sports training, spectator events and 'up-market' sports holidays – which, although proposed as relating to demand, essentially amount to a supply-side categorization of sports holidays. As such, these categories, with modification, can be useful in examining the range of provision and the types of providers for sports tourism. The 'activity holidays' category, while perhaps not initially intended to do so, has come to imply outdoor adventure or countryside pursuits such as rock-climbing, potholing, or hiking or trekking. It is useful to rename this category as 'sports participation holidays' to encompass the full range of sports activities that might take place as a prime purpose of a tourist trip. The 'spectator events' category is a useful one because it allows for the 'passive' aspect of sports tourism. However, other categories, such as general holidays with sports opportunities, may also include passive sports tourism. In addition, it is useful to allow for active involvement in sports events, particularly mass participation events such as the big city marathons. Consequently, this category is more usefully labelled as 'sports events'. The final category, 'up-market sports holidays' has been identified (Weed, 2001a) as being characterized not by the nature of the sports opportunities offered, but by the luxurious nature of the accommodation and attendant facilities provided. As such, it is perhaps useful to label this category as 'luxury sports holidays' to more accurately reflect this. In addition to the updating of the individual categories, one final modification is required to allow for the inclusion of day visits, which the vast majority of tourism definitions now include. This is achieved by simply replacing the word 'holidays' with 'tourism' where necessary in the categories. As a result, the updated sports tourism types are:

1 Tourism with sports content.
2 Sports participation tourism.
3 Sports training.
4 Sports events.
5 Luxury sports tourism.

The remainder of this chapter will now discuss the range of provision and types of providers within each of these sports tourism types, highlighting links between the categories, particularly in relation to providers that make provision in more than one category. The chapter will conclude with a model, derived from the analysis, illustrating the features of the sports tourism types.

Tourism with sports content

This category is the broadest of these sports tourism types, including not only the widest range of activities, but also the widest range of providers (Jackson and Weed, 2003). As earlier chapters have indicated, tourism that involves sport as an incidental activity rather than the prime purpose of the trip can often be sports tourism at its simplest and most unorganized. Consequently, the types of providers can vary considerably, from large-scale multinational operators such as Thomsons, to small leisure or sports centres that would not consider themselves to be part of the tourism industry. Providers in this category are certainly drawn from both the commercial and public sector, but there are also some examples from the 'not-for-profit' sector (Glyptis, 1982; Jackson and Glyptis, 1992). The defining characteristic, however, of this category is that sport is not the prime purpose of the tourism trip. Given such a defining characteristic, this category may overlap with 'Sports events' and 'Luxury sports tourism', where it may also be possible that sport is not the prime trip purpose

In exploring this category, it is perhaps useful to begin with the simplest form of sports tourism mentioned above, where sport is not an organized part of the holiday, where sports facilities or opportunities do not play any part in the choice of destination, and which would often take place spontaneously rather than being preplanned. Examples of such activities may be a trip to the local swimming pool, perhaps due to other activities being limited due to bad weather, or a trip to watch an ice hockey match as an alternative evening activity. As such, providers may be local public sector municipal provision (as in the case of the swimming trip), or a National Hockey League commercial franchise. In each case, the participation has not been preplanned, nor has it been part of the organized element of the holiday. Some research suggests (see Judd, 2002) that city breaks may often be most conducive to this element of sports tourism, as such breaks often involve a significant element of 'wandering around' the city and tourists may be attracted to events, activities or facilities that they previously had no knowledge of. The recent growth in 'sports museums' may be an example of this. Visits to such attractions, such as 'halls of fame' or 'stadium tours', as with many museums, can often be a spontaneous activity (Gammon, 2002; Snyder, 1991). Again, the providers may be commercial, public, or in some cases 'not-for-profit' in the form of trusts or charities.

Of course, the activities described above may, in other circumstances, be a planned, though not prime purpose, part of a tourism trip. Once sport becomes such a planned part of the trip, it is possible to examine the range of activities by reference to the importance of sport as a tourism decision factor. This is one of the categories used by Jackson and Weed (2003) in the Sports Tourism Demand Continuum described in the early part of Chapter 5, and subsequently used within the Sports Tourism Participation Model developed in that chapter. In illustrating this element, it is perhaps useful to begin with examples where sport can be a major tourism decision factor, despite not being the prime purpose of the trip. In such cases sport can be the deciding factor between a number of different tourism destinations, in effect, it is a 'unique selling proposition' for providers. As an example, a family may wish to take a beach holiday and, as described by Moutinho (1987), may have narrowed the choices down from a 'total opportunity set' of options, to a 'decision set' of three or four choices. However, this is but one element of the holiday decision-making process, comprising eight stages, described by Cooper et al. (1998):

1 Tourism need arousal.
2 Recognition of need for tourism.
3 Involvement and search for information.
4 Identification of alternatives.
5 Evaluation of alternatives.
6 Decision.
7 Purchase.
8 Post-purchase behaviour (anticipation and doubt).

The third, fourth and fifth stages listed above are those that correspond to the opportunity set reduction process described by Moutinho (1987). In many cases, if sport is perceived as important to the family, then the opportunities for activities such as water-skiing, scuba diving and other such activities may be the deciding factor between destinations in the fifth stage above. This is why the major tour operators' holiday brochures contain such a large number of photographs of sports activities and references to sports opportunities, and while some statistics suggest (Keynote, 2001) that the actual take-up of such opportunities may be low, that does not detract from their importance in the decision-making process, and therefore from the importance of sports provision to tour providers. Many hotels around the world use their sports facilities as a major factor in their marketing strategies, whether these are on the hotel's site, or provided by a local health club. In a number of cases in the UK, hotel chains have taken over or made strategic alliances with commercial health club providers to run facilities on their sites (Keynote, 2002). Hilton PLC, for example, bought Living Well Health and Leisure Ltd in 1999.

The Loughborough studies of sport at Butlins (McKoy, 1991; Reeves, 2000) described in Chapter 4, highlight how a British 'holiday camp' chain has attempted to use sport to revamp and refresh its product. Evidence from the tourists suggested that this had worked to a certain extent, as many said that sport had at least played a part in their destination choice. In many cases, it was the sports opportunities that existed for the children that were seen as important. Some families thought it was a useful way of keeping the kids occupied, while others were impressed by the opportunities for children to have some sports instruction. In fact, where instruction was available, a small but significant minority of adults took the opportunity to be introduced to new sports, something that has the potential to be a significant part of future sports tourism provision (Weed, 2001b). The provider here, similar to those discussed in the previous paragraph, is a commercial chain using sport to sell its holidays, and while the managing director knew that it was not sport alone that was bringing people to Butlins, he did feel that it was part of the mix of factors that affected choice, and also that it was a factor in generating repeat visits:

> To be honest, sport in general isn't at the top of our marketing agenda,
> but it's clearly part of the mix for families with children. I'm sure that
> the popularity of sport among the kids is one of the reasons that Butlins
> has a fairly loyal core market of returners. (From empirical data
> collected by Reeves, 2000, not quoted)

In other cases, sport can be a part of tourism planning once the destination choice has been made. In such cases there may be elements of sports participation or visits to events that are considered 'must see' or 'must do' activities when visiting a particular area. For example, for many non-American tourists visiting the USA, a trip to an American football or baseball game may often be regarded as such. As part of broader research on sports spectator motivations and behaviours at Loughborough University in 2002 (see Weed, 2003b), a number of focus groups and interviews were conducted with sports spectators, the following is an excerpt from one such focus group:

> *Interviewer:* . . . so what about sports spectating outside Europe? Has anyone travelled across the world to watch sport?
> *Responder:* Well, not specifically to watch, but I went to New York this year – my girlfriend and I went to visit a friend of hers who lives out there now. As soon as I knew we were going I wanted to see the (New York) Yankees play, I've never seen a baseball match, and don't really follow it, but it's something that you've got to do if you visit the States isn't it.
> *Interviewer:* What about your girlfriend, did she want to go to the game too?
> *Responder:* Yeah, that's the strange thing. She doesn't really follow sport at all over here, but as soon as I suggested it she was dead keen – she said going to a baseball match in New York was the same as visiting Buckingham Palace for American tourists in London. She didn't seem to think it was sports spectating in the same way as watching football is here, she'd never come to football with me in England.

There are three interesting things in this example. First, this example of sports tourism falls into the 'Visiting friends and relatives' sector which, similar to the city breaks described above, are often particularly conducive to incidental sports tourism (Jackson and Glyptis, 1992). Second, the visit to the baseball game became a part of the holiday plans from the first moment the destination choice was made as a 'must see/do' part of any visit to that city, but it was not a decision factor itself. Finally, the game was seen as more than a sports event, particularly by the responder's girlfriend, who saw it as a representation of the country's culture. While this is only isolated qualitative evidence, taken from a study that had other aims, it does give an indication of the types of factors that can be important in this type of sports tourism. It seems reasonable to assume that the 'Visiting friends and relatives' sector is important, that sports activities on general holidays can be an important part of pre-destination planning Cooper et al., 1998; (Moutinho, 1987), and that in some cases sport can be seen as a cultural representation of the destination.

The above discussions and examples can only be illustrative of this category of sports tourism. While this sports tourism type is defined by the fact that sport is not a prime purpose of the trip, it is virtually impossible to define or characterize provision in this area. This is because the range of potential sports activities that are not a prime purpose of the tourist trip are almost infinite. Many of the providers would not see themselves as part of the tourism industry, such as municipal sports facility providers or professional sports teams. These are, perhaps, 'incidental providers' and, along with the large-scale commercial tour operators, hotel chains, sports museums and small-scale destination sports providers, make up the eclectic mix of provision in this category.

Sports participation tourism

While the previous category is the broadest in terms of both range of activity and types of provider, the 'Sports participation tourism' category (where sport is the prime purpose of the trip) is perhaps the most obvious – essentially it refers to sports holidays, which is what most people would think of when they come across the term sports tourism. As with the previous category, there are some overlaps with other sports tourism types, particularly luxury sports tourism. Overlaps with other categories are best dealt with by exclusion. In this respect, active participation in sports events, except at the most basic level, is excluded from this category, as is any extended form of instruction or training. This category, therefore, encompasses the remainder of multi-sport or single-sport sports participation tourism and, with only a few exceptions, providers in this section tend to be drawn from the commercial sector.

A fairly obvious framework for examining this category is to consider multi-sport and single-sport trips. The most obvious single-sport is perhaps skiing, and entire texts have been dedicated to this topic by other authors (e.g. Hudson, 2000). Here, as with many aspects of the previous category, the major tour operators are the main providers, although they are obviously dependent on local destinations for much of their product. Probably almost as significant as skiing is golf, although providers are more likely to be independent courses and hotels, albeit often linked by producing or subscribing to golf holiday brochures to allow people to choose their own 'golf tour' if they wish (Jackson and Weed, 2003). Strangely for sports that are so different, there are two significant similarities between tourism trips to take part in these sports. First, there is often demand for some form of instruction, although where instruction is the prime purpose of the trip such holidays would fall into the sports training category. Second, the non-sporting aspects of the trips can be important and, while the sport provides the prime purpose and stimulus for the trip, the 'après-ski' and 'country club' experiences respectively often mean that these sports may often fall into the luxury sports tourism category (Weed, 2001a), a significant consideration for providers wishing to maximize profits.

At the more recreational end of the sports tourism spectrum are sports where the sport itself may be the method of transport for the trip, such as sailing, hiking and cycling. In the latter two cases, the not-for-profit sector is an important provider, with various hostel organizations such as the YMCA, which now exists in 122 countries around the world (WAYMCA, 1998), being important. In the UK, the Cyclists Touring Club, formed in 1878, provides advice and support for touring cyclists (Bull, Hoose and Weed, 2003), and other similar organizations, such as the Cascade Bicycle Club in Seattle, exist throughout the world, mostly linked to the International Bicycle Fund which acts as an international campaigning and umbrella organization for cycle transport and touring. Camp sites, usually very small independent commercial operations that subscribe to national 'guides' for promotional purposes, are also often a significant part of a cycling or hiking holiday.

The sport of sailing can be divided into two distinct categories: that where the boat itself is the transport and accommodation for the holiday; and that where the sailing takes place in the same place (e.g. at a lake venue) and the accommodation is provided nearby (Jennings, 2003). Sailing providers include commercial boat hire companies and marina developers, specialist commercial sailing holiday operators (that own a lake, equipment and accommodation) or networks of sailing clubs from the not-for-profit sector that organize exchange visits. In fact, across a range of sports, exchange visits, often organized independently between sports clubs, and sports tours, usually organized through commercial operators, are a further element of single-sports participation tourism. The most obvious examples are perhaps rugby and football tours, by professional, semi-professional, amateur and youth teams, often organized by commercial companies such as Travel International Sports, Harvard Sports Management Group and International Sports Tours (see Box 8.1). However, in almost any sport such tours or exchange visits are commonplace.

Box 8.1 Harvard Sports Management Group profile

Harvard Sports Management Group, Inc. was founded in 1991 by a group of corporate executives with the initial aim of providing sports tour experiences for their own children. Since then, the company's mission has been expanded to provide sports tours for all ages throughout the USA. Now the company offers 'sports tour experiences' for the first timer or the seasoned international traveller, the young player, or a young-at-heart adventurer, the youth league or the NCAA team.

As an example, youth football sports tour packages will typically include all aspects of tournament participation, including accommodations, meal plans, entry fees and transfers. The company will suggest possible tournaments, and advise on the expected standard of other teams to ensure a competitive experience. In addition to arranging tournament details, the company also offers pre-tournament activities including:

- the hire of a professional coach from the English FA, Dutch KNVB or Italian Serie A
- a tailored schedule of friendly games in the run up to the tournament
- tickets to see a 'professional' league match
- a 'behind the scenes' tour of a professional club.

Harvard Sports Management offers similar tours for a range of other sports, such as hockey, basketball and volleyball, as well as training camps and also 'familiarization' trips for coaches.

Bridging the division between single- and multi-sport participation tourism are outdoor adventure holidays. In some cases people will go on potholing or rock-climbing trips, and accommodation may be, like the cycling or hiking holidays described above, provided by hostels or camp sites. Similarly, some outdoor activity providers cater for single-sport holidays. However, the vast majority of such sites provide for the multi-sport adventurous activity holiday, including canoeing, climbing, kayaking, potholing and a range of other outdoor adventurous activities. Examples of such centres would be the Twr-Y-Felin Activity Centre in Pembrokeshire (discussed elsewhere in this text) and the National Mountain Centre at Plas-Y-Brenin, both located in Wales, a popular venue for activity tourism (see Chapter 12). Often such sites are independent commercial operators that generate much of their income through repeat business (Reeves, 2000; Weed, 2001a). Many operators also target children, providing either educational visits for schools or summer camps. PGL Activity Holidays, for example is a UK-based company that catered for over 130 000 guests in 2001 (PGL, 2002), the majority of which were in its core market of school trips. The company now operates in Europe, and offers skiing trips and environmental-based study trips in addition to its traditional adventure trips. In the USA, Camp America has long experience of providing summer activities for children, through both 'day camps' and 'on-camp' stays including both 'sporting and athletic' and 'creative and recreational' activities.

Increasingly the corporate market is becoming important, as centres that provide educational courses for schools are branching out into management training, using outdoor activities such as orienteering as team-building exercises because skills are thought to be transferable (Burke and Collins, 2002). While some of these companies, such as Ultimate Outdoor Adventures in British Columbia, offer corporate training alongside traditional adventure holidays and children's camps, others, such as Corporate Outdoor Training, based in Melbourne, Australia, concentrate on management training, offering activity programmes variously designed for 'team development', 'team-building' and 'leadership development'.

Multi-sport provision is also made by many hotels, although often a single sport, such as golf, is the primary sport on offer. Often such providers are 'country-house hotels' catering to the luxury market, and as such they will be discussed under luxury sports tourism. The number of commercial companies, mostly operating multiple sites, specializing in multi-sport participation tourism is increasing. The forerunner of this type of holiday was Club Med, which now attracts over 1.6 million 'clients' per year (Standeven and De Knop, 1999), however, other providers have emerged, particularly in Europe, that provide a 'subtropical pool' as the centrepiece of their facilities. Operators such as Center Parcs also provide for relaxing participation in sports such as tennis and snooker, alongside a range of restaurants and other facilities, usually set within a forest location (Keynote, 2001). Perhaps the final type of multi-activity provider is the 'health spa' concept, where the emphasis may either be on activity focused on weight loss, or on a more relaxing 'revitalization' visit. Providers here tend to be individual independent hotels, or small chains, however the growth of this market (Mintel, 2003b) means that some bigger players, such as the French Accor Group, are becoming involved (Weed, 2003e).

While this category of sports tourism is relatively wide-ranging, it is possible to identify some provider types involved in this market. Provision is largely by commercial companies, the only exception being the not-for-profit provision of accommodation and support by hostel organizations and cycle touring clubs. Within commercial provision for this category, it is only the multinational tour operators catering for the skiing market, and the multi-sport provider Club Med, that can be labelled as large-scale providers. Most other provision is by independent single-site operators, or small chains. There are perhaps two characteristics common to many of these independent sites. First, they often join together to produce, or subscribe to, guides or brochures to both market themselves and to help tourists to organize their own trip itinerary. The second characteristic, across a range of provision as diverse as adventure activity providers and health spas, is their reliance on, and ability to generate, repeat business (see Chapter 9).

Sports training

The sports training category is much narrower than the previous two sports tourism types discussed above. It comprises, quite simply, sports tourism trips where the prime purpose is sports instruction or training. This might range from a weekend instruction course for beginners on how to sail a dingy, to an elite training camp at altitude for a national athletics squad (Weed, 2001a). Provision can be by both the commercial and public sector, with public sector provision often being that for elite athletes.

It is possible to identify three areas within this category: 'learn to' courses, advanced instruction and elite training. In the first area, the purpose of the trip is to learn to play a sport. Sailing has already been mentioned as a good example, and within the UK the Royal Yachting Association (RYA) accredits residential courses at facilities throughout the country. Southwater Watersports, for example, offers residential instructional holidays in a range of water sports for individuals, couples, families and groups of adults or children. In addition to learning to play sports, coach education and training can also be included. Many courses to train coaches are residential, and as such should be considered as part of this 'learn to' category (Pigeassou, 2002). The similarity between coach education and learn to play is that in both cases some national governing body standard or certificate is often the end product of the course.

While any conceivable sport could be included in the 'learn to' category, another good example is golf, and here it is not just the technical skills needed to play golf that are important, but the cultural skills such as course etiquette (Bull and Weed, 1999). In this case, provision is usually by golfing hotels with a residential professional (Readman, 2003). In addition, the same sites would provide, also through a residential professional, advanced instruction in golf and, as with golf sports participation tourism, such holidays often are towards the luxury end of the market.

In the commercial sector, the same providers often cater for both advanced instruction and elite training. Club La Santa in Lanzarote is a good example of such a facility, with a range of sports on offer at top class facilities. In Reeves's (2000) study of elite British track and field athletes, Club La Santa was a regular training venue. However, a smaller, related study also described a trip to the facility by a small amateur squash club for 'advanced instuction'. The members of the club all contributed towards the cost of taking their own coach with them, and they emphasized that, while the purpose of the trip was squash coaching, all ability levels could join in and benefit from the trip. Similar facilities to Club La Santa exist around the world (e.g. La Manga in Southern Spain), while other popular sports training venues are focused on destinations rather than a specific site (e.g. Hilton Head Island in South Carolina and San

Diego in California) that have a concentration of top-class sports facilities and a favourable climate. In both cases, a significant proportion of business comes from repeat visits, particularly from elite athletes.

Sports training destinations may be in exotic locations, they may be linked to sports event venues, or they may be located where expertise exists. In the latter case, Loughborough University can be considered a sports tourism venue, regularly hosting training camps in a range of sports for both national and international teams. The sports training facilities have been subsidized by the UK National Lottery's Sport Fund for the specific development of elite sport (Sport England, 1999). Other sites in the UK have been similarly subsidized with some, such as the National Water Sports Centre at Holme Pierpoint, which has a 2000-metre rowing lake and slalom canoe course that can and have been used for international competition, being linked to event venues. However other centres, such as the picturesque Bisham Abbey, which often hosts England hockey and football team training and is home to the Lawn Tennis Association and English Hockey Association, are purely training venues. In such publicly subsidized facilities, the needs of elite training take precedence over any other use. Of course, the extent of publicly subsidized elite sports training provision in any given country will depend on the attitude of that country's government to the use of public funds for sports development purposes (Green, 2002).

The types of providers involved in catering to the sports training market are relatively simple to identify. 'Learn to' providers are largely small-scale independent commercial operations, but courses often work towards achieving ability levels or certification linked to national sports governing body standards in both participation and coach education. Commercial sector providers exist throughout the world for advanced instruction and elite training, and the same sites will usually cater to both markets. Similar to 'learn to' provision, which some of these sites may also provide, these providers are also often single-site operations. In some cases, elite training facilities may be subsidized by the public sector and, in these instances, it is unlikely that such sites would be available to any great extent to the advanced instruction market.

Sports events

As with the sports training category above, this sports tourism type is relatively easy to define. It refers to tourism where the prime purpose of the trip is to take part in sports events, either as a participant or a spectator. Provision may be by the commercial or public sector, or by a partnership of the two, and in most cases sports organizations are involved, so there can be voluntary sector involvement. Sports events can range in size from mega-events such as the Olympics and the football World Cup, to the smallest of local events, such as a 5-kilometre fun run. Regardless of size or importance, all events will attract both participants and spectators (Jackson and Weed, 2003).

Much has been written about the political and economic impacts of mega-events (e.g. Burbank, Andranovich and Heying, 2001; Fayos-Sola, 1998; Hall, 2001) and it would not be productive to repeat this material here – a brief discussion and reference to other sources can be found in Chapter 2. Needless to say, in order to stage an event of the magnitude of the Olympics, football World Cup or Commonwealth Games, partnership between the public, commercial and voluntary sector is required. For such major events, a country or city is nominally the provider as the named host, however this is far from the full story. Certainly government support is essentially to winning the right to stage such events, but even the most centralized of governments would not attempt to stage a wholly publicly funded mega-event. The last example of this would have been the Moscow Olympics of 1980, but at that time both world politics and the USSR's political system were very different to the present day. The commercial sector's involvement is likely to include, *inter alia, s*ponsorship, management expertise, facility provision and equipment supply (Getz, 2003). In addition, the voluntary sports sector, through sports governing bodies, will be needed to oversee the technical side of the sports competition. However, while the provision of such mega-events involves a complex set of partnerships among sectors, it is unlikely that the initial impetus to stage or bid for the games will come from the commercial sector, it will usually come from the city, country or, in some cases for individual sports, the national governing body for that sport.

Mid-size events, such as national championships or international championships in less high-profile sports such as judo, will generally gravitate to areas where suitable facilities exist, or to areas that have organizations that are prepared to host such events (Getz, 1997a). In many cases, mid-size events will be hosted in the run-up to, and the aftermath of, mega-events. The Sheffield case study in Chapter 11 highlights the way in which the facilities developed for the World Student Games in 1991 are still an important part of that city's event-based tourism strategy (Bramwell, 1997a). Similar to the mega-events described above, provision of mid-size events is often through a partnership of the three sectors, although public sector support may be less important. Most events depend to some extent on commercial sponsors, and almost all events involve some form of involvement from sports organizations, that will usually supply officials. Even the smallest of local fun runs will usually have some level of commercial sponsorship, will involve the public sector, if only in terms of permission to hold the event, and will be organized largely by volunteers (Stewart, 1993).

The events discussed above are mostly led by the voluntary or public sector, however, there are some events that are commercially owned. Examples would include some of the big city marathons, Major League baseball and, to all intents and purposes, Formula One motor racing. Here commercial companies own the patent to the event name, and while the public sector may be involved in terms of street closures or stadium subsidy, the events are organized along commercial lines for profit rather than any 'public benefit' (Getz, 2003).

While events attract commercial sponsors who get involved for the advertising and marketing benefits, it is important to highlight a further involvement of the commercial sector in relation to corporate hospitality. Such involvement may be through entertaining clients or providing incentive rewards for employees (Fraser, 1998). Corporate hospitality will obviously be most prevalent at more high-profile sports and at high-profile events, but to some extent corporate hospitality can exist, and can be important to providers, at many lower profile sports events (Lambton, 2001; Stewart, 1993).

Provision for sports events in the overwhelming majority of cases will take place through a partnership of the public, commercial and voluntary sectors. The lead sector may vary, depending on the event, but it is unlikely to be the commercial sector unless it is an event for which that sector owns the trademarks and rights, and thus can be exploited as it sees fit for commercial gain. Much that has previously been written on events has focused on their impacts, and such impacts are important to providers because in most cases they provide the motivation or impetus for provision.

Luxury sports tourism

Unlike any of the previous categories, luxury sports tourism is not defined by reference to the nature of the sport involved in the trip. Rather it is the quality of the facilities and the luxurious nature of the accommodation and attendant facilities and services that define this type of sports tourism (Weed, 2001a). Consequently, it overlaps with all the other categories, as it simply caters for the luxury end of the market in each case. As such it may seem a strange category to include, however, the nature of the clientele attracted, the tourism experience provided, and the aims and objectives of the providers themselves, mean that it is a useful and legitimate category. The nature of provision in this market is exclusively commercial.

As described earlier, golf and the country-house hotel, are high-profile examples of this type of sports tourism. In many cases, the luxury market is exploited by the addition of five-star accommodation to long established and renowned facilities (Readman, 2003). Golf provision in Scotland is a very useful example of this type of exploitation of historical facilities (see Box 8.2).

In addition to golf, some aspects of skiing provision might legitimately be labelled luxury sports tourism (Hudson, 2003a; Mintel, 2002b). In many cases this is as much a function of the exclusivity of the resort as the nature of the facilities, although five-star provision is still the defining element of this sports tourism type. The type of recreational sailing, involving luxury motor yachts, that might be a questionable inclusion as a sport, would also fall into this category (Jennings, 2003). Similar to the ski market, the luxury nature of motor yachting is defined by the exclusivity of the resorts visited, such as Monaco and St Tropez, where a marina berth would be prohibitively expensive for many aspirant tourists.

Luxury sports tourism can include the top end of the corporate hospitality market. The nature of the hospitality provided at many of top sports events, such as the Monaco Grand Prix, would certainly put such provision into the luxury category. Similarly, incentive packages for high achieving executives can quite often include a sporting break at the type of country-house hotel described in Box 8.2. Of course, some elements of elite training might also be described as luxury sports tourism, particularly for those at the very top of their profession travelling with national teams.

The nature of luxury sports tourism provision is exclusivity, or at least the perception of exclusivity. Such perceptions can be created by both the standards of facilities and the reputation of the resort. The need for exclusivity means that provision tends to be by independent operators – if the provider

---

Box 8.2 Golf tourism in Scotland

While clearly not all Scotland's golf tourism provision might be labelled 'up-market', the existence of commercial organizations such as Connoisseurs Scotland which seeks to cater for 'discerning travellers who expect the highest standards wherever they go' indicates that there is significant provision in this area. Such provision includes: the Turnberry Hotel, which has staged the British Open Golf Championship; the St Andrews Old Course Hotel, which hosts the home of golf – the Royal and Ancient Club; and Gleneagles, offering the Kings and Queens courses, and a further course designed by Jack Nicklaus. Golf tourism in Scotland has benefited from partnerships between sportsscotland and the Scottish Tourist Board which have, in partnership and independently, promoted Scotland as a golfing destination. The Scottish Tourist Board provides, in partnership with 'Golf Monthly' magazine, an annual guide to 'the Home of Golf', including where to play and stay, course listings and suggested itineraries for a golfing tour of the country, while sportsscotland maintains a published information digest on current provision and further opportunities to develop golf in Scotland. While neither of these initiatives is specifically aimed at promoting 'up-market' tourism, its impact on the Scottish economy means that such provision is promoted and encouraged. In highlighting the range of activities available at such country-house destinations, it is useful to consider Gleneagles. In addition to the three golf courses, Gleneagles provides for horse-riding, shooting, falconry, fishing and, a recent addition, off-road driving. The opportunity to 'enjoy virtually all Gleneagles has to offer for a single daily rate' is priced such that a couple taking up this opportunity would not have much change from £1000.

---

were part of a chain this would detract from the perception of exclusivity. In addition, provision is entirely commercial, and potential profits in this sector can be quite large (Lilley and DeFranco, 1999). Such large returns mean there is no need or desire for public sector investment or provision in this area.

Conclusion: features of sports tourism types

The discussion above has described five types of sports tourism, and examined an illustrative range of providers associated with those types. As a conclusion to this analysis, it is useful to identify, from both the discussion and the broader literature, key features of sports tourism provision, and to examine which features might be associated with each of the five sports tourism types.

First, and perhaps most obviously, sports tourism may involve multi-sport or single-sport participation. This is one of the dimensions identified by Standeven and De Knop (1999) in their catergorization of sports tourism, and as the discussions in this chapter show, all of the five types of sports tourism identified may involve either single-sport or multi-sport participation. Further features of sports tourism, identified by Glyptis in her 1982 categorization and

Jo Blackford

Data Co-ordinator

Elsevier

FREEPOST - SCE5435

Oxford

Oxon

OX2 8BR

Return this card today and enter £100 book draw

Select the subjects you'd like to receive information about, enter your email and mail address and freepost it back to us.

TECHNOLOGY

Architecture and Design:
- History of architecture ○
- Landscape ○
- Urban design ○
- Sustainable architecture ○
- Planning and design ○

□ **Building and Construction**

□ **Computing: Professional:**
- Communications ○
- Data Management ○
- Enterprise Computing ○
- IT Management ○
- Operating Systems ○

□ **Computing: Beginner:**
- Computing ○
- Programming ○

□ **Conservation and Museology**

□ **Engineering:**
- Aeronautical Engineering ○
- Automotive Engineering ○
- Chemical Engineering ○

- Health & Safety ○
- Environmental Engineering ○
- Plant / Maintenance / Manufacturing ○
- Marine Engineering ○
- Materials Science & Engineering ○
- Mechanical Engineering ○
- Petroleum Engineering ○
- Quality ○

□ **Electronics and Electrical Engineering:**
- Electrical Engineering ○
- Electronic Engineering ○
- Radio, Audio and TV Technology ○
- Computer Technology ○

□ **Film, Television, Video & Audio:**
- Audio/Radio ○
- Post Production ○
- Lighting ○
- Theatre Performance ○
- Photography/Imaging ○
- Radio ○

- TV ○
- Film/TV/Video Production ○
- Journalism ○
- Multimedia ○
- Computer Graphics/Animation ○
- Broadcast Management & Theory ○
- Broadcast & Communications Technology ○

□ **Security**

MANAGEMENT
- □ Finance and Accounting
- □ Hospitality, Leisure and Tourism
- □ HR and Training
- □ Pergamon Flexible Learning
- □ Knowledge Management
- □ Management
- □ Marketing
- □ IT Management

Name: _____

Email address: _____

Mail address: _____

Postcode _____   Date _____

Please keep me up to date by □ email □ post □ both

Science & Technology Books, Elsevier Ltd., Registered Office: The Boulevard, Langford Lane, Kidlington, Oxon OX5 1GB. Registered number: 1982084 used in much of the subsequent literature (Hall 1992a; Jackson and Glyptis, 1992; Standeven and De Knop, 1999), are its potential to be either active or passive. While each of the sports tourism types discussed here may be active, passive participation can only take place in the tourism with sports content (e.g. incidental spectating), sports events (as a spectator) and luxury sports tourism (e.g. as a corporate hospitality guest) types.

The four features identified so far exist on two binary dimensions; that is, they comprise two mutually exclusive pairs (multi/single sport and active/passive activities). Consequently, features are associated with sports tourism types in so far as each type of sports tourism may potentially display that feature, rather than the feature being a defining part of a particular sports tourism type. The remaining features identified do not exist to the exclusion of other features, but they are still associated with sports tourism types as potential features.

The discussions of sports training outlined how this sports tourism type is not only about elite training, but might also incorporate elements of 'advanced instruction'. However, instruction is also a potential feature of tourism with sports content (e.g. water-skiing instruction on beach holidays), sports participation tourism (e.g. advice about technique on cycling touring holidays) and luxury sports tourism (e.g. advice from a resident professional on golfing holidays). In each of these three cases 'instruction' is not the prime purpose of the trip as that would define the activities as sports training. Consequently, instruction might feature as part of four of the five sports tourism types. Sports training is also readily associated with elite sport although, as with instruction, this is not the only sports tourism type that might potentially involve elite sport. Elite sport may feature in both sports events (e.g. the Olympic Games) and luxury sports tourism (e.g. national squad 'get togethers' at luxurious facilities). Finally, involvement in sports tourism as part of a corporate group can be a feature of sports participation tourism (e.g. outdoor activity management training), sports events (e.g. corporate hospitality) and luxury sports tourism (e.g. a weekend in a country house hotel as a performance reward). A summary of the potential features of each sports tourism type is provided in Table 8.1, while Figure 8.1 presents a model of sports tourism types which illustrates these associations.

Each of the features described have recurred in relation to at least three of the sports tourism types, and three of them – multi-sport, single sport and active participation – may be a feature of every sports tourism type. It is perhaps

Table 8.1 Potential features of each sports tourism type

	Multi-sport	Single-sport	Active	Passive	Instruction	Elite	Corporate
Tourism with sports content	•	•	•	•	•		
Sports participation tourism	•	•	•		•		•
Sports training	•	•	•		•	•	
Sports events	•	•	•	•		•	•
Luxury sports tourism	•	•	•	•	•	•	•

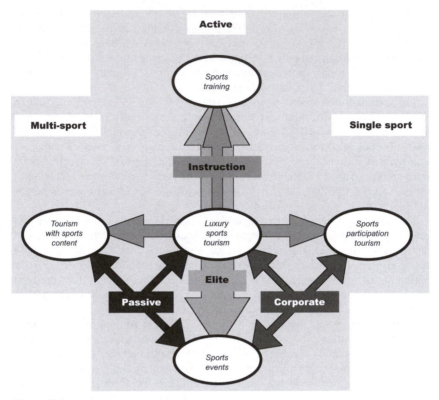

Figure 8.1 Model of Sports Tourism Types

useful to take one of the sports tourism types as an example to illustrate the potential features identified in the model. The model shows that sports events may be either multi-sport (e.g. Olympic Games) or single sport (e.g. football World Cup), may be active (e.g. as a participant in the Chicago Marathon) or passive (e.g. as a spectator at a New York Yankees baseball game), may involve elite sport (e.g. international championships) and may involve participation as part of a corporate group (e.g. the corporate hospitality boxes at Royal Ascot Horse Racing Events).

Developing a model such as this is useful in the context of studying sports tourism provision because an understanding of the nature and potential features of each sports tourism type can assist in examining the range of strategies used by sports tourism providers. As such, this model is used, in conjunction with the Sports Tourism Participation Model developed in Chapter 5, as the context for the analysis of provision strategies in Chapter 9.

9

Provision strategies

Throughout this book it has been maintained that the unique phenomenon of sports tourism arises from the interaction of activity, people and place. The participation chapters, particularly Chapter 3, 'Conceptualizing the sports tourist', discussed how activities, people and places contribute to the experiences of sports tourists. Such experiences, and the participation profiles discussed in chapter four, led to the development of a Sports Tourism Participation Model in Chapter 5 (see Figure 5.5). As noted in the previous chapter, this participation model is a useful tool in examining the provision strategies of sports tourism providers, as it assists in segmenting the sports tourism market and identifying key issues, such as the role of sports tourism in the holiday decision-making process.

However, the Sports Tourism Participation Model, while illustrating the range of sports tourist participants, does not allow for a similar illustration of provision. For such an illustration, it is useful to turn to the model of Sports Tourism Types, developed from the discussions in the previous chapter (see Figure 8.1). The use of these two models allows a discussion of provision strategies that can examine the ways in which providers match types of sports tourists with types of provision. In some places this may mean varying one or all of the activity, the people or the place, in others it may mean creating new sports tourists through, for example, converting intenders into actual participants.

A key consideration for the examination of provision strategies is the unit of analysis. Sports tourism providers come in all shapes and sizes, from an independent cycle hire firm that provides cycles and suggested routes for day hire, to large tour operating conglomerates such as Thomsons and First Choice, for whom sport is an important part of much of their product, and who operate on an international basis. Obviously the strategies of these firms will vary considerably as a result of their size. In some places, for example the Thrace region of Greece (Vrondou, 1999), an area, city or region may be attempting to promote itself as a sports tourism destination. In these situations it is likely that there will be some public sector involvement from local or regional government. Again the unit of analysis is important, because the focus could either be on the destination as a whole, incorporating a range of both commercial and public sector organizations, or on the strategies of an individual provider. Strategies at the 'destination' level, while not unrelated to those of individual providers, are likely to take on a different form, particularly in relation to marketing and promotion (Weed, 2003d). A further consideration is the nature of provision as ongoing, or as a one-off occurrence like the Olympic Games. Much research exists (Bramwell, 1998a; 1998b; Collins, 1991; Getz, 2003) detailing the importance of capitalizing on major events in attracting pre-event tourists, and continuing to attract tourists after the event. However, these strategies for provision are very different to those employed by providers, such as Club Med, that offer an 'ongoing' product.

The previous paragraph notes that, particularly at 'destination' level, some providers may be from the public sector, and this is perhaps particularly the case in cities such as Manchester and Sheffield (see case study in Chapter 11), where the public sector has had some role in relation to policy and planning, facility provision, marketing and promotion, or research. However, in many cases the role of the public sector relates to the support or facilitation of provision by others, and as such it is important to recognize the relationship of provision strategies to the role of policy-makers. The policy area matrix, discussed in Chapter 7 (see Figure 7.1), highlights the range of potential activities and issues for sports tourism policy-makers although, as the discussions in Chapters 6 and 7 show, collaboration on these issues is often not as developed as it might be. Nevertheless, the discussions in this chapter will, where appropriate, highlight the role of policy-makers in supporting provision.

The discussions in this chapter are organized around a range of provision strategies that are illustrative rather than exhaustive, and relate to the issues raised in the Sports Tourism Participation Model and the Model of Sports Tourism Types. These strategies are:

- converting intenders
- generating repeat visits
- expanding participation profiles
- co-operative marketing
- capturing incidentals
- creating competitive advantage
- exploiting intenders.

The extent to which varying the activity, the people or the place can be an effective way of expanding provision is discussed, and the relationship of provision to policy is highlighted. A key factor in the following discussions is the role of sports tourism in the tourism decision-making process.

Converting intenders

The concept of 'intenders' was drawn from work on arts audiences by Hill, O'Sullivan and O'Sullivan (1995). In Chapter 5 the concept was outlined as relating to those who are positively inclined towards sports tourism, and the idea of a tourist trip involving sport, but who never quite 'get round to it'. However, there is an important division in the intenders category, and this relates to the sports tourism types under discussion. The 'tourism with sports content' category relates to trips where sport is not the prime purpose, but may have been a factor, albeit one among many others, in destination choice. Here people may have undertaken the tourist trip with the intention of taking part in some sport while away, but in the event not actually done so (as evidenced by, *inter alia*, Keynote, 2001; Reeves, 2000; Tokarski, 1993). In such cases, the differentiation between intenders and participants is not apparent until the trip is undertaken. Issues relating to this category of intenders are discussed later under the 'Exploiting intenders' heading.

For most other sports tourism types, the differentiation between intenders and participants is apparent pre-trip, simply because participants will book a sports tourism trip while intenders will not. Often, because there is a positive attitude towards the idea of a sports tourism trip, intenders will appear on providers' mailing lists because they are likely to have sent off for brochures or registered an interest in sports tourism. Converting such intention into actual participation is clearly one potentially productive strategy for providers.

The potential type of sports tourism that intenders are considering will obviously affect the way such strategies are followed. For providers in the 'sports participation tourism' category, it may be that special discounts for 'first-time' sports tourists are offered, or 'taster' days or weekends with other newcomers where all equipment, instruction and accommodation is provided on site. A useful example of such provision is provided by the National Mountain Centre at Plas-Y-Brenin in Wales. Alongside provision for more experienced and advanced sports tourists, introductory two-day courses are offered in rock-climbing, mountaineering, kayaking and canoeing. These courses include on-site accommodation, all necessary equipment, and training and supervision by qualified instructors. Specially tailored versions of these 'taster' courses are run to cater specifically for families and, as discussed in the next section, further 'intermediate' or 'technique development' courses are offered to encourage repeat visits.

In these cases the strategy is similar to that followed by those tourism companies that offered the first overseas package holidays to tourists that had never travelled abroad before. The strategy is to make booking the trip as easy as possible, and as everything is provided through one contact, the customer will feel comfortable and at ease with trying a new activity (Holloway, 2003). Such feelings of comfort and safety are further enhanced by the involvement of policy-makers who draw up 'safety codes' and 'accredit' providers, particularly for the types of outdoor and adventurous activity sports tourism described in the above example.

Simple targeted marketing is one way in which intenders are converted. The discussions in Chapter 5 highlighted the importance of identity to understanding sports tourism participation. These discussions also noted that it is possible for intenders to be highly identified with an activity, without actually participating in it. One such example is sports spectating. For many intenders, watching sport on television is an important part of their lives, although they may never have actually attended a live event (Weed, 2003a). The targeting of such people by sports event providers is one key way in which intenders may be converted. This may be through advertising the event on television during another televised event, through targeted mail-outs to those subscribing to satellite or cable channels or, in cases where intending spectators are also active participants in the sport in question, by targeting clubs. Athletics provides a useful example of two of these strategies. In Britain, the ticket office for forthcoming athletics events is often advertised during televised athletics events broadcast by the British Broadcasting Corporation (BBC). This is almost unique, as the BBC is a publicly funded broadcaster that carries no commercial advertising. Addresses of athletics clubs are also often passed on to event promoters by UK Athletics, the sport's national governing body, who are then targeted to receive ticket offers for forthcoming events.

Of course, the targeting of clubs is also a strategy for both sports events and sports training providers to generate new custom. For many sports participants, the idea of combining active participation in a sports event (such as the New York Marathon) with a holiday may be attractive, as may the prospect of a sports training trip with friends and training partners. There are a number of companies who specialize in offering trips to sports events and sports training venues, and while much of their advertising is done through sports specific magazines such as *Runners World*, *Adventure Kayak* and *Triathlete*, they also target sports clubs with special offers for group bookings. The Volcano Triathlon Training Camp at Club La Santa in Lanzarote, for example, has been specifically targeted at triathlon club secretaries, and can incorporate participation in the Volcano Triathlon, which in 2003 was in its nineteenth year.

The market for corporate hospitality is also about converting intenders, but here the intenders are companies requiring a unique venue to entertain clients, and increasingly to reward and entertain their own employees in what is being termed 'participative hospitality' (Lambton, 2001). A key element in converting such companies to hospitality participants is the extent to which they can be convinced that the sports venue and event in question is congruent with their corporate image and target audience. A successful hospitality operation at a sports venue can provide a significant income – research from the Corporate Hospitality and Event Association showed that the UK hospitality market was worth £650 million in 2000. However, Lambton (2001: 56) believes that there is no question of hospitality making or breaking an event financially, rather it 'is there to reflect the event's inherent qualities' and is a key part of brand-building. As such, the decision as to which type of corporate 'intenders' an event or venue seeks to attract is important, and should be aimed at generating a truly mutually beneficial and complementary relationship between event organizer and hospitality client.

In a similar way that sports participation tourism providers may offer 'taster' weekends for 'first-timers', luxury sports tourism providers may attempt to capitalize on their corporate conference or incentive market to encourage guests to return on another occasion with friends or families (Fogelman, 1992). Many country house hotels, such as Pawleys Plantation Country Club in Myrtle Beach, South Carolina, have both extensive conference and sports and leisure facilities. Complementary access to sports and leisure facilities for conference guests is one way in which such providers attempt to covert such participants, who may fall into the intenders category, into participants with their families.

Strategies aimed at converting intenders for whom sport is usually the prime purpose of the trip, tend to relate to individual providers, or groups of providers packaged together by the specialist sports tour operating firms described above. In many cases, strategies at the destination level, while sometimes relating to the conversion of intenders, largely fall within the other categories discussed below.

Generating repeat visits

The generation of repeat visits is a provision strategy that is inextricably inter-linked with the conversion of intenders. The offers and incentives used to attract first-time sports tourists described above are made because it is hoped that having got a taste of sports tourism, guests will return for another, longer, higher-priced stay. Here sports tourists are being offered a sports tourism experience that they know and that, in many cases, they cannot get at home. As discussed in Chapter 4, sports participation tourism based around such activities as mountaineering and kayaking often cannot be accessed in the home environment, due either to lack of resources, lack of equipment, lack of like minded people, or lack of place experience. While a lack of resources and equipment can prevent the activity from taking place, a lack of like-minded people and imposing or extraordinary places can detract from the experience that is a key part of sports tourism (Weed, 2002d). Activity centres such as Plas-Y-Brenin described above, and Twr-Y-Felin in South Wales, provide not only the necessary equipment and resources for the activity, but also the people and the places necessary for the experience. Consequently, as described in Chapter 4, much of their trade comes from repeat visits. The study of Twr-Y-Felin (Reeves, 2000) showed that 45 per cent of visitors had previously visited the centre within the last six months, while 44 per cent indicated their intention to 'definitely return'.

The role sports tourism can play in generating both visits and repeat visits for family groups should not be underestimated. For many families, the avail-ability of activities that will keep the children occupied can be a central factor in destination choice. The study of Butlins Hoiliday Worlds in the UK (Reeves, 2000) provided evidence of this, with 73 per cent of respondents being on holiday with their children, and 85 per cent having previously visited Butlins in the last three years. The sport and leisure element had played some part in determining holiday choice for 69 per cent of these holiday-makers, with the following comment from a focus group being representative of many others in emphasizing the importance of sport in providing activities for children: 'We weren't really bothered about the sports and recreation facilities for ourselves, but we have two young children and they get bored very easily, so this was an easy choice to keep them out of trouble and in one place.'

Similarly, the availability of sport on beach holidays has been shown to be a factor in generating repeat business (Jackson and Glyptis, 1992), although the repeat business in such cases is more likely to be to another destination owned by the same tour operator. This is because holiday-makers come to recognize certain brands as providing a certain type of product (Morgan and Pritchard, 2000), in this case good sports opportunities and facilities.

At the driven end of the Sports Tourism Participation Model, the subcategory of elite athletes is a lucrative market for providers. Evidence of the importance of repeat visits in this sector is evidenced by the fact that a number of destinations have almost cornered the market in this area (examples being La Manga in Southern Spain, Club La Santa in Lanzarote and San Diego in California) although, as discussed by Delpy (1999), some of the bigger players such as Disney are now moving into provision in this area. However, the nature of the product can be very different to that of other sports tourism types. The elements of the place that are important are less related to experience, and more related to quality of facilities and support, and climate (Jackson and Reeves, 1998). Consequently, some elite sports training venues, such as Club La Santa in Lanzarote, also provide for sports participation tourism, and non-elite training and instruction trips. However other venues, such as Bisham Abbey and Loughborough University, both in the UK, where the emphasis is on facilities and sports science support and the trips are usually more intense training days or weekends, only provide for the elite element of sports training. As such, their ability to attract repeat visits has been based on the quality of service they are able to offer to elite athletes. In fact, in recent years, in recognition of the quality service such venues provide, their development has been publicly funded as a result of government policy initiatives related to the development of elite sport and the provision of a network of facilities and services comprising an English Institute of Sport (Shakespear, 2002).

In relation to sports events, there has been some research on customer loyalty, particularly in relation to football (King, Crabtree and Alexander, 2002), focusing on the utility of relationship marketing, which Clowes and Tapp (1998) suggest may be a more appropriate approach than a price or promotion response to the need to fill seats. A specific study of stakeholders at Nottingham Forest Football Club in the UK (Hearne, 2003) suggests that the relationship approach has worked in developing a good rapport with supporters groups. However, despite these specific examples, there must be some doubt as to the extent to which this approach is as useful as in other areas where there is not such an emotional attachment to the teams and clubs in question.

Some sports events are used as a way to introduce tourists to a particular area, and to generate repeat visits, either to other sports-related events and activities or to other tourist related aspects of the destination. One of Manchester's policy goals in hosting the Commonwealth Games was to introduce visitors to Manchester as a broader urban tourism destination, and to showcase other elements of Manchester's tourism product, some of which involve sport (Regan, 1999). Lancashire's County Cricket Ground, which is also a venue for Test Match cricket, and Manchester United's Old Trafford stadium, which contains a Museum and visitor centre, were both prominently promoted in Common-wealth Games material, as was the city's range of cultural attractions, theatres and bars. In addition to introducing visitors to the broader tourism product on offer, strategies such as this may also play a role in expanding the participation profile of sports tourists.

Expanding participation profiles

One of the strengths of the Sports Tourism Participation Model is that it can be conceived as a three-dimensional model including an individual's participation across a range of sports tourism activities. An individual may be a driven football spectator, but an incidental or sporadic participant in water sports on tourist trips. While the generation of repeat visits discussed above often relies on providing an experience of activity, people and place that cannot be attained in the sports tourists home area, repeat visits can also be generated by strategies that attempt to expand the sports tourists participation profile, thus offering a similar place experience, but through a different activity that will often be experienced as a different type of sports tourist.

A useful example of this type of strategy comes, initially, from the elite-training sports tourist. During warm weather training trips, athletes often have long periods of rests between training sessions and, within the constraints of avoiding injury, other sports often provide a useful diversion, both physically and mentally. Evidence from Reeves's (2000) study of elite athletes illustrates this, with athletes making the following comments:

> I play a lot of golf. When we went to La Manga the camp was actually situated on a golf course. We also take part in activities such as water skiing and swimming. It is like a half holiday, so we try and do as many activities as possible. We have to be careful of injury, but we must make sure that we are able to relax as well. The best way for me to do that is through playing sport. (Emma Merry, 21, GB and England Intermediate International, Discus and Shot Putt)

> We play anything to take the monotony out of athletics training all the time. We might go cycling or swimming, just to get out of the complex. When you are away training you tend to eat, breath and talk athletics. So for example when I was in Lanzarote in January, we went swimming, played badminton and basketball and joined in with the aerobics. (Jackie Agyepong, 26, GB and England Senior International, 100m hurdles)

> We have bicycles and we tend to play a lot of basketball. We do a lot of go-karting in Benidorm as they have brilliant facilities out there. Anything at all to stop the boredom whilst you are out there training hard twice a day. (Paul Hibbert, 30, England Senior International, 400m hurdles)

The extent to which this recreational participation is likely to translate into subsequent sports tourism trips in these activities is debatable because such activities are undertaken largely as merely a diversion from elite training. There may, however, be opportunities to encourage athletes to return with their families, or to develop broader sports tourism interests once their elite athletic career has come to an end.

The previous section described Manchester's strategy of exposing sports event tourists to the Commonwealth Games to other aspects of the city's tourism offering in order to generate repeat visits. At the city level, specific policy has been developed aimed at using a profile of sports events as the hook on which city visits can be generated. Consequently, the place experience of Manchester is similar, but the central activity – a test match, European football tie, athletics meet or other sports event – is different. This is a strategy that Sheffield has also used to good effect (see Bramwell, 1998a; 1998b; and the case study in Chapter 11).

Perhaps the most obvious areas in which participation profiles might be expanded are in sports participation tourism and luxury sports tourism. This is because in most cases providers of these types of sports tourism offer a range of activities. Some visitors to outdoor activity and adventure centres will be committed sports tourists across a range of activities, and for such multi-sport participants the expansion of the participation profile is unlikely to be a fruitful provision strategy. However, for those sports tourists for whom the prime purpose of the trip is to participate in a single sport, at whatever level, opportunities exist for providers to expand their participation profile through a number of strategies. Several examples of such strategies are related to the use of space. Henderson and Frelke (2000) discuss the close association of space with the activities and practices of those who use it, and therefore the provision of social spaces, such as bars and/or restaurants, at multi-sport activity centres where sports tourists participating in different activities can mix will often be one of the most effective ways of expanding participation profiles. Simply talking to people taking part in different activities may be enough to encourage people to try something new. Similarly, if activities take place in relatively close proximity to each other, then seeing others take part in activities may also encourage new activity take-up. Providers may try to capitalize on this by offering short supervised 'come and try it' sessions in different activities for those on a single sport trip, or may offer similar taster weekends as might be offered when trying to convert intenders as discussed above. Plas-Y-Brenin, the National Mountain Centre in North Wales, does this, offering 'have a go' multi-activity weekends which provide 'a whirlwind tour of canoeing, orienteering, climbing/abseiling, and skiing' (Plas-Y-Brenin brochure, 2003). All of the above also applies to the luxury end of the market, although strategies for such providers can often be more focused on capturing incidentals, particularly in country house hotels with extensive spa facilities (Weed, 2003e).

For some providers, the provision of opportunities to take in a number of sports at a relatively introductory level is the central tenet of their product. Here, the pre-trip decision is to engage in sports tourism that allows a wide range of activities to be undertaken, thus the participation profile is expanded at a relatively introductory level. Examples of such providers would be Center Parcs and Club Med, both of whom offer a range of leisure sport activities in a relaxed environment. The Center Parcs villages are largely sited in Northern Europe in forest locations, and are each centred around an indoor simulated subtropical pool environment, with the further provision of, among others, tennis, badminton, cycling, health centre and spa activities. In contrast to Center Parcs, Club Med villages are largely located in warm locations and so there is no need for an indoor pool environment. Club Med also employs 'animators' or activity leaders who tend to the needs of guests, not only in relation to their sports and recreation activities, but also to virtually any other holiday requirement.

While the strategies discussed under this heading have focused on varying the activity at a particular place, a further strategy may be to vary the place. This may be done by large tour operators who can offer a range of activities at a range of places, but can also take place through arrangements for co-operative marketing of sports tourism opportunities.

Co-operative marketing

A variation in activity and/or place experience is perhaps an obvious way to expand sports tourism take-up. In many cases, co-operative marketing is a sensible way forward because the sports tourism activities generated by such variations are often supplementary or complementary to current participation, rather than being replacement activities. Even where there may be some displacement of sports tourists, the reciprocal benefits of co-operative marketing can far outweigh the disadvantages (Selin et al., 1993).

Co-operative marketing may take place at a number of levels, but at its most straightforward it simply involves mutual promotion of activities and facilities at a particular destination (Briggs, 2001). This is often led or supported by local or regional policy-makers who may develop 'destination' marketing strategies and promotional materials. The cases of Manchester and Sheffield in relation to sports events are one example, but there are many others in relation to other sports tourism products. The 'Melbourne Now' campaign by the Victoria Tourism Commission in Australia was seen as effective in collectively marketing parks and recreational facilities as tourism attractions (D'Abaco, 1991), while co-operation among tourism firms on the Waterfront of Wellington in New Zealand (Doorne, 1998) have seen that area emerge as a recreational sports tourism destination.

An example of national level co-operative marketing from the luxury sports tourism type can be found in the promotion of golfing breaks in Scotland. As discussed in Chapter 8, policy partnerships between the Scottish Tourist Board and sportsscotland have promoted Scotland's golf tourism product as the 'Home of Golf', while the commercial consortium, Connoisseurs Scotland, specifically targets the 'discerning traveller' demanding the highest standards of both accommodation and facilities. A similar national level example, although not from the luxury end of the market, is provided by Vrondou's (1999) work on sports tourism policy and promotion in Greece, where there has been a deliberate policy of marketing a range of areas in Crete as 'soft' sports tourism destinations as a strategy to diversify away from the traditional mass tourism product.

Co-operative marketing is a strategy usually aimed at sports tourists from the centre of the Sports Tourism Participation Model, the regular and committed participants who may be seeking to expand their portfolio of experiences. This may be related to 'collecting places' (Urry, 2002) as discussed in Chapter 3, or to expanding the participation portfolio, as discussed above. For active sports event tourists, providers of other events see each event as a prime marketing opportunity to promote travel to their event (Green, 2001). The trade exhibitions that accompany large mass participation events, such as the London and Chicago marathons, will always contain a considerable number of stalls promoting other events such as running races, triathlons and endurance cycling, all of which might be seen as appealing to the type of sports tourist who would take part in a marathon. On a smaller scale, cars parked at local 10-kilometre running races, to which people may have travelled as a day trip, taking in lunch with family and friends after the event, will always attract a number of flyers for other events under the car windscreen.

There is a great deal of co-operative marketing that takes place between outdoor activity providers. Centres that specialize in some sports may contain material for other centres that provide related and complementary activities. In other cases, instructional centres will provide information on where sports tourists can continue their activity once they have developed the required competences. Skiing providers may also organize some cross promotion of facilities and destinations. For example, 'Top Ski Austria' is a marketing alliance of the country's top eighteen ski resorts (Hudson, 2000) which, in addition to the mutual promotion of facilities, also aims to organize the type of joint marketing activity described above. While in some of these cases, the cross-promotion may appear to be of competing resorts, this may still be an efficient business strategy given the motivations of many sports tourists. Notwithstanding the importance of generating repeat visits discussed in a previous section, many sports tourists are motivated, as described above, to 'collect places' (Urry, 2002), and as such will demand new place experiences. If resorts accept that certain sports tourists will not return year after year, then it makes sense to promote other destinations in return for reciprocal promotion of their resort (McDonald and Milne, 1999)

Capturing incidentals

One type of co-operative marketing described in the previous section – that of cross-promotion at the destination level – can aid considerably in capturing incidental sports tourists, those for whom sport is not the prime purpose of the trip. The capturing of incidentals relates largely to tourism with sports content, but can also be a productive strategy for providers of luxury sports tourism and sports events.

While for some forms of tourism with sports content, the availability of sports tourism activities plays a part, albeit a small one, in destination choice, for many other forms, incidental sports participation on tourism trips is the result of decisions made once the destination choice has been made. At some destinations there may be some incidental sports tourism that might be considered 'must see' activities, such as a trip to see the Yankees play baseball during a visit to New York, or a visit to the Australian Gallery of Sport or a cricket international at the Melbourne Cricket Ground on a visit to Victoria. At other destinations, incidental participation in sports tourism is an opportunistic decision, often made on the spur of the moment while at a destination. This is where strategies aimed at capturing incidentals, particularly co-operative marketing, are important.

The capture of potential incidental participants is largely about ensuring that information is available to such participants in the right place at the right time (Jackson and Glyptis, 1992). This may mean leaflets and posters in local accommodation, information in strategic places around the destination, and an awareness of the availability of sports tourism products among those working in other areas of tourism within the destination. For example, the Royal Malta Golf Club, part of the Marsa Country Club in Malta, runs an 'affiliate' programme among hotels on the island whereby hotels can become affiliated to the Royal Malta Golf Club, and display the club crest in their foyer. This has been shown to be an effective strategy in capturing potential incidental golf tourists, aided by the ease with which a round of golf can be booked through the hotels (Bull and Weed, 1999).

In many cases, potential incidental sports tourists may simply 'come across', for example, sports events while 'wandering around' an area, particularly more low-key local events in urban areas (Law, 2002). Alternatively, visits to indoor sports events or fixtures, such as ice hockey or basketball games, may take place because bad weather has precluded participation in activities that might have been preplanned. Similarly, the day hire of cycles, along with information regarding routes and potential stopping-off points, can also be a spontaneous, unplanned activity, although many hire centres are promoted in local guides (Koorey, 2001). In such cases, the type of destination-level co-operative marketing and information provision described above are key elements in strategies aimed at capturing these incidental sports tourists.

Finally, at the luxury end of the market, country-house hotels with extensive sports and spa facilities may often generate repeat visits by capturing incidental participants on a trip on which they originally had no intention of utilising such sports and spa facilities. A pilot study at one such hotel by Weed (2003e) showed that a significant group of 'incidental' participants in the health/spa activities on offer decided to take up such participation opportunities upon arrival at the hotel, rather than the facilities playing any part in their pre-trip planning. A significant minority of this group stated that their experience of the facilities at this hotel would lead them to consider such provision when considering future holiday plans for similar trips to country-house hotels.

Creating competitive advantage

While strategies aimed at capturing incidental participants can be productive at destination level, the provision of sports opportunities in the luxury sports tourism, tourism with sports content and sports events areas can be part of a wider strategy to create competitive advantage over competitor organizations or destinations. Sports facilities and events are now being used by a considerable number of tour operators, accommodation providers and destinations to 'add value' to their tourism offering (Standeven and De Knop, 1999).

Many hotels now have their own health and fitness suites, either through direct provision, or through strategic alliances with health club chains. Related to such provision, the health/spa/wellness concept is an area that is seen to offer considerable growth potential in the hotel sector. This is something that has been recognized by the French Accor hotel group, which has invested substantially in a wide range of health and wellness facilities across all of its hotel brands in the last decade (Reznik, 2003). Such health, fitness and wellness facilities are also important in creating advantages over competitors in relation to business tourism. As noted in Chapter 2, if a hotel wishes to attract the lucrative conference market, top-class conference, meeting and exhibition facilities must be complemented by similarly luxurious leisure facilities.

The study of sports tourism in Malta (Bull and Weed, 1999) revealed an interesting way in which sports event provision might be used to create competitive advantage. Some mass-participation sports events, such as the Malta Marathon and Masters Open Swimming Meets, were attracting participants who were combining their trip to the island for the sports event with a family holiday. Malta had been selected as the destination for a package holiday at a time when it was possible for a member of the family to participate in a sports event. Here, the sports tourism participation was only a small part of the holiday, but had been a key factor in destination choice. Research on both sides of the Atlantic (Dobson, Gratton and Holliday, 1997; Marsh, 1984; Yardley, MacDonald and Clarke, 1990) indicates that sports events and tournaments, for junior or adult participants, can be the excuse for a longer family holiday at the destination in question

Discussions in Chapter 8 outlined the extent to which sport and leisure opportunities are used by the big tour operators to add an additional dimension to their traditional tourism offering, although increasingly at this level the provision of this type of incidental sports tourism is necessary to maintain pace with competitors, rather than create an advantage. Similarly, the Butlins Holiday Worlds studies (McKoy, 1991; Reeves, 2000) show how Butlins initially used sport and leisure provision to update and refresh their product, and to create an advantage over competitor providers. However, as time has moved on, almost all 'holiday village/camp' providers have some level of sport and leisure provision (Mintel, 2002a). Furthermore, the arrival of the sport and leisure village concept, exemplified by Center Parcs, has raised the stakes in this area of provision.

Despite the investment by a number of the large tourism firms in provision for incidental and sporadic sports tourists, evidence suggests (Keynote, 2001) that take-up of such provision is relatively low. Why, then, have providers invested so much in the promotion of such opportunities? The answer lies in the final provision strategy to be discussed in this chapter, the exploitation of intenders.

Exploiting intenders

Discussions under the 'Converting intenders' section of this chapter described a division in the intenders category between those intenders taking a tourist trip that they intend to fall into the 'tourism with sport content' category, and those for whom the conversion from intender to participant takes place with the booking of a trip on which sport is the prime purpose. The latter category was discussed under the 'Converting intenders' heading; however, the former category, where intenders and participants are indistinguishable pre-trip, is the focus of this section.

Research at Butlins Holiday Worlds in the UK (McKoy, 1991; Reeves, 2000) provides primary evidence of the existence of intenders for whom sport is a part of the holiday decision-making process, but for whom participation never actually materializes. The following quote, from a focus group of Butlins holiday-makers, is representative of this behaviour: 'I must admit, I had all these great ideas of taking advantage of the facilities both indoors and outdoors, and in ten days all I've managed is a couple of games of snooker with a guy I met on the first day.'

The use of sport and leisure facilities as a marketing strategy has been discussed under the previous heading, but a comparison of activity take-up with the priority given to sports and leisure provision in marketing and promotional material reveals that the intention to use sport and leisure facilities on tourist trips where sport is not the prime purpose is far greater than actual participation. Furthermore, a cursory inspection of the actual facilities offered at some hotels, and a comparison of their capacity with expressed participation intentions (cf. Keynote, 2001; Mintel, 2002c), leads to the conclusion that many providers are banking on take-up being low, because if the level of participation matched intention to participate, then the level of provision would be woefully inadequate. Thus, intenders are exploited by providers whose market research tells them that sport and leisure provision sells holidays, but also tells them that activity take-up is comparatively low.

Conclusion: provision overview

The discussions of provision in this chapter have been intended to be illustrative of the strategies of providers, rather than provide an exhaustive coverage of such providers' behaviours. The chapter is not intended to be a 'how to' guide for sports tourism managers (see Turco, Riley and Swart, 2002 for that type of material), but offers an insight into the behaviours and objectives of those concerned with sports tourism provision.

The conceptualization of sports tourism as being derived from the unique interaction of activity, people and place has, once again, been useful in appreciating aspects of provision behaviour. Some strategies, such as the generation of repeat visits, aim to create a unique experience of activity, people and place that cannot be accessed at home, while others, such as creating competitive advantage and exploiting intenders, use the image associated with such experiences to sell various types of sports tourism trips. Variations in the nature of this interaction are also part of provision, with the expansion of provision profiles being related to the variation of activity, while co-operative marketing strategies are largely about varying the place. Finally, strategies aimed at converting intenders and capturing incidentals attempt to introduce potential sports tourists to this unique interaction in the hope that they will subsequently return as a more committed sports tourist type.

As the last substantive chapter before the case studies in Part Five, the material presented does provide a useful overview of the interconnected nature of knowledge about participants, policy-makers and providers. The Sports Tourism Participation Model, developed in Chapter 5, is useful in informing the strategies of providers, while the Model of Sports Tourism Types, derived from the discussions in Chapter 8, provides a useful context for understanding provision strategies. In addition, the chapter has highlighted key areas where the work of policy-makers, in both supporting and making provision, can be important. The final part of the book now examines the behaviours, motivations and strategies of sports tourism participants, policy-makers and providers in relation to four very different sports tourism products.

Part Five: Case Studies

Preface

The final part of this volume has been included to provide practical illustrations of the issues discussed in the earlier parts of the text. The cases have been selected to cover a range of sports tourism types, but also to illustrate a range of issues. As such, they each relate to varying extents to different parts of the earlier discussions.

However, these chapters are also intended to 'stand alone' and to be full discussions of the areas and types of sports tourism in question. Consequently, the chapters each locate the cases within their broader context, and highlight the nature of the impacts of the particular area sports tourism under discussion, in addition to providing an illustration of various issues associated with participants, policy-makers and providers.

The four case study chapters relate to sports tourism as a diversification strategy, urban sports tourism, activity tourism and winter skiing, in relation to Malta, Sheffield, Wales and the European Alps respectively. This range of areas and sports tourism types is intended to cover a range of aspects of sports tourism, and to specifically illustrate its nature as derived from the unique interaction of activity, people and place. The discussions of Malta and Sheffield both highlight how specific strategies are being pursued to develop the destination as a sports tourism place, although the nature of the activities and the types of people attracted are very different. The Welsh and Alpine cases perhaps focus more on the nature of the people involved, and how particular activities can interact with places in a way that provides an experience that cannot be replicated through the provision of artificial facilities in the sports tourists' home area. In terms of illustrating the material discussed earlier in the text, the Malta case relates largely to the provision chapters (8 and 9), while the Sheffield case highlights some of the issues discussed in the policy chapters (6 and 7). Both the Wales and European Alps cases are illustrative of the behaviours, motivations and profiles of participants discussed in Chapters 3, 4 and 5. However, each of the cases is intended to allow some level of reflection on the range of issues discussed throughout the book.

10

Sports tourism as a diversification strategy in Malta

The earlier chapters of this book have documented the increasing recognition, by participants, policy-makers and providers, of sports tourism as an important sector of the tourism industry and Chapter 2 described the range of areas in which sport and tourism might be linked for mutual benefit. Furthermore, Chapters 5 and 8 highlight the nature of sports tourism as a heterogeneous area, with a range of different markets offering potential to a destination seeking to diversify in this area. It would appear that the Mediterranean island of Malta possesses a number of advantages that would enable it to exploit some of these markets, perhaps particularly those relating to sports training, sports participation tourism, tourism with sports content and sports events identified in the Model of Sports Tourism Types in Chapter 8. This case study examines the development and potential of sports tourism as an important niche market in Malta, together with various problems which may constrain such development. It is based on an analysis of key documents, correspondence and interviews with Ministry officials, interviews with key personnel at a number of important sports facilities, as well as personal observations gained through several visits to the island.

The tourism product on Malta

One of the key problems relating to tourism development is that, despite its undoubted economic benefits, overreliance on this one industry are can be problematic (Bull, 1997; Buswell, 1996; King, 1982; Lockhart, 1997a). Small islands such as Malta are often regarded as particularly vulnerable because tourism can totally dominate the overall economic structure, in some cases accounting for well over 50 per cent of export earnings (Hutchings, 1996; Lockhart, and Drakakis-Smith, 1997; Shaw and Williams, 1994). Apart from the general problems of market fluctuations linked to a range of external factors, there are often problems associated with the precise nature of the tourism involved. Many small islands have allowed mass tourism to develop with scant regard to planning and long term, sustainable development. Apart from the usual vulnerability of such destinations to changes in fashion and the possible desire of tourists to extend their 'gaze' to new places, mass tourism development also brings additional problems which may ultimately lead to decline, such as poor quality accommodation, inadequate infrastructure and degradation of the environment. In addition, many places which embraced rapid tourist development often concentrated on limited markets and may have provided few alternative attractions beyond the basic sun, sand, sea and hotel facilities. While there may be little scope for significant development of other economic sectors, which is why tourism has been encouraged to such an extent in the first place, there is growing recognition that the tourist industry itself might be less vulnerable in such places if it were able to diversify (Lockhart, 1997a).

Malta has experienced many of these problems and has recently sought to establish new markets and attractions. Tourism began to develop in Malta from the mid-1960s and experienced spectacular growth in the 1970s with tourist arrivals increasing from 170 800 in 1970 to 705 500 in 1981; numbers then dropped back to approximately 500 000 for several years but built up again in the late 1980s, reaching nearly 1.2 million in the mid-1990s (ITR, 1996; Lockhart, 1997b; Lockhart and Ashton, 1987; 1991). One of the key factors in the rapid growth of tourism in Malta has been its dependence on a single market. In 1972 British visitors accounted for 50 per cent of all arrivals and by 1980 this had risen to over 76 per cent. The British legacy on Malta, the use of English, a readiness to respond to a demand for low-cost, self-catering accommodation, a favourable exchange rate boosted by exchange rate subsidies, and successive schemes to support British tour operators have all helped to encourage British visitors (ITR, 1996). The British market has thus not only been welcomed in the past but positively encouraged. But such dependence is double edged; it has seen Malta through some difficult times but it has also made Malta's tourism industry particularly vulnerable. While the UK share of the market has now dropped to just over 40 per cent, it is still high, and the problem of such an unhealthy dependence has been demonstrated at various times in the past. For example, in the early 1980s it was the large numbers of British holiday-makers transferring to Spain that was responsible for the substantial decline in overall tourist arrivals and, more recently, in 1995 a new decline was attributable to British tourists going to Turkey.

The problem of relying on a single country for a major proportion of visitors is further aggravated by the fact that much of Malta's tourism has also catered for the cheaper end of the market – a market which is likely to be much more sensitive to price competition. In fact this was the reason for British tourists transferring to Spain and Turkey. In addition, a high reliance on such a market has meant that greater numbers of tourists are needed than would otherwise be necessary to maintain a given level of income and these large numbers have at times led to tourist facilities being overstrained. Inadequate water supply, traffic congestion, waste disposal and general environmental degradation are all problems which have resulted from the rapid development of low-cost mass tourism, problems which further reduce the island's attractiveness and threaten tourism's long-term sustainability. As the Structure Plan for the Maltese Islands (Government of Malta, 1990) states, 'Malta has now reached the point at which tourist infrastructure is destroying the very features which attract tourists in the first place.'

As a result of these problems, Malta has been seeking to counter its reputation for providing a low-quality product by upgrading facilities and has also been attempting to reduce its reliance on its traditional mass tourism (Inskeep, 1994; ITR, 1996). As part of this process it has been encouraging diversification and the development of niche markets (Lockhart, 1997b). A number of alternative forms of tourism development have been suggested, one obvious example being that of cultural tourism which the National Tourist Organization (NTO) has been promoting explicitly in the 1990s. According to Boissevan (1993) this policy has been responsible for the growth of tourism in the off-peak period; whereas in the mid-1980s 70 per cent of tourist arrivals were between June and September, by 1992, although overall arrivals had nearly doubled, only 40 per cent were visiting during this period. A further example of diversification is the growing conference market which, in addition to being less seasonal, is also linked to a policy of upgrading hotel accommodation and only allowing the building of new hotels if they have a four- or five-star rating. However, a key area that has clearly been identified by the Maltese authorities as an important market is sports tourism (Brincat, 1995; Inskeep, 1994; Lockhart, 1997b; UNDP and WTO, 1989). Certainly the Maltese NTO is promoting a wide range of sports events and activities – both for participation and spectating – to foreign tourists (National Tourist Organization – Malta, 1997). Diving, yachting, power-boating, golf, football and swimming are just a few examples from a wide range of sports which are seen as having a great deal of potential in this respect.

The potential market and the current extent of sports tourism

Opportunities to be gained from the development of sports tourism in Malta relate to the growing importance of sport within society and increasing participation rates in a range of European countries for which Malta provides a convenient location and relatively short flying distances. An analysis of sports participation in such countries – for example Britain, France, Germany, Spain and Poland – shows that general participation in sport has been steadily increasing. While these countries use different definitions of sport and a range of survey methods to measure participation – see Cushman, Veal and Zuzaneck (1996) for a discussion of this – it is possible to identify general increases in participation in cycling, football, golf, tennis and a range of water sports over the last two decades.[1] Such increases are highly significant for Malta's development as a sports tourism destination because it already possesses the resources to provide these sports to foreign tourists and has long identified much of Europe as a major target market and, indeed, has existing links with many of these countries, especially the UK. Furthermore, the sports identified have been shown, both in Chapters 3, 4 and 5 and in studies elsewhere, to be mainstays of the sports tourism product (Jackson and Glyptis, 1992; Standeven and Tomlinson, 1994). In addition Malta's Mediterranean location provides a climate which is suitable for much of this sporting activity throughout the year but especially during the winter months when climatic conditions make the pursuit of sport difficult in many parts of Europe. Consequently, not only has Malta demonstrated the ability to attract the people element of the sports tourism experience, but it is also very well placed to provide for both the activity and place elements.

As the Model of Sports Tourism Types in Chapter 8 shows, the market for sports tourism is not homogeneous and a wide range of differentiated areas can be identified. At its simplest 'tourism with sports content' involves sport as part of a general holiday undertaken on a casual, informal basis and this has been a part of holiday-making in Malta for many years, just as it has been elsewhere. However, there is growing evidence to show that it is being seen as a more important part of the general holiday with travel brochures and hotels specifically promoting sporting opportunities. Certainly the better quality hotels are highlighting sports facilities. For example, several hotels advertise gymnasia and opportunities for water sports, with the Mellieha Bay Hotel listing, among other things, an 'independently run watersports centre' offering a range of opportunities including windsurfing, dinghy sailing, and water-skiing together with a 'PADI Five Star Dive Centre offering professional instruction in scuba diving for beginners to experts'. Similarly, the five-star Hotel Bay Point in St George's lists 'watersports including canoes and scuba-diving . . . golf at the Marsa Sports Club 8 km away . . . and supervised gym (in fitness centre)' (Thompson Summer Sun, 2000). A number of hotels on Malta are 'affiliated' to the Royal Malta Golf Club which is part of the Marsa Sports and Country Club and, as a result, are allowed to use the Club logo on their notepaper and display a plaque on the wall in their reception areas. In addition to golf being arranged for guests through the hotels, a 'pay-as-you-play' facility is also available for the incidental or sporadic sports tourist who may wish to play golf but for whom golf is not the main holiday purpose. As an official of the Marsa Club commented: 'no one will leave Malta having been unable to have a game of golf', a situation in stark contrast to that experienced at many other golf courses in Europe.

While golfing opportunities clearly exist for the general holiday-maker, Malta also caters for the golfing holiday, just as it provides for other types of 'sports participation tourism'. However, unlike golfing holidays in many other destinations, the market in Malta does not primarily fall within the 'luxury sports tourism' category. Malta's tradition of catering for 'cloth cap' tourism has helped to bring a golfing holiday within the reach of the 64 per cent of golf players in the UK who are skilled working class and there is every likelihood that this market will continue. However, the policy of promoting higher-quality hotels and the possibility of providing additional golf courses may well lead to a shift in the social balance in future. In contrast to golf, it is perhaps the case that much of Malta's provision and potential for water sports does fall more clearly into the 'luxury sports tourism' type. Malta's situation as a small island with a great deal of interesting coastline means that such water sports as scuba-diving, windsurfing and windsailing are an important part of its sports holiday market. Further to this, the development of the Marina at Msida has meant that yachting, both competitive and recreational, has become a significant contributor to the Maltese tourism industry. In fact yachting and scuba-diving, along with golf, have been the subject of specific development plans that aim to develop their potential as niche tourism markets.

'Sports training' in Malta is already provided for in a number of different sports. Once again golf provides a good example in this respect. Golf raises 40 per cent of the Marsa Sports Club's income, around half of which is from tourists, with golf schools being the major contributor. These schools usually involve a week's stay, with Scandinavia, especially Sweden and Norway, being a particularly important market. Not only does Malta provide physical opportunities to play golf which do not exist in these countries during the winter months, but it also provides an opportunity to learn how to play, something that is not always easy to achieve as a result of 'the snobbery of many golf clubs at home' (Marsa Club official). The Marsa Club employs a full-time resident professional who is primarily responsible for holding classes for visiting tourists (*Golfing in Malta*, undated). As a result, Malta enables such tourists to acquire the skills necessary to allow them to play golf on their return – thus providing the important 'foundation' stage of the sports development continuum, and providing sports tourists with an additional leisure opportunity that they would not have possessed prior to such a holiday. In this respect, the provision of golf in Malta is a good example of the sports development potential of sports tourism highlighted in Chapter 2.

Another important area of sports training is that of football. Indeed, the Malta Football Association has a German firm that advertises Malta in northern Europe as a place for training camps (Brincat, 1995). Teams from Scandinavia, Switzerland and Germany regularly use Malta for their pre-season training, taking advantage of the mild winters. In 1994 a team also came from South Korea to train (Brincat, 1995). The training camps are usually held at the Malta Football Association Technical Complex which, in addition to incorporating the National Stadium and possessing training grounds with the lushest and greenest grass on the island, also contains on site accommodation for up to twenty-four people, a restaurant catering for up to fifty people per sitting, a food technologist available for special menus, a gymnasium, sauna, sports injuries clinic (including fitness testing), lecture theatre, conference room, games room, television lounge and bar. These facilities have recently been expanded as part of the ongoing Ta'Qali Action Plan (Maltese Planning Authority), which is developing the area surrounding the Technical Complex as a National Recreation Centre including an indoor and outdoor sports complex, a basketball stadium, a cross-country/jogging track and further opportunities for informal recreation together with some additional accommodation. These developments increase the potential to develop this area of Malta as a major focus, not only for sports training trips, but also for less formal sports-tourism opportunities in the 'sports participation tourism' and 'tourism with sports content' areas. Swimming provides a further example of sports training linked to tourism with the Tal-Qroqq Swimming Pool and University Sports Complex providing an Olympic-size pool and a range of associated facilities for visiting groups including sports injuries clinic, underwater viewing facility, conference hall and seminar rooms. This facility is currently very popular with swimming clubs in the UK, with specialist sports tourism operators such as Toucan Tours and Track and Field liaising with the pool, the university and local hotels to provide a complete package to these clubs.

Despite its strengths in relation to golf, and in other areas of sports tourism that fall into the 'luxury' category, 'sports participation tourism' is currently perhaps the weakest area of the Maltese sports tourism product. However, Malta does have potential to develop this market. The landscape to the west of the island, away from the main urban areas surrounding the capital Valletta, provides opportunities for walking and hiking, and particularly mountain biking. This, combined with the proposed developments in the Ta'Qali area, particularly those for more informal recreation, enhances Malta's potential to develop sports participation tourism.

Finally, Malta has demonstrated an ability, despite its size, to make some provision for sports events. In recent years Malta has hosted a number of international events including the World Offshore power-boat racing grand prix, a senior APT tennis tournament, the Malta Marathon, the World Paralympics, the Small Nations Games and several editions of Jeux Sans Frontiers. Participation in the qualifying rounds of the football World Cup has also brought visiting teams to Malta together with their supporters, the Malta v. Ireland match in 1994 having attracted 3000 visiting spectators to the island (Brincat, 1995). But, as Chapters 4, 8 and 9 demonstrate, it is not just the more prestigious events that are important in this respect. The Tal-Qroqq pool, for example, is an important venue for Open Meets and Masters Events and this has a wider tourist impact as competitors will often bring their families with them and combine an event with a holiday. In fact, Malta hosts a number of events where visits by competitors' extended families can have a significant effect on tourist numbers. In order to capitalize on this, the NTO produces a comprehensive calendar of such events each year. The commercial potential of such events is further evidenced by the existence of such companies as Sportsmans Travel Malta, a UK-based firm which arranges visits for competitors and their families to such events.

Thus it is possible to see that Malta has already begun to exploit the undoubted demand for sports tourism but, while the potential market would appear to be growing inexorably, the extent to which Malta can take full advantage of these opportunities is dependent upon overcoming a number of resource constraints. Part of the solution to this rests with tourism planners and their ability to recognize the opportunities and their willingness to provide positive commitment to ensuring that development will occur. However, as discussions in Chapters 6 and 7 have shown, such recognition and commitment among policy makers and planners is not often easy to develop.

Resource constraints on sports tourism development in Malta

Despite the attractions of its accessible location and mild climate, a number of resource factors combine to constrain the development of sports tourism on Malta. Apart from the general problems of water supply, degraded landscape, and poor transport infrastructure, there is also the problem of limited land resources which have to cater for a wide range of demands. Malta involves a relatively small area of only 316 square kilometres and, as outlined earlier, has already experienced substantial tourist development. In addition, its own domestic population of approximately 350 000 is also making increasing demands on the land resource as living standards increase and the need for more housing and other facilities grows. Not only does this mean that land for additional sports facilities is becoming increasingly scarce but any new development has to be able to overcome strict planning controls which now operate. Golf provides a useful illustration of these problems as at present the Marsa golf course is the only course on the island. In the late 1990s the membership of the club was reaching saturation point with members often antagonistic towards large groups of visitors. However, the club needs the tourist income, without which it would either have to double its membership (which would not solve the saturation problem) or double membership fees. In any case, because the land on which the club is situated belongs to the government, and because the government recognizes the importance of golf tourism, there is little prospect of a change in the status quo. Consequently, in order that both domestic and tourist participation can flourish in Malta, an additional course is clearly required. However, two potential sites have already been refused planning permission partly because of landscape/environmental considerations but also because they would have impinged on high-quality agricultural land, something else that is becoming increasingly scarce. The large land requirements of golf, together with the need for substantial amounts of water on an island where water supply is problematic to begin with, mean that finding an additional course will not be easy.[2]

A further issue which complicates the facilities problem is the development of domestic sport. At present sport is not particularly well developed on the island, something that is due in large measure to what the former Maltese National Football Coach referred to as 'a gross lack of culture for sport' (Pippo Psaila, *Malta Football Association Quarterly Review*, December 1996). The Ministry of Education and National Culture is attempting to remedy this with discussions currently underway to establish 'how sports, culture and the arts may be promoted further both in the school curriculum, as well as extra curricular activities' and has talked about 'a concerted effort (being) made to see that sports' amenities in schools are upgraded together with their general maintenance' (discussion with Ministry official). In some ways, a general lack of participation in certain sports may have provided more opportunities for visitors. This would certainly appear to have been the case with golf in the past and also at the Tal-Qroqq Swimming Pool where there would appear to be spare capacity with no problems in programming the various user groups. In fact, the operations manager claimed that he could programme time for all user groups (when required) throughout the day, all year round. However, as sport becomes more popular on the island, the demands of the domestic population for access to sports facilities could have two very different consequences for sports tourism. On the one hand, the development of a sports culture could well lead to increasing demands for more and better facilities, which could enhance opportunities for sports tourists. On the other hand, it could place substantial pressure on existing sports resources and ultimately reduce availability to sports tourists. This would certainly seem to be happening in golf as well as other sports at the Marsa Country Club. For example, the club has 1000 tennis-playing members which certainly reduces the market for sports tourists who are only allowed to play on weekdays before 3.30 p.m.

In addition to providing new facilities, there is also the problem of accommodation. In order to attract the higher spending sports tourist, improvements in hotel accommodation are required, with possibly investment needed in the development of more five-star hotels. More hotel development, however, will inevitably involve further loss of land as well as landscape impacts and thus developers may find planning permission difficult to obtain, especially given the background of an apparent surplus stock of accommodation. The whole question of increasing the stock of five-star hotel accommodation has been the subject of considerable debate, with the issue often arising in the *Maltese Times* and including contributions from both the Minister of Tourism and the Shadow Minister. While the overall consensus appears to be supportive, there is still a hint that planning policies could impose constraints.

The role of government in sports tourism development

Chapters 6 and 7 show that the future direction and success of sports tourism can, in part, be determined by the policies and commitment of the relevant government departments. Malta is no different to any other country in this respect, and the government has an important role to play in a number of areas. First, it is responsible in large measure for some of the key infrastructural requirements of sports tourism such as the quality of transport facilities and provision of an adequate water supply. Second, through its environmental planning policies it can influence both the quality of the physical environment, and thus the attractiveness of the places in which sports tourism operates, and also through its development control mechanisms the extent to which sports facilities are permitted to develop. Third, through both its sports and tourism policies it can specifically encourage sports tourism development and, finally, through its relevant agencies it can promote its attractions abroad.

For several decades successive Maltese governments have attempted to promote tourism but, while espousing the principles of effective tourism planning, policy goals have not always been realized. Since the late 1980s a clearer recognition of the problems has emerged and, according to Lockhart (1997b), evidence of recent progress has been made regarding diversification, niche markets and an improvement in the seasonal spread of arrivals. However, as Chapters 6 and 7 highlight, the development and implementation of policies involving the integration of sport and tourism may be more difficult to achieve. Work in a range of countries has shown that, despite the undoubted advantages of linking the two, the respective sport and tourist bodies have often pursue independent policies with little attempt at integration. A useful comparison is with the situation in

Britain where evidence (Weed and Bull, 1997b) suggests that the lack of integrated policies may be due to the specific organizational arrangements that operate there. In particular it appears that such problems may be associated with the historically separate development of the two sectors. Unfortunately, in Malta the sport and tourism sectors have also developed separately.

The administrative arrangements in Malta are similar to those that existed in Britain prior to the creation in 1992 of the Department of National Heritage (renamed the Department for Culture, Media and Sport in 1997). Tourism responsibility rests with the Ministry of Tourism while responsibility for sport is located in the Secretariat for Youth, Sport, Art and Culture within the Education Ministry. Although in Britain the Department for Culture, Media and Sport (DCMS) notionally brings sport and tourism within the same Ministry, the various policies that the DCMS has pursued (with the exception of those relating to major events) appear to have actually weakened the potential for integration rather than strengthened it. Weed and Bull (1997b), identify the reduction of funding to the national and regional tourism agencies allocated to core functions, the adoption of increasingly narrow definitions of sport, and the cutting of the only statutory link between sport and tourism agencies in the abolition of the Regional Councils for Sport and Recreation, as DCMS policies that have limited the extent to which integration is likely to occur. A paradox is revealed between a government department structure that would appear to encourage sport-tourism relations and a set of policies that seems to do the opposite. The situation in Malta, of course, is slightly different and there may be opportunities to learn from the British experience.

Perhaps the most obvious difference is Malta's position as a small island state. Consequently, it has no regional structure of sport or tourism agencies nor does it need the large-scale bureaucracy that exists in Britain to co-ordinate matters at a national level. In this respect, the historically separate development of the two spheres may not be as problematic as in Britain, as large-scale readjustment would not be required for greater integration. Furthermore, the small-scale nature of the Maltese administration should make it easier and simpler to co-ordinate things on an informal level between the individuals involved. However, during discussions with officials of the Maltese government in the course of preparing this case study, it became apparent that in a number of cases such informal co-ordination did not appear to be occurring. Informal lines of communication between the planning department (responsible for the Ta'Qali Development Plan) and officials in the government responsible for sport had not even reached the point where the officials concerned knew the names of their colleagues in the other department. This example appears to be indicative of the situation across the Maltese government. In Britain, as elsewhere (see Chapter 7), the inclinations of key staff to develop links across sectors has been identified as one of a number of important factors affecting sport-tourism liaison (Weed and Bull, 1998). It would appear that this is also the case in Malta. It further appears that the attitudes of key staff may be of greater importance in the Maltese situation where there is greater latitude to develop links through informal co-ordination as a result of its smaller scale. In view of Malta's previously identified potential to further develop its sports tourism market, the obstacles that its government faces in assisting such development would not appear to be insurmountable.

Conclusion

While the inexorable growth of tourism means that on a world scale it is likely to remain the single most important industry well into the foreseeable future, the prospects for tourism within individual countries may not be so secure. Not only do countries need to ensure that the product they provide is not forsaken for a new product somewhere else, as tourists become increasingly fickle in their desires and requirements, they may also have to improve and rethink their product as a result of the legacy that initial, unplanned tourist development may have caused. These problems are particularly acute in many countries whose economies are especially reliant on mass tourism and one response to this has been the attempt to develop niche markets in order to diversify the tourism sector and possibly also attract visitors with a propensity to spend more.

While Malta is characterized by a number of unique circumstances, it also encounters many of the problems that beset other countries and, like many of them, it too is attempting to diversify through the establishment of niche markets such as sports tourism. This case study chapter shows that not only does Malta possess considerable scope for the development of a wide variety of different types, but that some of this potential is already being realized. There are, however, considerable opportunities still to be realized but it is also clear that, despite possessing a number of distinct advantages, various constraints could seriously hinder future progress. The resource constraints of land and water shortages, inadequate transport infrastructure, and large areas of unattractive landscape may pose substantial limits on future growth, while the lack of high-quality accommodation and the related image problem are also significant hurdles to be overcome.

In addition to resource and environmental problems, the future success of sports tourism development will also depend to a large extent on the attitude and commitment of the Maltese government. The government's involvement in improved infrastructure and environmental planning is obviously an important factor, but so too is its commitment and ability to develop and implement specific sport tourism policies. While successive Maltese governments have embraced the principle of tourism planning, related policy goals have not always been realized and, in the area of sports tourism, additional obstacles may hinder progress towards effective policy development and implementation. Both Chapters 6 and 7 and studies elsewhere have shown that this may be far more problematic than might be imagined, especially where the two sectors of sport and tourism involve separate departments and agencies. While sports tourism is highlighted in a number of policy documents, it would appear that the policy process has not involved the integrated involvement of both the sport and tourism sectors which, as in Britain and many other countries, operate independently. However, despite this, Malta also possesses an important advantage in overcoming such lack of integration, namely, its small size. The interest and enthusiasm of key staff is often a crucial factor in joint policy initiatives and the opportunities for joint action, if only on an informal basis in the first instance, must be greatly increased given Malta's situation as a small city-state. The growth of sport and the increasing way in which it is becoming involved with tourism provides substantial opportunities for places like Malta but, in overcoming the various constraining problems, such development needs to be planned, resourced and promoted by means of a clear policy.

Notes

1 The way data is collected across different countries varies significantly (see Cushman, Veal and Zuzaneck, 1996). The dates and methods of collection also vary. The estimates of trends quoted in the text were based on the following sources:

   (a) Office of Population Censuses and Surveys (1985–92). *The General Household Survey.* London: HMSO.

   (b) Institut National de Statistique et d'Etudes Economiques (INSEE) – see Garrigues (1988).

   (c) National Institute for Sport and Physical Education (INSEP) – see Erlinger, la Louveau and Metoudi (1985).

   (d) Israel Institute of Applied Social Research (IIASR) – see Katz (1992).

   (e) Uczestnictwo w kulturze (1992). Cultural Participation Surveys. Warsaw: GUS.

   (f) Foundation for the Development of Social Studies and Applied Sociology (1976–94). *Informe Sociologico Sobre la Situacion Social en Espana.* Madrid: Euroamerica.

2 The Marsa golf course occupies a unique site in the Wied Il-Kbir valley, which means that it is only a metre above the water table. Consequently, it does not experience problems of watering greens and fairways that might be expected of a golf course in Malta, an island with no surface water, where water is obtained from underground aquifers and expensive desalination plants.

11

Urban sports tourism: the case of Sheffield

Like Alpine skiing which will be examined in Chapter 13, another well-established example of sports tourism is that associated with large urban areas. However, unlike skiing where the principal involvement is active participation, in urban areas the main emphasis is with spectator sports. Cities exhibit a number of attractions for the development of this form of sports tourism. Given their size and market influence, they inevitably possess high-quality facilities and stadiums, established initially for their own residents and sports teams. However, domestic and subsequent international competitions have encouraged substantial numbers of people to travel to cities either to support their teams or to experience the sporting spectacle. In addition, cities are increasingly hosting mega-sporting events, using their existing facilities as well as creating new ones specifically for such purposes. While perhaps not as obvious as alpine regions, cities are, nevertheless, important sports tourism places, possessing distinctive sports tourism landscapes (Bale, 1994).

As outlined in Chapter 1, many sports teams have attracted a substantial following of supporters who are prepared to travel to watch their team play away from home, in both domestic and international competitions. Those teams with the greatest level of success are invariably associated with larger cities. For example, in the English Premier soccer league during the 2002–03 season, all the teams were located in urban centres with populations over 100 000 and 75 per cent were from cities with populations over 200 000 including six from London, three from Birmingham, two from Manchester, two from Liverpool and one each from Leeds and Newcastle. Similarly the two most successful Scottish teams – Rangers and Celtic – are located in Glasgow, Scotland's largest city, while in European football the teams that dominate European competitions are usually those associated with large cities (e.g. Real Madrid, Barcelona, Ajax of Amsterdam, Inter Milan and AC Milan, Roma and Lazio, Bayern Munich and Paris St Germain). This success is clearly attributable to their larger potential support and subsequent income which itself attracts financial investment from both local and external business, thus helping to maintain future success and support. This clear advantage of larger cities is further reinforced through the infrastructural and other peripheral facilities that such urban centres provide. Transport media, for example, are focused primarily on the major cities (e.g. motorway networks, inter-city train services and international and regional airports) and thus sports tourists can travel more easily to such destinations. In addition, given that cities are major locations for other forms of tourism means that they can also provide accommodation, restaurants, bars, clubs and various forms of entertainment for the visitor beyond the immediate attractions of sport. Not only are cities able to accommodate travelling supporters but, as outlined in Chapter 1, part of the attraction of travelling away to support the team may also include experiencing the nightlife and other facilities available to the mainstream tourist.

The large local catchments, transport foci and general tourist infrastructure also mean that large cities, and especially capital cities, are the logical locations for national stadiums. Various sports have their respective national stadiums in London with Wembley (currently being rebuilt), Twickenham, Lords and Wimbledon being obvious examples, although other UK cities are also capable of hosting national and international events (e.g. the Millennium Stadium in Cardiff, Meadowbank in Edinburgh and the Don Valley Stadium in Sheffield).

While the sports tourism associated with inter-city competition is well established, sports tourism in cities has become much more important in recent times as a result of two overlapping influences. The first involves a recognition of the importance of mega-events (including major sporting events) in the shaping of both the national tourism product and the long-term city product (Getz, 1991; Hall, 1992b; Ritchie, 1984; Tyler, Guerrier and Robertson, 1998) and the second is the way that sport in general has been used as part of tourism's role in urban regeneration. Each of these areas is recognized within the Policy Area Matrix for Sport and Tourism (Figure 7.1) discussed in Chapter 7. Aside from the identification of 'spectator events' within the 'sports holidays' category, issues surrounding provision for sports events are a feature of the 'facility issues' category, while 'economic and social regeneration' is a specific subcategory under 'resources and funding'.

According to Law (1993: 97) the term 'mega-event', in an urban context, describes 'large events of world importance and high profile which have a major impact on the image of the host city'. They are 'usually viewed as a highly significant tourist asset with the event directly attracting participants and the resulting raised profile of the area also indirectly encouraging increased general visitation' (Bramwell, 1997b: 168). Roche (2001) distinguishes between 'mega',

Table 11.1 Types of mega-event

Type of event	Example of event	Target attendance/ market	Type of media interest
Mega-event	Olympic Games; Football World Cup	Global	Global television
Special event	Grand Prix (F1); World regional sport (e.g. Pan-American Games	World regional/ national	International/ national television
Hallmark event	National sport event (e.g. Australian Games)	National	National television
	Big city sport/festivals	Regional	Local television

Source: Based on Roche (2001).

'special' and 'hallmark' events on the basis of the target attendance/market and the type of media interest involved (see Table 11.1), although other writers use the terms interchangeably which is the approach adopted here.

Special sporting events have emerged as major tourism policy instruments for governments keen to boost local business as a result of visitor spending (Mules, 1998). The economic benefits from mega-events are substantial. The total economic impact of the Montreal Olympic Games in 1976 was reckoned to have generated between US$77 million and $135 million (or between US$124 million and $216 million if multiplier effects are included), while the estimated total impact of the Los Angeles Olympic Games was US$417 million in value-added terms (Collins and Jackson, 1999). The 1996 Atlanta Olympics generated £645 million. Such figures may be exaggerated and, of course, do not reveal the extent of municipal debt and written-off capital involved (ibid.). The Atlanta Olympics cost £557.9 million. However, there are other reasons why such events have become increasingly attractive to both local and national governments. They are seen as a means of changing the image of both the city and the state as a whole (Robertson and Guerrier, 1998). In fact, Weiler and Hall (1992: 1) argue that 'Hallmark events are the image builders of modern tourism' while Waitt (1999) suggests that the Olympic Games as a spectacle is the ultimate tourist attraction. Such events can enhance the status of smaller states as in the Seoul Summer Olympic Games and also non-capital cities as in the Barcelona and Los Angeles Olympics, the Adelaide Grand Prix, the Calgary Winter Olympic Games or the Victoria, British Columbia, Common-wealth Games (Collins and Jackson, 1999). The Barcelona Olympic Games also helped Spain demonstrate an alternative tourism product to the mass tourism of the 'costas' (Robertson and Guerrier, 1998) and the city has subsequently become one of the top European tourism destinations, being ranked fifth in terms of visitor numbers in the late 1990s after London, Paris, Rome and Dublin (Wöber, 1997). More recent work by Waitt (2003: 112) who examined the social impacts of the Sydney Olympic Games, has also suggested that such impacts are positive and can 'generate patriotism and a sense of community or belonging, particularly among the young and ethnic minorities'. He believes that such 'global sporting events provide the opportunity for government and city authorities to (re)establish or increase the attachment and identification of people to place'. Whatever the overall benefits, there is intense competition among nations to host such prestigious events and governments are willing to help finance bids and fund the building of stadiums and related infrastructure as well as send delegations on 'charm offensives' in order to help secure them. Sport England invested £3.4 million in the bid for the 2006 Football World Cup, a decision which the government fully endorsed (DCMS, 2001).

As highlighted in the Policy Area Matrix for Sport and Tourism (Figure 7.1) discussed in Chapter 7, hallmark events are also part of sports tourism's wider role in helping urban regeneration. The idea of using tourism as a spur to urban economic and environmental regeneration originally came from North America but has now been adopted in many towns and cities throughout the developed world (Law, 1992; 1996; 2000; Swarbrooke, 2000). Various dockland areas such as Liverpool and London are classic examples of this, influenced to a large extent by the success of similar developments in the city of Baltimore (Shaw and Williams, 2002) and sport has often played a prominent role. London Docklands now contains the Docklands Sailing Centre, Surrey Docks Water Sports Centre and the London Wetbike Club, and has become an important tourist destination (see also Hall and Page, 2002). The 1992 Barcelona Olympic Games led to US$8 300 million of public and private sector investment in the area, including a new airport, a ringroad and clearance of a derelict waterfront area for the construction of an Olympic village (Chalkley et al., 1992; Stevens, 1992). Some cities have specifically marketed sports tourism as a central feature of their tourism-led regeneration. Manchester's failed bid for the 2000 Olympic Games acted as a catalyst for a 'vision' for change and expansion (Shaw and Williams, 2002), creating investment and development opportunities and allowing linkages and partnerships to flourish. Sport has subsequently become a crucial part of a central marketing initiative involving its football teams, cricket, the new swimming and diving complex at the university, the velodrome and the Commonwealth Stadium which hosted the Commonwealth Games in 2002. Birmingham also failed in bids for previous Olympics but, like Manchester, gained in civic reputation and sports facilities which included an indoor arena with 20 000 seats, a 50-metre pool and a refurbished stadium (Collins and Jackson, 1999). Likewise Glasgow and Sheffield have used sport as part of their regeneration attempts (see below).

Sports tourism in Sheffield: a case study

The city of Sheffield provides an interesting case study for the issues discussed above. While not a capital city, it is nevertheless a large urban centre with a population of 530 000. As such it possesses a variety of sports facilities consistent with its size and boasts a number of stadiums linked to domestic sports teams. It contains a range of world-class spectator sports venues including Bramall Lane and Hillsborough, the respective homes of the city's two football teams, Sheffield United and Sheffield Wednesday, the Sheffield Arena (for ice hockey and basketball) the Don Valley Stadium (athletics and rugby league), Ponds Forge International Sports Centre (ice hockey, basketball, swimming and aquatic sports) and Owlerton Stadium (speedway, stock cars, greyhound racing). In addition to spectator sports, the city also possesses various facilities for active sport including various leisure and sports centres, climbing centres, an ice centre with facilities for ice skating and speed skating, a ski village (Europe's largest artificial ski resort), golf courses, tenpin bowling venues and a laser zone. In addition, the new Phoenix Centre, being built with the help of a Lottery award, will include a 200-metre indoor athletics track and straight, sports hall, dojo, sports science and medicine services. Sports competitions not only attract substantial numbers of spectators to the city but a range of sports facilities is thus also available to general tourists.

But it is the way sport has been used in conjunction with tourism as part of Sheffield's regeneration process that is the major interest of this chapter. As such, it is illustrative of many of the potential linkages identified in the Policy Area Matrix for Sport and Tourism (Figure 7.1) in Chapter 7, and also of the importance of specific 'regional contexts' (see, again, Chapter 7), in this case Sheffield's decaying manufacturing industry and employment base, in overcoming many of the barriers to policy liaison. Sheffield built its reputation on its steel and cutlery industries but, like many cities in the developed world, it has seen its traditional industries decline in recent years such that steel now employs less than 10 per cent of its former workforce. In 1971 almost half of the workforce was engaged in manufacturing industry, but this had fallen to 24 per cent by 1984, with job loss in the metal-based manufacturing sector between 1981 and 1984 being double the rate for the UK generally and the city also suffered from a relatively poorly developed service sector (Dulac and Henry, 2001).

The development of sports tourism in Sheffield and its political context

The development of sports tourism in Sheffield did not simply develop by accident or as a result of market forces but rather as the direct result of specific decisions by local politicians to use sport in this way. Up to the mid-1980s investment in sport in Sheffield had been very low, much lower than in the majority of other cities in the UK, with the city council placing far more emphasis on cultural aspects rather than sport. However, as Dulac and Henry (2001) explain, a change in the political make-up of the ruling Labour group on the council and a worsening unemployment situation led to an acknowledgement that finance and other resources had to come from sources other than local taxation (which had been effectively capped by central government legislation) or financial transfers from central government. Partnership with local capital provided one of the few ways forward and, as a result, Sheffield adopted a series of partnership projects with local capital from the late 1980s.

In 1986 the Sheffield Economic Regeneration Committee in the City Council's Department of Employment and Economic Development was established (Strange, 1993, quoted in Dulac and Henry, 2001) which brought together representatives of the City Council, the business community, trade unions, higher education institutions, central government agencies and local organizations. As Dulac and Henry (2001: 66) explain:

> The aim of the group, as stated in the principal planning document it
> produced, *Sheffield 2000* . . . was to develop a long-term economic

regeneration strategy for the city, with a particular focus on the Lower Don Valley in which most of the old steel plants had existed and which was now largely derelict. As part of the regeneration process and following the recommendation of commercial consultants that a flagship project was required to spearhead the drive for regeneration, the city developed a successful bid over the period 1986–8 to stage the 1991 World Student Games.

According to Dulac and Henry (2001) the staging of the Games had several objectives: to reorient the image of Sheffield from 'City of Steel' to 'City of Sport'; to promote tourism in the city; to erode central government antagonism to the city and thus improve the city 's financial standing with central government; to generate a range of new and exciting facilities for local people to use after the Games, and which would allow, in the post-Games era, the staging of international sporting events; and, finally, to enhance the derelict environment of the Don Valley.

The city invested £147 million in sport venues for the 1991 World Student Games, and these were designed for a range of uses to attract visitors to the city following the Games event (Bramwell, 1998a). These venues included the £34 million Sheffield Arena (now called the Hallam FM Arena) 11 000-seat indoor facility which now hosts sport, concerts, exhibitions and shows; the Ponds Forge complex of Olympic standard swimming and diving pools, leisure pool, sports hall and night club; and the £28 million, 25 000-seat Don Valley Athletics Stadium, the Hillsborough Leisure Centre and the Lyceum Theatre (which was refurbished).

The strategy to host the 1991 Games has attracted much criticism. Sheffield's initial decision to bid for the Games did not involve much formal strategic planning but, instead, relied in its early decision-making on 'muddling through' (Bramwell, 1997b: 174). This lack of a final plan and insufficient research was probably a factor contributing to the Games being depicted as crisis ridden, incompetent and financially highly questionable (Roche, 1994). Bramwell (1997b: 174) also believes that the city has missed some city development opportunities by being slow to have a clear and adequately funded strategy linking the Games investment with tourism and city development. He cites the example of the city's Visitor and Conference Bureau and Events Unit being quite slow to assemble a range of accommodation packages with events in order to promote staying visits, although they have collaborated successfully later in the 1990s on subsequent major events. As outlined in Chapters 6 and 7, there are very few significant examples of partnerships between agencies in the area of sports tourism, and certainly no longer-term strategic collaborations. It is perhaps not surprising, therefore, that collaboration was lacking in the early stages; the fact that it occurred at all is unusual.

Another criticism has been the lack of public consultation, with the consequence that the local public did not feel that it 'owned' the project (Roche, 2001), a problem with added emphasis given the amounts of public funding involved, the related opportunity costs and the fact that the Games made an actual financial loss of £10.4 million. Critcher (1991), for example, has criticized the lack of consideration of alternatives while Dulac and Henry (2001: 68) are sceptical of the Games' value in terms of meeting the social needs of the local

169

population. For instance, in 1987, at the same time that the project was being planned, the City Council argued it needed £650 million to modernize its public housing and over £70 million to refurbish educational facilities (Bramwell, 1997a). As Collins and Jackson (1999: 191) comment 'the aftermath of debts and recrimination left a sour taste in the electorate's mouths and impoverished the image of the city's managers rather than enhancing it'.

Longer-term benefits

While there have clearly been many criticisms in relation to what some would describe as short-term failure (Collins and Jackson, 1999; Roche, 2001) it could be argued that in the medium and longer term the commitment to use sports tourism as a vehicle for urban regeneration in Sheffield has brought various benefits. The World Student Games was the largest multi-sport event in the UK since the 1948 Olympic Games and the facilities originally developed for the Games helped attract 250 major sporting events to the city between 1990 and 1996, including ten World and six European championships (Bramwell, 1998a). While no substantial research on the actual economic and social impacts was conducted after the Games – another key criticism – there has been some limited monitoring of the economic effects of events held in the new venues based on event attendances and simple estimates of spectator expenditure (Bramwell, 1997b). For example, numbers in 1994 totalled 900 000 at Sheffield Arena (indoor arena), 880 000 at Ponds Forge and 239 726 at the Don Valley Stadium. By the mid-1990s the city's sport programme was estimated to have added £31 million to the local economy and gained television coverage worth £85 million (Bramwell, 1997a; 1997b). Individual events like the European Swimming Championships and the UK Special Olympics in 1993 are calculated to have generated £1.7 million of expenditure in the city and more detailed work has shown that the three Euro '96 football matches held in Sheffield produced a substantial economic impact, boosting the city's economy by £5.83 million and generating 157 full-time employment jobs (Dobson, Gratton and Holliday, 1997). This event attracted 61 323 visiting supports and 5 400 accredited visitors (mainly media). Hotels, guest houses, pubs, restaurants and shops all benefited economically. The event was also an organizational success, and brought media attention to the city from across the world and, according to Dobson, Gratton and Holliday (1997), Destination Sheffield, the city and tourism promotion arm of the City Council, used the success of the tournament to market its short-break city trips to the Danes, the major group of visiting supporters. During June/July 1996, four other major sporting events injected an additional £4.1 million into Sheffield's local economy, economic impact figures which, as Dobson, Gratton and Holliday (1997) suggest, appear to justify the policy of urban regeneration that uses major sporting events as an economic catalyst. Another key international sporting event is the Embassy World Snooker Championships which up to 2003 had been held twenty-seven times in the city. While the event and its famous venue, the Crucible Theatre, existed well before the 1991 Games, it is nevertheless now part of the overall sports tourism strategy. The championship attracts thousands of visitors to Sheffield every year, including many from abroad, and it is estimated that it generates

£1.2 million for the local economy. It is therefore perhaps not unreasonable to believe city officials who reckon that the benefits of the Games now outweigh their costs sevenfold (Collins and Jackson, 1999: 191). In fact, in an enquiry into the future of major sporting events in Britain, a central government, all-party National Heritage Select Committee concluded that, despite the resulting burden of debt for the city, the Games investment did appear to be successful (quoted in Bramwell, 1998a).

It is not just the specific economic benefits from sporting events that are important, however, but also the re-imaging involved and its impact on the wider economy. As mentioned in the previous section, one of the key objectives of the initial project was to create a new image for Sheffield based on sport and leisure. Although at first little was done to develop specific strategies aimed at using sport explicitly in this way, this changed substantially in the mid-1990s. Following a report by Friel, a consultant employed to advise on Sheffield's marketing, strategies were formulated specifically linking the Games investment with the development of tourism as a means of promoting city development (Bramwell, 1997b). Friel's report also led to greater co-operation between sports event organizers and tourism staff in the Visitor and Conference Bureau, with the Events Unit moving into the same building as the Bureau. The formal strategic plan of 1995 (Destination Sheffield, *An Event-Led City and Tourism Marketing Strategy for Sheffield*) involved the use of 'profile' events using the venues built for the 1991 Games (Bramwell, 1997b). Such venues are not only used for prestigious sports events, but also for high-profile concerts. The Arena has been successful as a venue on the circuit of major European and world pop concert tours, while in 1995 100 000 people attended two outdoor concerts by Bon Jovi and the Rolling Stones at the Don Valley Stadium (Bramwell, 1997a).

The 1995 event-led city and tourism marketing strategy was also developed in the context of a strategic plan for Sheffield's wider economic regeneration, *The Way Ahead*, published in 1994 (SCLG, 1004), which also contained elements of sport, tourism and city marketing (ibid.). The conventional wisdom of the urban regeneration process (see Law, 1992) suggests that a city with high profile sports and leisure facilities marketed as key elements of a vibrant and exiting place in which to live is one means of attracting new businesses and Sheffield has clearly adopted this thinking. As Steve Brailey, chief executive of Sheffield International Venues and a member of Sheffield First Partnership commented in a press release issued in 1999:

> important as the cash into our economy is, there is an even more
> important factor for Sheffield in the provision of sports and leisure
> facilities. The key issues identified by Sheffield First Partnership when
> we consulted the people of Sheffield included attracting and keeping
> business in the city and updating the city's image. The presence of
> quality sports teams and leisure facilities will do that, along with regular
> staging of prestigious events – from Euro '96 to the world snooker finals,
> from the world masters swimming to the speed skating championships
> heading to the Arena early next year. The range and diversity of what
> Sheffield offers will also help persuade people this is a location to be
> considered for their expansion plans. There are many factors a business

171

will take into account when deciding on location. Naturally great weight will be given to the skills of the labour force and the cost of premises. But research has shown that the standard, range and variety of sporting and leisure facilities is a significant factor. Sheffield needs new investment, new jobs, and new businesses. It needs improved education results and improved health. But it also needs a high quality of life – and on the sport and leisure front the city has every right to be extremely proud of what it provides.

Another key part of the urban regeneration process is that of environmental improvement and its effect on improving a city's image. The sports facilities developed for the Games certainly had a very positive effect in this respect as they created a sport and leisure 'corridor' through the Don Valley, the area of the city most affected by de-industrialization (Dulac and Henry, 2001).

An examination of current marketing initiatives clearly illustrates the continuing importance of sport being used as a key vehicle to market the city and its tourism. The Sheffield City Council website, Welcome to Sheffield, highlights the fact that Sheffield was Britain's first National City of Sport, designated as such by the then Sports Council in 1995. The Destination Sheffield website also lists 'City of Sport' as one of its eight principal web links and the subsequent web page further promotes its sporting excellence in terms of being 'chosen as one of the main regional centres for the UK Sports Institute', having 'Britain's best array of international sports venues' and possessing Sheffield Ski Village, 'Europe's largest artificial ski resort'. In 2003 the Welcome to Sheffield website had the World Snooker Championships as its initial item and was also highlighting the 'wealth of fun events happening in the city centre as part of the "Sheffield on Cue" festival 2003' which the city had organized to celebrate the hosting of the championship. Furthermore, the sheffieldscene2 website was also highlighting the British Open Show Jumping Championships being held at the Hallam FM Arena (formerly known as the Sheffield Arena) in late April, and promoted as 'the biggest international show jumping event in England for over 30 years'.

Another objective of the Games was to provide sport and leisure facilities for the city's population, reflecting a continued concern for social welfare issues (Bramwell, 1997b). The city has certainly gained many high-quality sports facilities and more people now see these as assets. However, according to Dobson and Gratton (1995, quoted in Collins and Jackson, 1999: 191) 'the degree to which (the) commitment to sport has benefited the community's quality of life, patterns of sporting participation and social regeneration remains unanswered'. Dulac and Henry (2001: 68) also suggest that the Games' legacy in terms of meeting the social needs of the local population has been problematic. They believe that this is due to the management of the new facilities being placed in the hands of a City Trust, contracted by the local authority to meet certain standards of financial performance with no significant social goals specified by contract. As a result social goals have been de-prioritized. They argue, for example, that the policy of centralizing swimming provision in a large city-centre facility of international competition standard has radically affected those neighbourhoods which lost their swimming pool to permit this centralization and quote Taylor (1998) who has shown that participation in swimming in the city has actually declined since the introduction of the new facility, against the national trend. As Dulac and Henry (2001: 69) conclude:

> The overall outcome in terms of sport policy might be characterized therefore as a two tier policy, with an increase in consumer rights for those who can afford to pay private sector or near private sector rates, with some lower level welfare rights (subsidized sports development) for others who do not have the financial resources to benefit from consumer choice.

Nevertheless, despite such criticisms, there is some evidence that local people are pleased with the new sports and event facilities and see them positively, at least as tourism assets. A small survey of residents' satisfaction with Sheffield's tourism products undertaken in 1996 (Bramwell, 1998a) showed that, while people still had doubts about the merit of the original decision, many in the sample agreed that the city's new sport and event facilities were 'a great benefit to the city as they attract tourists' (74.8 per cent 'agreed' or 'strongly agreed'), that they 'improved the image of Sheffield' (85.6 per cent) and they are 'something to be proud of' (81.9 per cent).

Conclusion

This chapter has outlined the importance of sports tourism in cities and used a case study of Sheffield to illustrate some of the salient issues. Like most urban centres Sheffield possesses a range of sports teams and associated venues which provide the basis for a sizeable number of visitors who travel to the city to support their teams in domestic, and occasionally international, competitions. As such, it has been a sports tourism place for many years. In more recent years, however, Sheffield has also developed a substantial array of sports venues linked to mega-events as part of a regeneration process involving a conscious effort to promote itself on the basis of a new image linked to sport, leisure and tourism. As the history of this development has shown, this was not an automatic process and involved key decisions being made by city councillors and other prominent players, considerable risks being taken, both economically and politically, specific organizations and, especially, partnerships, established to facilitate the process, and a considerable amount of marketing and promotion. As such, it provides a useful illustration of many of the key issues and linkages suggested in the Policy Area Matrix for Sport and Tourism (Figure 7.1) in Chapter 7. However, it also shows that many of the tensions in the sport-tourism policy process identified in Part Three of this volume can be overcome, particularly if there is a specific focus for liaison. In the Sheffield case this was provided by the 'regional context' (see Chapter 7 for a discussion of this and other influences on collaborative sport-tourism policy) of urban decay and unemployment, and became strategically focused in the mid-1990s following the hosting of the World Student Games in 1991. While these policy directions did not attract universal support and clearly involved some problems, not least the £147 million cost of hosting the World Student Games and the lack of an initial strategy to capitalize on this event, there are many who would now admit the overall idea has been a success. As a result Sheffield has become a much more prominent sports tourism location than it was hitherto. Rather than simply being a city possessing some sports tourism, it is clearly a specific sports tourism place which is marketed as such. Not only is sport a key part of the overall tourism product but tourism has also been an instrumental element in the city acquiring so many prestigious sports facilities. Given the recognition of the clear benefits to be gained from the integration of sport and tourism, a claim discussed in earlier parts of this text, it is likely that Sheffield's position as a distinctive sports tourism location is assured.

12

Activity tourism in Wales

The countryside has a long history of receiving tourists but its significance has become increasingly important in recent times (Butler, Hall and Jenkins 1997; Page and Getz, 1997; Sharpley and Sharpley, 1997). According to the English Countryside Agency, in 1998, 1253 million day visits were made to the English countryside involving 66 per cent of the English population with several national parks recording over 20 million visitors a year. It is estimated that rural tourism contributes about £12 billion to local rural economies in the UK, its overall economic importance being especially highlighted, ironically, by the 2001 foot-and-mouth crisis (ETC, 2001; Sharpley and Craven, 2001). Furthermore, its significance for local employment has been illustrated by Leslie (2001) who estimated that half the Lake District National Park's population (approximately 42 000) is directly supported by tourism.

Much of the tourism associated with the countryside has been largely of a passive nature, involving such activities as walking, pleasure motoring, sightseeing, picnicking, nature study and fishing (Butler, 1998; Glyptis, 1991b; 1992; Harrison, 1991). However, more recently there has been a discernible growth in participation in active pursuits, a trend acknowledged by the Sports Council (1992) in its policy document, *A Countryside for Sport*. Clark et al. (1994) also highlight the growth of countryside sport as part of the increasing specialization and diversity of leisure, and cite the evidence of the growing range of related niche/specialist magazines as testimony to this. They also identify further specialization in the holiday market, especially in relation to short breaks and list, among others, specialized sports holidays (e.g. skiing, walking and canoeing) and activity holidays (see, e.g. Mintel, 1999).

Apart from the more traditional forms of outdoor pursuit involving hiking, climbing, caving and various water sports such as sailing and canoeing, some totally new forms have emerged such as snow skiing, snowmobiling, mountain biking, orienteering, survival, windsurfing, endurance sports and paragliding (Butler, 1998). Some are developments of existing activities, while others have been influenced by new technology, such as lower-priced and more friendly equipment, allowing easier, safer, and more comfortable operation than in the past, and many of these new activities have become accessible and popular with a vast new market (ibid.).

In the context of the particular concerns of this volume, activity tourism, as a particular form of sports tourism, is characterized by a number of key issues, including the nature of the market and the particular profile of the participants, the nature of the places involved and associated environmental impacts and, finally, the organization of the activities and the businesses involved. It is the intention of this chapter to consider these issues and illustrate them in the context of the UK and, more specifically in the later part of the chapter, in relation to rural Wales.

The activity tourism market and its socioeconomic profile

As outlined above, the term 'activity tourism' includes a wide range of outdoor pursuits undertaken for physical pleasure. The activities include highly popular pursuits such as cycling and hiking and hill walking together with those requiring special skills and equipment involving very few participants. It may be organized as a specific adventure and activity holiday, involving specific accommodation and/or itineraries, or it may be pursued more informally. All activities, however, are linked together by the enjoyment of natural landscape features and simply being out in the 'open air' (Mintel, 1998). In addition, given that the majority of resources are located at some distance from where people reside, travel and possibly a stay of one or more nights is often involved.

According to Mintel (1999) specific activity holidays account for just under 17 per cent of the domestic market (11 million activity holidays) and just over 9 per cent of holidays abroad (3 million). Growth in the 1990s has been steady with the number of domestic activity holidays increasing from 10.5 million holidays in 1994 to 11 million in 1999 and this domestic market is worth an estimated £1.9 billion (ibid.).

In terms of outdoor pursuits generally, cycling is the most popular activity with 25 per cent of the population taking part at least occasionally and half of these (12 per cent in total) doing so at least once a month (Mintel, 2000). This is followed by hiking and rambling involving 17 per cent of adults (just under 10 per cent doing so regularly). Most outdoor pursuits provide the basis for activity holidays as well as day-to-day leisure. In terms of activity holidays *per se*, the most popular pursuit is walking (in its various forms) followed by water sports (see Table 12.1).

Table 12.1 Activities as main purpose of a domestic activity holiday

	Long holidays		Short breaks		Total	
	000s	%	000s	%	000s	%
Walking, hiking, hill or fell walking, rambling, orienteering	1 300	26	1 400	23	2 700	24
Sailing, boating, canoeing, water sports	900	18	1 200	20	2 100	19
Swimming	800	16	800	13	1 600	15
Fishing, hunting or shooting	500	10	700	12	1 200	11
Golf	400	8	500	8	900	8
Cycling	400	8	350	6	750	7
Climbing	300	6	350	6	650	6
Other sport and multi-activity	400	8	700	12	1 100	10
Total	5 000	100	6 000	100	11 000	100

Source: Mintel (1999) Activity Holidays.

According to Mintel (1998) research for the UK tourist boards shows that 15 per cent of holidays taken in the UK by the British involve walking (or hiking etc.), although other forms involve much lower participation rates – cycling (3 per cent), water sports (3 per cent) and climbing (2 per cent). Mintel's (1997) report, *Activity Holidays, Leisure Intelligence* (cited in Mintel, 2000) found that 37 per cent of adults had, at some time in their lives, taken an activity holiday of one sort or another, led by walking or climbing holidays (12 per cent), holidays based around ball sports (including football, golf and tennis), cycling and water sports.

It is difficult to identify a particular socioeconomic profile for outdoor pursuits as the different activities display different characteristics. While under two-thirds of all regular cyclists are male and 53 per cent are aged under thirty-five, the demography for hiking/rambling is very different (Mintel, 2000). Here the gender balance is more even (52 per cent male compared with 48 per cent female) and hiking and rambling are one of the few groups of sporting activities in which regular participation is biased towards those aged over thirty-five. In water sports the gender distribution is more similar to cycling with males clearly more numerous (male:female ratio of 60:40) but the age distribution is even more dominated by the younger age groups, with nearly two-thirds of participants under the age of thirty-five, and 35 per cent aged under twenty-five (ibid.). In terms of activity holidays these demographic patterns are similar. Men are more interested in activity holidays than women (60 per cent compared with 44 per cent respectively) with youth especially important. One key difference is that there is not quite the same bias in favour of older age groups in relation to walking holidays as there is in relation to walking as a whole. The dominance of youth is also reflected in Table 12.2 which also highlights the constraints of family life for such activities.

Outdoor pursuits tend to be pursued primarily by those in the top three socioeconomic groups. The Mintel (2000) report shows that with cycling there is a slight bias in terms of those in groups ABC1 but hiking/rambling is predominantly an ABC1 pursuit with three-quarters of regular participants coming from these groups, four in ten being ABs. With water sports again there is a preponderance of ABC1s but this time over 40 per cent are in the C1 category

Table 12.2 Participation in various activity holidays by life stage

	Multi-activity	Walking etc.	Water sports
All	5	12	9
Life stage:			
Pre-family	13	15	22
Family	5	10	7
Empty nesters/no family	3	16	9
Post-family/retired	1	8	3

Source: Based on Mintel (1999).

(ibid). In relation to specific activity holidays, ABs show the most interest, especially in relation to walking holidays, although the appeal, if not actual participation, still remains strong among C2s and Ds (Mintel, 1999). Nevertheless, there are certain other groups who are prominent by their absence, in particular inner-city sixteen to twenty-five year olds and those from the black community (Logan, 1991). In fact, low participation rates for such groups are the case for countryside recreation as a whole, where problems of travel, the unwelcoming nature of the countryside, or at least a perception of such, and the low importance of the countryside in their cultural experience produce significant barriers (Agyeman, 1990; Harrison, 1991).

Those who regularly take part in outdoor pursuits do not just participate in one particular activity but also engage in several. Overall they are more likely to participate in other sports than other sports persons. According to Mintel (2000) nearly 10 per cent of those who regularly go hiking or rambling also climb on a regular basis (compared with only 2 per cent of all sports participants) and 7 per cent regularly go skiing or snowboarding. Similarly, 60 per cent of water sports participants swim on a regular basis, while a third cycle regularly. Outdoor pursuits and activity holidays would thus tend to be part of a particular lifestyle which emphasizes the active, usually linked to fitness and health, although such lifestyles are not uniform and may embrace different values. The degree to which fitness is pursued varies between different pursuits with some activities having far higher proportions of what Mintel (2000) refers to as 'fitness fanatics'. The Sports Tourism Participation Model discussed in Figure 5.5 accounted for the fact that certain sports tourists would be multi-activity participants and in relation to activity tourism they tend to be 'committed participants' across a range of activities.

'For most people, a holiday offers the chance to unwind, to relax and "do nothing". A typical holiday is usually an "in-active" one' (Mintel, 1999: 5). Activity holidays thus appeal to a specific niche within the overall tourism market where the motivations of participants would appear to be different to those more normally associated with holiday-making. However, as Chapter 3 pointed out, motivations are far from simple and relaxation is not necessarily synonymous with inactivity. In fact, as will be pointed out in the Wales case study later in this chapter, those engaged in activity holidays also see such active pursuits as relaxing. Thus, while it may not be possible to identify particular socioeconomic and demographic profiles among activity tourists, it is possible that they may be distinguished by certain behavioural and motivational charac-

Table 12.3 Characteristics of rural leisure activities

Traditional activities	*New activities*
Relaxing	Individualistic
Family/group orientated	Competitive
Non-competitive	Active
Passive	High cost
Non-mechanized	Relatively high per capita impact
Rural landscape complementary	Mechanized
Rural land use complementary	High technology
Low cost	Prestigious
Low per capita impact	Fast paced
Low technology	Rural landscape irrelevant
Non-urban	Rural land uses competitive
Minimum skill or training required	Urban related
	Skill demanding

Source: Butler (1998: 216).

teristics associated with activity and place. In addition, many individual outdoor activities are associated with specific subcultures, as discussed in Chapter 4.

Outdoor pursuits have also become fashionable, especially among the young, with the new and better quality clothing and footwear becoming fashionable items in their own right. Butler (1998) also identifies some different values in relation to the newer forms of rural activity that were mentioned earlier in this chapter and these are illustrated in Table 12.3. Whereas he is comparing all forms of countryside recreation, it is still possible to see how the more traditional outdoor pursuits such as rambling and walking, which tend to be non-competitive, non-mechanized, basically sympathetic to rural land uses and the landscape and can be group orientated, are very different from many of the newer forms. Butler (1998: 215) suggests that the development of these new activities is linked more readily to urban lifestyles and that many of them have 'no specific rationale for being located in rural areas except that they require considerable expanses of land and water'. The fact that they tend to be competitive with rural land uses and that the rural landscape may be irrelevant can thus lead to negative environmental impacts, an issue which will be considered in the following section.

Environmental impacts

Although many rural sites offer opportunities for outdoor pursuits, the areas offering the greatest potential are those associated with the more remote parts of the countryside, often areas of upland or less developed coasts. These are the places that have the specific resources that different pursuits require, such as cliff faces for climbing or rugged terrain for mountain-biking, or they are areas of wild, open landscape providing at least a semblance of the great outdoors, if not actual wilderness. In Britain such areas relate most closely to the national park areas in England and Wales and the upland areas of Scotland. But the remoteness and physical attributes that provide the distinctive attractions for outdoor pursuits also provide the potential for conflict. Many of these areas are the least able to sustain the impacts of sporting activity because they contain relatively fragile ecosystems which are both easily damaged and slow to recover. In addition, such areas often possess rare wildlife species and communities. The growth of outdoor pursuits clearly puts pressure on such resources but, in addition, such pressure is more acute due to the growing concern in society generally for the environment. As Standeven and De Knop (1999: 236) point out 'sports tourism is nowadays putting intense pressure on the natural environment, endangering it, and because of that sports tourism is also in danger'.

The various impacts that countryside recreation, including outdoor pursuits, can have on the environment have been discussed by many authorities over the years (Croall, 1995; Glyptis, 1991b; Mathieson and Wall, 1982; Patmore, 1983; Selman, 1992; Standeven and De Knop, 1999). A few studies have looked specifically at the impacts of outdoor pursuits, one such being that of Sidaway (1988) on the impacts on wildlife. His work involved a detailed analysis of various pursuits including caving, climbing, hiking/rambling (upland access), orienteering, subaqua diving, and water sports. His overall conclusions were that 'problems of conflict are localized and should be put into the wider perspective of more widespread habitat losses and damage from pollution and agriculture, and increasing numbers of examples of creative conservation' (ibid.). He also acknowledges, however, that there are 'some sites of such value to both sport and nature conservation that each interest is unwilling to concede priority to the other' (ibid.) and here planning and management will be necessary.

The importance of using the countryside for sport was spelled out in the Sports Council's policy document, *A Countryside for Sport*, published in 1992. The document stated the Council's belief that it had 'a significant role to play in encouraging the co-ordinated development of countryside activities' (ibid.: 3) and, as part of its 'sport for all' policy, its belief 'that everyone should have the opportunity to take part in countryside and water activities and to improve their level of skills and confidence' (ibid.: 5). Nevertheless, while on the one hand encouraging growth, on the other it was also conscious of the need to balance such growth with the need to protect natural resources and thus it argued that such promotion must be sustainable. However, Clark et al. (1994: 103) criticize the policy for, among other things, failing to 'acknowledge the variety of countryside activities and their widely different impacts on the environment, through identifying the term "countryside activity" as a singular category'.

Subsequent joint efforts by the Sports Council and Countryside Commission produced the publication, *Planning and Management for Sport and Active Recreation in the Countryside* (Elson, Heaney and Reynolds, 1995). This involved a study of the impacts of sport and recreation on sensitive environmental sites with attempts to demonstrate good practice in accordance with the principles of sustainable development. Six principles of good practice were identified, including systematic knowledge on the state of the environment; clarity of purpose (establishing goals and objectives); participatory management (involving voluntary agreements, multiple-use agreements, partnerships, negotiation and liaison); the voluntary approach involving the governing bodies of sports organizations; local involvement and consultation; and monitoring and review. While the need for good management is clearly an essential issue, and there is no doubt that serious impacts do occur at certain sites, some writers have suggested that the overall level of impact can be overstated (CRN, 1995; Sidaway, 1988; 1997; Sidaway and O'Connor, 1978). It can be severe in specific localities and along certain footpaths and bridle paths but is not extensive.

In some respects the impacts are as much the result of perceptions of the role of the countryside and conflicts between different recreational groups wanting to use the same space as they are about actual physical damage. The countryside is a contested space with many different groups and individuals, often with different values and perceptions, claiming it as their own (Harrison, 1991; Urry, 2002). Even among those seeking to use the countryside for recreation and sport, there exist different views as to the nature of the countryside and what activities it should support – for example, between those seeking peace and tranquillity and those wanting to practise noisy pursuits (Butler, 1998). Outdoor pursuits and activity tourism are clearly involved in this contest, especially where some of the newer forms are felt to be somewhat alien to broader consensus of what constitutes appropriate activity. Consequently, 'environmental, countryside and water issues' was one of the six main areas for joint policy attention highlighted in the Policy Area Matrix for Sport and Tourism (Figure 7.1) discussed in Chapter 7.

Organization and facilities

As outlined at the outset of this chapter, the rural economy has become highly dependent on tourism, and in many upland areas and remoter parts of the countryside it offers one of the few alternative economic enterprises to agriculture, itself a rather marginal activity. Outdoor pursuits and activity holidays form an important part of this economy and a number of different forms of facility and accommodation are involved in its operation. These range from specialized centres run by local authorities, schools, and voluntary organizations as well as the private sector, to small private concerns involving guesthouses, farm-based accommodation and caravan and camping sites. Nevertheless, despite this variety, there are some distinctive elements.

In addition to the specific forms of accommodation, there also exist a number of specific tour operators that have emerged to cater for activity holidays. The limited scale of demand for most activity holidays means that specialists come to the fore ahead of major travel groups (Mintel, 1999). It is estimated that around 120 members of the Association of Independent Tour Operators offer some type of activity-themed holiday, although many of these also offer conventional holidays (Mintel, 1999).

One particular characteristic of activity tourism is that outdoor pursuits/activity holidays have been promoted as appropriate forms of leisure for young people for well over half a century. Such activity was encouraged by the establishment of the Outward Bound Trust in 1946 and later by the Duke of Edinburgh Award Scheme, and has also been a key feature of the Scout movement. The same ideals have been echoed more recently by the Hunt Report (1989), in particular the recommendation that 'every young person in the United Kingdom (should have) the opportunity to take part in adventurous activities'. This report led to the immediate establishment of the Foundation for Outdoor Adventure committed to the promotion of the values of outdoor and adventurous experiences for young people. And, in 1990, the Countryside Recreation Research and Advisory Group (CRRAG) devoted its annual conference to the theme, 'Young People, Adventure and the Countryside' (CRRAG, 1991).

As part of the above tradition, although of slightly longer origin, the Youth Hostels Association (YHA) has for over seventy years encouraged the use of the outdoors and helped young people, and others, of limited means by providing suitably priced accommodation. The YHA has 300 000 members and 228 hostels throughout England and Wales (YHA website, May 2003) and, in addition to providing accommodation, it also advertises activity holidays at some of its hostels. Such holidays embrace family breaks, training, special interest, caving, climbing, horse-riding, multi-activity, hill- and mountain-walking, water sports and cycling. Its hostels at Edale and Okehampton are particularly important in this respect but other activity holidays are also advertised at hostels in Wales, Cornwall and the Lake District.

The most unique characteristic of activity tourism is the specialist activity centre, which exists to facilitate this form of sports tourism. According to Clark et al. (1994) multi-activity centres provide a wide range of activities, the average number being eleven, with the four most common being rock-climbing, orienteering, skiing and canoeing. Examples of such centres in Wales are described below.

Activity tourism in Wales

Wales contains a wealth of resources for outdoor sport and activity holidays. It possesses three national parks (Snowdonia, the Brecon Beacons and the Pembrokeshire Coast), five areas of outstanding natural beauty and a varied coastline, including 300 miles of Heritage coast. In the Wales Tourist Board's (WTB, 2000: 39) tourism strategy such areas are highlighted as one of the principality's strengths along with its ability to cater for activity holidays. As a result, the WTB has engaged in the proactive marketing and development of campaigns specifically promoting a number of activities including walking, adventure activities, cycling, fishing and riding, and in 2002 produced tourism strategies on each of these five activity products.

The Welsh activity tourism market

According to the walking strategy (WTB, 2002a) walking as a holiday and day-visit activity is clearly very popular in Wales with research showing that almost three-quarters of UK holiday visitors, and two-thirds of overseas holiday visitors to Wales go walking at some point during their stay, and over half of all-day visits in Wales include walking. Walking tourism offers considerable economic benefits to Wales with spending by walking visitors estimated to bring over £550 million into its rural and coastal economies. While walking is by far the most significant, other activities are also important. An estimated 800 000 horse-riding occasions are taken by visitors in Wales each year with an estimated direct expenditure of £18.55 million. Riders comprise three broad groups:

1 Holidaymakers taking a horse-ride as one activity during their stay – *c.* 55 per cent of riding occasions.
2 Between 30 000 and 40 000 people take a riding holiday – accounting for 15–20 per cent of Wales' tourism riding occasions.
3 Day visitors (excluding local riders regularly exercising their horse close to stabling) – *c.* 25 per cent of riding occasions (WTB, 2002b).

Cycle tourism also offers considerable economic benefits and, like horse riding, this involves cycling holidays as well as those participating in cycling as a holiday or day-visit activity. This represents a growing and valuable tourist market for Wales with estimates suggesting that cycle tourism is currently worth as much as £18 million, and that it could be worth over £34 million by 2007 (WTB, 2002c).

A wide range of other pursuits, grouped together as 'adventure tourism' by the WTB also take place in rural and coastal Wales. In their adventure tourism strategy (WTB, 2002d: 1), adventure tourism is defined as 'holiday and day visits that involve participation in active or adventurous outdoor activities, either as a primary or secondary purpose of visit' and the following varied activities are identified:

1 Climbing – mountaineering, rock climbing, abseiling, bouldering, sea level traversing, coasteering.
2 Caving and potholing
3 Non-motorized water sports – sailing, windsurfing, kitesurfing, canoeing, kayaking, white-water rafting, surfing.
4 Motorized water sports – jet-skiing, water-skiing, ribbing, wakeboarding.
5 Diving.
6 Motorized land sports – 4 × 4 driving, trail-biking, quad-biking.
7 Airsports – hangliding, paragliding, microlighting, gliding.
8 Mountain-biking – trail riding, downhill riding.
9 Hill-walking/trekking.
10 Other land-based activities – orienteering, gorge-walking, skiing, snow-boarding, land-yachting, parakarting, bungee-jumping, paintballing, archery, clay pigeon shooting, rope courses.

According to the strategy:

> Adventure tourist visits involving these activities either as their main or a secondary purpose of visit, currently account for at least 1.25 million visits to Wales per year, and in the order of £180 million of direct visitor spending. They make up approximately 13 per cent of domestic trips, nights and spend in Wales. Adventure holidays (where participation in adventure activities is the main holiday purpose) account for about 4 per cent of the domestic holiday market for Wales – a figure almost comparable to walking holidays (which account for around 5 per cent of domestic holidays in Wales). (Ibid.)

The most popular adventure activities are non-motorized water sports and climbing, with hill-walking and, to a lesser extent, mountain-biking, also being popular. Most of the other activities appeal to particular niche markets which, by comparison, tend to be minority pursuits.

As with other forms of sports tourism considered in this volume, people with a wide range of experience levels, motivations and interests participate in such adventure activities. They range from the very experienced and highly skilled adventure sports enthusiast, to the beginner learning an adventure sport with a view to future independent participation, or somebody on holiday who decides to try out an adventure activity during their stay. They thus range from the 'incidental' participant to the 'driven' in terms of the Sports Tourism Participation Model developed in Chapter 5 (Figure 5.5) and, given that the 1999 Mintel report also records that there are many people who have not participated expressing a desire to do so, there are also significant numbers of 'intenders'.

Reeves (2000) examined the profiles of activity holidaymakers visiting the Twr-Y-Felin outdoor activity centre and St Davids area of Pembrokeshire in Wales and identified various types of participants. There was a varied age and sex distribution as well as significant variation in socioeconomic status, with a relatively high number of respondents in the lowest income category, no doubt reflected by the not insignificant numbers of retired people, students and those in part-time employment. A wide range of different activities were undertaken, with swimming followed by walking and canoeing being the most popular, although such activities were influenced by the particular coastal location. While 31 per cent of those surveyed engaged in activities by themselves, the vast majority were involved with others, either with partners or with larger groups, including some involving club, school or college groups. This is related to the reasons for undertaking an activity holiday as that of companionship was ranked second in importance (see Table 12.4). What is interesting in these results is the fact that this social dimension along with that of relaxation were the two most highly ranked motives for holiday choice, rather than the physical and mental challenge posed by the activity and the adventure inherent in such participation (Reeves, 2000: 181). Motives more readily associated with mainstream tourism would appear to be more important here than those more normally associated with mainstream sport. This not only emphasizes the complexity of motivation in sports tourism but also lends support to the ideas discussed in Chapter 3 that sports tourists are distinctly different from those who pursue sport *per se*.

Table 12.4 Ranked importance of factors in holiday choice: Twr-Y-Felin Activity Centre

Factor	Ranking
Relaxation	1
Companionship/social dimension	2
Physical fitness/wellbeing	3
Novelty of experience	4
Challenge (physical and mental)	5
Adventure	6

Source: Reeves (2000: 181).

Resources and organization of activity tourism in Wales

According to the adventure tourism strategy, Wales has some of the finest natural resources for adventure sports of anywhere in the UK and, coupled with its ease of access from English markets, these make Wales one of the leading UK destinations for many adventure activities (WTB, 2002d: 2). Snowdonia, for example, is one of the best and most accessible climbing and mountaineering destinations in the UK; half of all UK caving trips are taken in Wales; the Gower is one of the best places in the UK to learn to surf; Wales is one of the best locations in the UK for scenic diving; Wales boasts three or four of the top ten UK sites for paragliding; and the National White Water Centre at Tryweryn near Bala provides international standard white waters for canoeing and rafting (ibid.). The WTB's promotional guide, *Cycling Wales*, lists thirty-four traffic-free rides, twenty-six lane network areas/rides (roads where traffic is minimal) and twenty-seven mountain bike areas/rides.

In addition to the natural resources, there is also a well-developed supply of activity centres, operators and freelance instructors, including three national centres of excellence – Plas-Y-Brenin (climbing), Plas Menai (watersports) and the National White Water Centre at Trywryn (WTB, 2002d). According to the strategy:

> 183 adventure activity operators are currently licensed by the Adventure Activities Licensing Authority (AALA), or accredited under WTB's Activity Holiday Accreditation Scheme. In addition there are many other operators and training schools that are accredited through appropriate national governing body inspection schemes. The activity operators sector is highly independent, fragmented, and weakly organized, with no tradition of joint working, Activity operator networks have, however, recently been set up in Snowdonia, the Brecon Beacons, Pembrokeshire, the Gower, and the Llangollen area. Waterfront Wales also exists as a national private sector led organization to promote Wales as a sailing and watersports destination. (Ibid.: 3)

Although certain centres specialize in particular activities, they also offer opportunities for a much greater range. Plas-Y-Brenin, for example, which is run by the Mountain Training Trust on behalf of the Sports Council, boasts a training wall, an artificial ski slope and a canoe pool, and offers courses in rock-climbing, summer mountaineering and hill-walking, winter climbing and mountaineering, alpine skiing and mountaineering, mountaineering qualifications and awards, kayaking and canoeing, paddle-sport qualifications, alpine paddling as well as various course relating to personal and professional development. In addition to providing courses, it also offers accommodation for those who wish to visit the area and make their own activity arrangements. In addition to activity centres there are also more specialist centres – for example, the WTB guide, *Riding Wales*, lists twenty-two accredited equestrian centres.

As outlined earlier in the chapter, the YHA also provides opportunities for activity holidays which extend beyond simply that of accommodation, and in Wales these are promoted at four of its hostels – hill and mountain award and assessment weekends at Lywyn-Y-Celyn in the Brecon Beacons; trail-riding in

Table 12.5 Activities available at Black Mountain Activities

Land-based activities	Water-based activities	Activities available on multi-activity breaks	Team-building events	Activities available to schools, youth groups and colleges
Climbing and abseiling	Kayaking	Hill-walking	Development training	Kayaking
Caving and potholing	Open canoeing	Gorge-walking	Black Mountain challenge day	Canoeing
Mountain-biking	Wye expeditions	Caving		Rafting
Clay pigeon shooting	Raft-building	Potholing		Raft-building
Archery		Mountain-biking		Hot-dogging
Orienteering		Clay pigeon shooting		White-water rafting
Land carting		Kayaking		Caving
High-level ropes course		Canoeing		Mountain-biking
		White-water rafting		Archery
		Orienteering		Orienteering
		High-level ropes		Land carting
		Climbing tower		High-level ropes
		Archery		Climbing
		Raft-building		Abseiling
				Hill-walking
				Mountain expeditions

the Brecon Beacons and riding courses in the Black Mountains at Capel-Y-Ffin; navigation and walking courses at Poppit Sands, Cardigan Bay; and cycling in Snowdonia at Conwy.

Twr-Y-Felin outdoor activity centre, the subject of Reeves's (2000) study, is one of the largest centres of its kind in West Wales, in terms of volume and diversity of courses offered. The company organizes management development courses, children's activity holidays and courses for groups and individuals of all standards who wish to participate and/or gain the relevant coaching/leadership qualifications. Another such centre is Black Mountain Activities, established in 1992, which organizes a wide variety of outdoor pursuits and activity courses for individuals, families, social groups, businesses, schools, colleges and youth groups (see Table 12.5). Situated on the edge of the Brecon Beacons National Park and very near the banks of the River Wye, the centre uses adjacent resources rather than having significant facilities of its own. It does not provide accommodation, although it does advertise a variety of accommodation in the vicinity on its website, and is prepared to organize accommodation for its clients. As a non-residential centre it has no significant overheads and no fixed programmes, and its principal activity is thus bringing visitors and training staff together. It offers two-, three- or five-day holidays and emphasizes weekend breaks in its promotions. This sort of activity holiday is a good example of the tourism product highlighted by the Wales Tourist Board (2000: 25) 'which closely matches the needs of the short-break market, offering diversity in a naturally inspiring landscape that is within easy reach of large centres of population'.

Environmental impacts on the Welsh coast and countryside

The general issues associated with the environmental impacts of activity tourism have already been addressed in an earlier section of this chapter and apply equally to the various resources found in Wales. It is worth noting that in the study by Sidaway (1988) a number of the case studies examined involved activities at locations in Wales. One involved caving, a popular activity in outdoor pursuits centres which frequently include a day's caving in their courses. Given the large number of such centres in Wales, the pressures on popular, accessible caves from this source are considerable. Damage from cavers included litter, physical damage such as the removal of stalactites and the removal of mud deposits, disturbance to wildlife such as hibernating bats, and graffiti. Other Welsh case studies in the Sidaway report included the impacts of climbing on cliff-nesting birds such as peregrine falcons and various seabirds, and the impacts of subaqua diving on marine wildlife. Specialist activity sports involve a greater range of environmental impacts than simply the erosion of surface vegetation and damage to routeways.

Apart from the more direct impacts arising from such activities, the other impact is that of the car. As mentioned above, one key characteristic of adventure tourism in Wales is its appeal to the short-breaks market, and much of this activity is based on car travel. Much of rural Wales is within easy travelling distance from key population centres, such as the West Midlands conurbation, Merseyside and Greater Manchester, the Bristol area as well as the urban areas of South Wales, and the car is the obvious mode of travel given its speed and convenience, the need to transport equipment and the extensive system of minor roads enabling cars to reach relatively inaccessible locations. Cars cause a variety of problems including congestion, air pollution, visual impact, danger to vulnerable users and wildlife on narrow roads caused by speeding traffic, noise and loss of tranquillity, and loss of countryside character (Speakman and Speakman, 1999). The impact of the car is highlighted in a study by Owen, Bishop and Speakman (1999) who report that 90 per cent of Snowdonia's 6.6 million visitors a year arrive by this form of transport with their vehicles polluting the environment and producing substantial congestion along the roadsides, given that roadside parking is freely available. Although much of this car use involved passive recreationists, activity tourism, which is expected to expand in the coming years, still makes a significant contribution to the problem. In fact it is worth noting that the problem was also cited at several of the sites examined by Sidaway (1988) in the 1980s.

While the impacts can be overstated, as mentioned earlier, there is no doubt that at certain popular locations they can be severe and the need for management linked to sustainable tourism policies is required. The Northern Snowdonia study (Owen, Bishop and Speakman, 1999) is one such attempt to suggest more sustainable solutions to the car problem involving increasing transport options and greater use of public transport. Some of the options involve improving walking and cycling opportunities and, thus, activity tourism can actually play a role in helping to develop sustainable tourism. The question of improved access arrangements for many adventure sports has also been cited as a key development requirement by the WTB adventure tourism strategy (WTB, 2002d).

187

Conclusions

This chapter has examined activity tourism, a further form of sports tourism that involves a distinctive interaction of activity, people and place. The places and environments are characterized by areas of scenic landscape and often rugged terrain – in Britain areas most typified by the national parks and heritage coasts. The activities themselves are highly dependent on such resources as well as specific facilities such as activity/adventure centres and various types of accommodation. As with the Alpine skiing environments examined in the following chapter, such places produce distinctive sports tourism places and, although the demographic and socioeconomic profiles of participants may vary, due to the very different activities involved, they all nevertheless seek enjoyment of natural landscape features and, with the exception of cavers, being in the 'open air'. In addition, the chapter has demonstrated how a particular form of sports tourism accords with the sports tourism participation model discussed in Chapter 5. Activity tourism is to a large extent a multi-activity form in which participants are often 'committed' but where, nevertheless, some participants will range from the 'incidental' to the 'driven'. In addition, within the general population there are also many non-participants who express an interest to participate and who can be clearly seen as 'intenders'.

As a specific case study for activity tourism, Wales possesses a wealth of suitable resources and has established a substantial collection of varied facilities to aid its development. The importance of activity tourism to the overall tourism product has been highlighted in the most recent tourism strategy for Wales (WTB, 2000) where it is regarded as having significant future potential and is being marketed vigorously through specific guides and websites. As *Time for Action – an Adventure Tourism Strategy for Wales* (WTB, 2002d: 4) makes clear, the vision is to see 'Wales as a world class Adventure Tourism destination offering the widest choice, the highest quality, and the best managed and promoted adventure activity experiences of anywhere in the world'.

13

Winter skiing in the European Alps

Skiing is perhaps the best known and most developed form of sports tourism. As outlined in Chapter 1, Alpine skiing dates back to the late nineteenth century and by the early decades of the twentieth century a significant tourism industry was in place with Switzerland possessing several clusters of ski resorts serviced by a well-established infrastructure. Today the ski market is extremely large and accounts for a substantial segment of all tourism. The snow-sports market in Britain, for example, breaks down into three categories: inclusive tours or skiing packages (accounting for around 588 000 holidays), independently organized skiing trips (243 000) and school trips (123 000) (Mintel, 2002b). Skiing accounts for about 20 per cent of the total European holiday market with the European Alps attracting 40–50 million visitors to the 40 000 ski runs (Standeven and De Knop, 1999); while in America the 490 ski resorts attracted 57.3 million skier/snowboarder visits in 2000–001 (Hudson, 2004).

Skiing provides the classic form of sports tourism. It is a typical sport involving physical activity and physical skill, and it can be pursued at various levels of competence, competitively or otherwise. At one level it is an Olympic sport, at the other it involves families with young children pursuing it for fun. Like many other sports it involves goals, challenge, stimulation and, in some cases, risk. Apart from a few artificial ski slopes and more recently developed snow domes (such as the facility at Milton Keynes), it is a sporting activity that is dependent on specific natural resources found only in certain locations. Thus the vast majority of participants have to travel significant distances and stay for several days or longer in specific resorts. No matter which definition of tourism is adopted, they are thus tourists and therefore also sports tourists.

Attempts to conceptualize sports tourism in the first part of this text suggested that it might be defined as a social, economic and cultural phenomenon arising from the unique interaction of activity, people and place and, while Chapter 3 considered the uniqueness of sports tourism places, the way it was organized and the motives of participants, Chapter 5 developed a Sports Tourism Participation Model (Figure 5.5) as a means of understanding the phenomenon. How then does alpine skiing relate to these aspects?

The skiing environment

As mentioned above, skiing requires a particular type of upland environment with appropriate physical conditions, namely, snow cover and slopes. Snow cover is the main determinant of the length of season and related aspects such as duration, earliness of first snow, quality of snow cover and reliability of snow cover from year to year are all key factors in establishing the quality, and hence success, of a particular location. Slopes are also important, as a range of slopes is needed to provide for a variety of skiers, from novices who need gentle slopes, to advanced skiers who need exhilarating runs. But the unique environment that is the modern ski resort is much more than simply a natural phenomenon – it involves a combination of both natural and human attributes. In addition to there being sufficient natural environment, ski resorts also require a collection of built features such as ski lifts, ski schools, equipment shops, hotel accommodation, restaurants, car parking and possibly other leisure facilities to provide après-ski entertainment. Thus there is a need for flat land as well as slopes to enable such facilities to be provided.

Apart from the basic requirements of slopes and snow, there are also several other factors that influence the quality and viability of ski resorts. Avalanche risk may restrict skiing to a limited number of slopes; wind can affect the functioning of ski lifts and produce significant wind chill; and natural features may provide opportunities for cross-country ski trails. The quality of accommodation and après-ski facilities are also important, as is the extent to which resorts are fashionable (see discussion on motives below).

Despite the need for specific requirements, skiing is well established in many mountainous areas and, in the European Alps alone, for example, there are an estimated 40 000 ski runs with 14 000 ski lifts that are capable of handling 1.5 million skiers an hour (Ward, Higson and Campbell, 1994). Alpine ski resorts have clearly been socially constructed as mass tourist destinations – as recognizable places for the tourist gaze through various markers and signposts (Urry, 2002). In the latter half of the twentieth century the tourist image creators have promoted ski resorts along with seaside resorts and, to a lesser extent, rural idylls such as national parks, as the rightful objects of the tourist gaze (Shaw and Williams, 2002: 218). Although the Alps had originally been an area of summer tourism, related to the romantic tourist gaze through the attractions of climbing, walking and viewing the scenery (see Chapter 1), writers and other image creators subsequently re-imaged the Alps as a highly desirable winter tourist destination.

Although there is a tendency for uniformity in terms of the production of mass winter sports tourism, it is possible to discern a degree of differentiation among resorts. Barker (1982, cited in Shaw and Williams, 2002), for example, identified differences between the eastern and western Alps. The former have been developed at lower altitudes and are more integrated with the economic and cultural lives of the indigenous communities than are the high altitude resorts of the western Alps where more external capital and labour are involved. Some resorts have also developed a significant summer season based on warm-weather pursuits or developing means to transport tourists to high-altitude skiing areas (Shaw and Williams, 2002). Table 13.1 describes a continuum of skiing resorts based on these differences and, whereas those at the low altitude end of the continuum have a varied function, it is clear that those at high altitudes are distinct sports tourism places.

Table 13.1 The continuum of characteristics of Alpine resorts

Low altitude	High altitude
Integrated settlement	New settlement
Local capital	External capital
Local labour	External labour
Cultural exchanges	Cultural islands
Environmental pressures	Environmental pressures
Temporal polarization	Temporal polarization

Source: Shaw and Williams (2002: 236).

The French resorts, in particular, have been developed for the mass market. As the Mintel (2002b: 24) report points out they are:

> mostly purpose built and provide a high level of convenience for the skier. They are designed for the maximum number of skiers to be able to ski to and from their accommodation to the ski lift system. Overall convenience has been provided at the expense of ambience and the French resorts tend to lack the Alpine charm of the more traditional resorts found in Austria and Switzerland. The extensive lift systems in French resorts have opened up glacier skiing; attracting tourists throughout the year and investment in snowmaking equipment and snow management has enabled resorts to remain open despite unpredictable snow conditions.

Another feature characteristic of mass tourism generally is that of accommodation. While France offers a wide range of accommodation, much of it is provided in apartments rather than hotels. The apartment blocks, built during the early development of the mass-market ski industry were cramped and now fall short of the expectations of today's tourists (Mintel, 2002b), a feature reminiscent of much apartment development in many coastal Mediterranean resorts.

Another key aspect of quality is the extent to which resorts can cope with environmental impacts. Alpine environments are fragile and in the last few decades there have been increasing concerns from a growing environmental lobby about the impacts that skiing produces. According to Ryan (1991: 95) 'previously unvisited areas are continually being made accessible' and this is producing a range of different problems. The alteration of traditional Alpine land for construction of dams, skiing facilities and hotels has led to both widespread deforestation, soil erosion and alteration of drainage patterns with the resulting increased risk of both avalanches and landslides as well as the disappearance of rare habitats (Hudson, 2000; Ryan, 1991; Standeven and De Knop, 1999). It is estimated that in the early 1990s some 100km^2 of forest had been removed throughout the Alps for tourism development (Shaw and Williams, 2002) and deforestation also releases destructive geomorphological processes that have impacts on local communities. For example, in the Austrian Alps it is believed that the creation of 0.7km^2 ski runs for the Winter Olympics contributed to a major mudslide in 1983 (Jenner and Smith, 1992). There is also some evidence that in the French Alps the impact of ski tourism has affected the black grouse population (Jenner and Smith, 1992). While the exact causes are still uncertain, they may well include the growth of extensive off-piste skiing, an increase in predators attracted by litter and waste produced by tourists, and the displacements of the grouse by ski activities. Furthermore, skiing in sparse snow conditions contributes to the significant damage of sensitive vegetation (Selman, 1992; Shaw and Williams, 2002). To many the new built environment appears unsightly and there are also problems of pollution from car exhausts, from chemicals used to manufacture snow and noise pollution from snow guns, the latter two stemming from attempts to extend the season (Standeven and De Knop, 1999).

The skiing market and economic impact

The ski market was estimated to comprise 65–70 million skiers worldwide in the mid-1990s, with Europe accounting for approximately 30 million, North America 20 million and Japan 14 million (Cockerell, 1994). According to figures published in the *Ski and Snowboard Industry Report* (quoted in Mintel, 2002b) the UK market involved 954 000 overseas ski and snowboard trips made by UK residents in the 2001–02 season. This compares with 720 000 trips made in 1980–81 and thus represents a moderate average annual growth rate of 1.6 per cent over that twenty-one year period (see Table 13.2).

As outlined in the introduction, the market can be segmented into the tour operator market, independently organized holidays and the school trip sector. UK statistics for each of these categories are also provided in Table 13.2 and show that while there has been a modest overall growth since the early 1980s, there has been a marked change in the type of consumers. The most dramatic change has involved the number of school trips which have declined by over 400 000 during this period. Whereas in 1980–81 school trips accounted for over 76 per cent of all trips, in 2001–02 they accounted for only 13 per cent (Table

Table 13.2 The UK ski market size, by tour operators, independent travel and schools, 1980–81–2001–02

	Tour operator 000s	Independent travel 000s	School trips 000s	Total 000s
1980–81	150	20	550	720
1990–91	278	90	110	478
1995–96	430	190	140	760
1996–97	475	205	150	830
1997–98	510	210	145	865
1998–99	515	215	145	875
1999–2000	452	199	119	770
2000–01	560	231	130	921
2001–02	588	243	123	954

Source: *Ski and Snowboard Industry Report, 2001*, cited in Mintel (2002b).

Table 13.3 The UK ski market share, by tour operators, independent travel and schools, 1980–81–2001–02

	Tour operator %	Independent travel %	School trips %
1980–81	20.8	2.8	76.3
1990–91	58.1	18.8	23.0
1995–96	56.6	25.0	18.4
1996–97	57.2	24.7	18.1
1997–98	59.0	24.2	16.8
1998–99	58.9	24.6	16.6
1999–2000	58.7	25.8	15.5
2000–01	60.8	25.1	14.1
2001–02	61.6	25.5	12.9

Source: *Ski and Snowboard Industry Report, 2001*, cited in Mintel (2002b).

13.3). The decline has resulted in part from a change in UK local authority funding for extracurricular activities, which has shifted the burden of payments to parents, and also from the necessity for risk assessments and increasing risks of litigation which has reduced the willingness of teachers to lead such trips (Mintel, 2002b). In addition, however, the growth of tour operators, the rise of real incomes, the role of skiing as part of a fashionable, healthy lifestyle and a growing belief that skiing holidays are great for families have also contributed to this decline. As can be seen in Table 13.3, as the proportion of school trips has declined so the proportions accounted for by both tour operators and independent travel have increased.

A further factor influencing the skiing market is accessibility. One of the key attractions of the European Alps is its location in relation to substantial population centres. It is no surprise, therefore, to find that the European Alps is the most developed area for skiing in the world. Concentrated primarily in France, Italy, Austria, Switzerland and Germany, countries which themselves possess substantial affluent populations, the region is also within easy travelling distance from other densely populated countries of the EU and beyond. This proximity has meant that a variety of travel options – road, rail and air – are available and also the short travel times provide opportunities for weekend trips as well as longer stays. The influence of accessibility is illustrated in relation to the travel characteristics of UK skiers with France, the most accessible location, dominating the market. France accounts for 36 per cent of all UK skiing holidays, followed by Austria (19 per cent) and Italy (14 per cent). While other factors have played a key role, such as purpose-built resorts with substantial accommodation geared to the mass market and the establishment of a large number of tour operators specializing in these resorts, the ease of access to the French resorts does attract independent holidaymakers who can travel by train or car or fly cheaply with the low-cost carriers (Mintel, 2002b).

Another key feature of the skiing market is the way tourism developers and tour operators have promoted skiing as a form of mass tourism (see previous section). As Shaw and Williams (2002: 234) point out 'mass winter sports tourism shares many features in common with mass beach tourism'. While the origins of the winter sports tourism market lie in the nineteenth and early twentieth centuries, mass international winter tourism developed only in the 1950s and 1960s (Barker, 1982). The necessary conditions were similar to international mass coastal tourism involving the reconstruction of the tourist gaze, rising real disposable incomes and car ownership levels, and falling real costs allied to increased tour company activity (Shaw and Williams, 2002). As with coastal tourism, the industry is characterized by a high degree of external control and its promotion has, of course, been encouraged for two important economic reasons. One is the fact that skiers tend to be reasonably affluent and are more likely to spend more than most other types of holidaymaker. In addition, given that most mass tourism involves sun-seeking and takes place primarily during the summer months, the fact that skiing takes place in the winter months is a useful counter to the problems of seasonality.

The organization of the industry and the resorts

As outlined in Chapter 3, one of the key aspects of the conceptualization of sports tourism is the way it is organized. If it is distinctly different from more general forms of tourism, this may be where differences are encountered, in that as a specific niche or, more accurately, a collection of niches, it has particular requirements that can only be provided through particular organizations. This would be partially true of skiing in relation to what Hudson (2000b) refers to as 'channels of distribution'. Skiing holidays are organized primarily through a very limited number of operators. While around 200 operators trade in the snow-sports market, six operators – Crystal, Inghams, Thomson, First Choice, Neilson and Airtours – account for 83 per cent of package holidays sold, with the majority of small specialist companies serving the needs of particular niche groups (Mintel, 2002b). Crystal Holidays, owned by TUI UK (formerly Thomson Travel Group), retains a quarter of the market which, when added to Thomson's own market share of 14.3 per cent gives TUI UK a total market share of 38.5 per cent. While some of these companies are clearly major players in the overall tourism industry, they have developed specialist sections of their companies to cater for skiing, acquiring specialist ski operators as part of the process. In addition to Crystal Holidays, TUI UK promotes its skiing operations through Thomson Ski and Snowboarding Holidays as well as owning the more specialist snow-sports company, Simply Ski, which runs catered chalets in the Alps. The Thompson Ski and Snowboarding programme for 2002–2003

> aims to have appeal to skiers from all sectors and offers group discounts, free pre-season skiing trips for group leaders, special party holidays, family holidays with children's clubs, a nanny service and ski and board guides/rangers. Accommodation options include hotels, apartments, chalets, chalet hotels, club hotels and the transport options are for flights, ski train or self-drive. Increasing flexibility is being built into the programme and special packages allow the consumer to book ski weekends and short breaks, ski weddings, twin-centre holidays or tailormake a holiday with accommodation only, scheduled flights or car hire. (Mintel, 2002b: 35)

Although the four major UK travel companies dominate the general snow-sports market in terms of volume, there are many other independent companies that play an important role in supplying the market with niche products, and several of these have a large and loyal consumer base, usually specializing in a particular region. For example, independent companies are particularly numerous in France where in one case 'more than 20 independent operators are dedicated to a single French resort' (Mintel, 2002b: 25).

The profile of the Alpine skier

Despite the large number of participants, skiing, nevertheless, tends to be associated with a more restricted profile of sports tourist. For example, according to Mintel (2002b) 85 per cent of UK residents have never skied and those who do so are concentrated in the ABC1 socioeconomic groups with over one-quarter of the ABC1 fifteen to fifty-four age group being skiers. In fact 98 per cent of the C2DEs aged over fifty-five years have never skied.

The Mintel report on snow sports (Mintel, 2002b) identified both those who had skied at some time in their lives (15 per cent) and potential skiers (18 per cent) the latter being those who had stated that, while they had never been on a skiing trip, were either planning one or would consider going on one. The demographic details for these two groups are listed in Table 13.4. Skiing is clearly an activity pursued primarily by relatively young, affluent consumers and is also more attractive to males with 18 per cent of male respondents being recorded as skiers compared to only 10 per cent of women. With the potential skiers, however, the gap between the two is considerably smaller.

The concentration of skiers among the more affluent socioeconomic groups is not surprising given the various constraints of cost, perception of danger and the degree of difficulty involved (Williams and Basford, 1992). Cost is clearly a major factor deterring those with limited incomes who might consider skiing. In fact, almost a quarter of consumers think that skiing holidays are too expensive. Unlike most other forms of tourism, and even various forms of sports tourism, skiing involves additional costs of equipment, special clothing, entry

Table 13.4 Skiers and potential skiers by demographic subgroup, 2002

Base: 976 adults aged 15+	Skiers %	Potentials %
Men	18	19
Women	10	16
15–24	25	29
25–34	16	27
35–44	23	19
45–54	11	12
55–64	4	12
65+	4	5
AB	21	18
C1	22	20
C2	9	18
D	6	12
E	4	15
Socioeconomic age groups:		
ABC1 15–34	28	35
ABC1 35–54	25	14
ABC1 55+	7	6
C2DE 15–34	11	21
C2DE 35–54	9	18
C2DE 55+	2	9

Source: BMRB/Mintel (Mintel, 2002b).

charges to the slopes and, for the beginner, the costs of acquiring the necessary skills, in addition to the normal costs of travel and accommodation. It is likely that the lower proportion of skiers in the 25–34 age group in Table 13.4 is constrained by costs, as this is the age group where young families produce additional expenditures and possibly reduced incomes. In addition to cost, various risks and perceived dangers such as speed, steepness of the slopes, fear of being out of control, chances of injury and fear of ski-lifts, together with the physical demands and necessary skill acquisition, also pose significant constraints for many people and especially those with family commitments and older age groups. It is probably these constraints which account for the substantial number of potential skiers listed in various categories in Table 13.4. (For a more detailed discussion of the socioeconomic and demographic characteristics of skiers and the various constraining factors for non-skiers see the work of Carmichael, 1996; Hudson, 1998; 2000; Williams and Basford, 1992.)

Despite a more restricted profile, however, alpine skiers do not constitute an entirely homogeneous group. Hudson (2000: 65), for example, highlights a number of differences between Alpine skiers in the USA and those visiting European ski resorts based on data from the National Sporting Goods Association (in relation to American skiers) and a Mountain International Opinion Survey (MINOS) conducted in European ski resorts in the mid-1990s. In the USA skiers are predominantly male (60 per cent), thirty-five years old and have a median household income of $56 614 a year. They are college educated and tend to have managerial and professional jobs. Besides skiing, they participate in tennis, cycling and racquetball, and are twice as likely to buy wine, invest in real estate and travel overseas as the average person. Among European skiers, incomes tend to be lower, age is younger and self-ranked skier ability levels are lower. In addition, European ski resorts attract a more cosmopolitan clientele from around the world than do the US resorts. Another key difference, according to Hudson (2000), concerns the different requirements of the respective groups. Those at European resorts are far more interested in snow and sun, whereas Americans are more interested in the terrain. These differences are clearly linked to motivations (see below) and the fact that most of those at European resorts are intermediate skiers with many northerners tending 'to balance their downhill participation with a keen interest in basking in the sun, having a good lunch with a bottle of wine, and enjoying the conviviality of friends' (Hudson, 2000: 65).

Motivations

As suggested in the previous paragraph, the type of sports tourist who participates in skiing must in part be identified on the basis of motives. However, motivation is a particularly complex issue, as outlined in Chapter 3. Pearce (1987: 24–5) reports the findings of a survey of Grenoble skiers by Keogh (1980) who found the 'physical sporting experience' (57.6 per cent) and the 'aesthetic outdoor experience' (33.6 per cent) were the prime motivations in influencing the decision to go skiing, with the opportunity to participate in an activity with family or friends coming a distant third (7.7 per cent). On the basis of these motivations Keogh then identified three groups of skiers – the 'sporting', 'contemplative' and 'social' – and found that statistically significant differences occurred between the groups in terms of the resorts they frequented. As Pearce (ibid.: 25) points out, however, 'while this study provides some original insights into skiers' motivations, it does not tell us why those interviewed were seeking either a "physical sporting" or "aesthetic outdoor experience" in the first place'.

Keogh's study is perhaps somewhat dated now and more recent studies have suggested that a more complex set of motivations are likely to be involved with social motives in particular being more important. According to Hudson (2000), who reviewed various studies of North American skiers, several basic motivations have been identified over the years, including personal achievement, social reasons, enjoyment of nature, escape and thrill. In the context of the discussion in Chapter 3, while skiing is clearly a sport, which may also embrace some of these motives, all of these motivations can also be found embedded within the classic tourism literature. For example, Boon (1984, quoted in Hudson, 2000) in a study of the benefits sought by skiers at Ski Beech in North Carolina identified various 'push' factors as being important, such as 'getting away from the usual demands of life', 'having a change from your daily routine', 'giving your mind a rest' and 'experiencing new and different things'. The sociability factor was also found to be important in Boon's study; in fact, the benefits of 'being with friends' and 'being with others who enjoy similar things' obtained the highest rankings. Such benefits have also been identified among European skiers. The Mintel (2002b) study found that the second most popular statement chosen from a group of attitudinal statements regarding snow sports was that 'it would be fun to go skiing with a group of friends' followed by the perception that 'skiing holidays are great for families'. An earlier Mintel report (1996, quoted in Hudson, 2000) also suggested the importance of social benefits together with that of skiing offering 'pleasant and attractive surroundings'. As with the findings for other activity tourists, reported in the previous chapter, these motives are not those that are most readily associated with sport *per se* and, thus, this provides yet further support for the contention proposed in Chapter 3 that sports tourism is unique and distinct from the single activities of sport and tourism. Such motivations are clearly consistent with the guiding theme of this volume that sports tourism is a unique interaction of activity, people and place. Not only is the place essential for the activity, but some of the principal motives of participants would seem to involve social interactions that are only possible through such activities at these locations.

One relatively recent study of UK skiers by Lewis and Wild (1995, quoted in Hudson) identified four specific types of skier – expert, sports skier, recreational skier and novice – based upon level of skill and experience combined with behavioural and attitudinal aspects of skiing. As Hudson (2000: 76) points out, both the recreational skier and sports skier may be capable of skiing the most difficult runs but the reason why they ski such runs will be totally different. This typology can be linked to the Sports Tourism Participation Model outlined in Figure 5.5. Given the nature of skiing discussed earlier as requiring significant investments of time and money, each of the groups are likely to fall towards the outer end of the participation triangle, with the expert likely to be 'driven' and the sport skier likely to fall into the 'committed' category. Recreational skiers could, in theory, be placed in any of the other groups depending on their motives, although in practice they are more likely to be located in the regular category as they are characterized by regular repeat visits.

The future of the industry

According to Tuppen (1998) the ski market in Europe has reached a mature phase with increasing problems of saturation and oversupply of facilities. 'Resorts have been forced to invest and innovate to remain competitive; new ski lifts, snow making machines, cultural, sports and entertainment facilities and refurbished buildings are all part of the armoury of measures employed to render resorts more attractive' (ibid.: 260) with the large, internationally renowned, often high altitude locations, with resources to invest, more likely to retain their competitiveness. Global warming and the uncertainty of snow cover have also contributed to a slow down, especially for those resorts at lower altitudes, while the growth of other areas, such as in Eastern Europe, has also been a factor. European skiers have also been attracted increasingly to North America as have Japanese skiers (Hudon, 2000).

According to Hudson (2004) today 'visitors to winter resorts are seeking a variety of niche options' with 'the trend back towards the early days of winter sports, with a diversification of activities'. As with the outdoor pursuits discussed in Chapter 12, there is also a range of new winter sports which are gaining popularity and competing with traditional ones (Table 13.5).

Table 13.5 The diversification of winter sports activities

Traditional winter sports activities	Contemporary winter sports activities
Skiing	Snowboarding
Cross-country skiing	Snowmobiling
Telemarking	Snowshoeing
Cat-skiing	Heli-skiing
Winter sports events	Parapente/handgliding
Ice-skating	Tubing
Horse-drawn sleigh	Dog-sledging
Curling	Snowcycling
Toboganing	Thrill-sleds/extreme sledding
Ice-climbing	
Ice-driving	
Ice-sculpting	
Snowskating	

Source: Hudson (2004).

This diversification has been partly encouraged by the resorts as a response to the declining ski market, especially as an increasing proportion of those who take winter sports holidays in both North America and Europe do not ski at all (Hudson, 2000). In addition, 'even avid skiers are typically skiing less' as the average skier tends to be getting older and is thus switching to more gentle winter sports. As Hudson (2004) points out 'the more progressive resorts are now treating skiing as a form of entertainment by establishing more off slope diversions' and, although he is referring primarily to resorts in North America, such developments can also be seen in Europe.

The other key development affecting the skiing market has been the massive growth of snowboarding. According to Hudson (2000) it is probably the biggest winter sport in the USA and its popularity in Europe is also burgeoning. It has the advantage over skiing in that it is easier to master the technical skills and thus may be far more appealing to the recreational winter sports enthusiast who can confidently take to the slopes far more quickly than with skiing. It is particularly popular among young people and thus has substantial potential for growth in the future, with some projections suggesting that it may overtake skiing as the most popular winter sports activity in the next ten to twenty years (Scott, 1995, cited in Hudson, 2000)

While the European Alps may have experienced some decline, according to Mintel (2002b) the UK skiing and snowboard market will continue to experience a steady year-on-year growth for the foreseeable future, with the number of trips breaking the 1 million barrier for the first time in 2003–04 and reaching 1.08 million by 2005–06. The growth will essentially follow the pattern of the 1990s, with trips organized through tour operators and those organized independently continuing to grow while schools trips continue to decline. A number of factors are likely to contribute to the growth of skiing and snowboarding, including the continuing growth of personal disposable incomes, especially among the young, the popularity of short-break holidays and the accessibility of the Alps, the fashionability of skiing and the perceived health benefits of both holidaying and physical exercise.

Conclusion

This chapter has sought to provide a further example of sports tourism to illustrate the various themes and concepts that are the central concerns of this volume. Skiing represents not only one of the largest segments of sports tourism but, in many ways, provides the classic form of sports tourism, given its precise environmental requirements, its distinct organization of tour operators and its unique interaction of activity, people and place. Like the vast majority of people who pursue other forms of activity tourism, the overwhelming majority of skiers have to travel and thus, by definition, become tourists. But, unlike the typical tourist who seeks an 'inactive' holiday, the skier is involved in an active pursuit. Nevertheless, as has been illustrated above, some of the key motives that drive such activity are not necessarily those immediately associated with sport and active pursuits but include various sociability motives, enjoyment of the natural environment and those of escape. Thus skiers are neither tourists specifically nor sportspersons, but clearly a unique combination of the two. As with many other forms of sports tourism, skiers do not constitute a homogeneous group but differ to some extent in terms of their socioeconomic and demographic characteristics and their levels of skill and commitment. However, they do tend to have more in common than other groups being dominated by the relatively young, affluent consumers and characterized by regular levels of participation. Thus as a distinct form of sports tourism, skiing provides a further illustration of the utility of the Sports Tourism Participation Model illustrated in Figure 5.5 in Chapter 5, with different levels of activity and importance, a growing diversification involving multi-activities, and a clearly identifiable group of potential participants who might be seen as 'intenders'.

Epilogue: the development of research and practice

The prologue to this text identified a paper by Don Anthony in 1966 as one of the earliest writings in the field of sports tourism. However, Sue Glyptis's (1982) study of sport and tourism in five European countries was identified as marking the beginning of a growth of interest and research in the area. It is perhaps a useful exercise to return to Glyptis's (1982) paper and examine the three 'needs' for the field that she identified over twenty years ago, these being:

1   A recognition of the tourist potential of sport and the sports development potential of tourism.
2   The establishment of working partnerships between sport and tourism policy makers and providers at national, regional and local level to develop facilities and services for active holidays.
3   Undertaking more detailed market research to establish consumer profiles and satisfaction, and potential market sectors. (Ibid.: 70)

Much of the literature in the field since Glyptis's (1982) paper has focused on the first 'need', and might be identified as 'advocacy' work that argues and makes the case for the links between sport and tourism. This was a key part of the 1992 report to the GB Sports Council from Loughborough University (Jackson and Glyptis, 1992) and the earlier chapters of Standeven and De Knop's (1999) text, as well as having been the focus for numerous other articles and conference presentations. As noted in the prologue, such links have now been broadly established by previous work, and further replication of such material does little to advance knowledge in the field.

The focus of this text, therefore, has not been on 'evidencing' the relationship between sport and tourism, as this has been covered in considerable detail elsewhere (see the studies noted in the prologue). Some evidence relating to the nature of the sport-tourism link was presented in Chapter 2, but the substantive content of the book has been concerned with examining the actors involved in sports tourism. In doing so it has noted that the 'working partnerships' between policy-makers for sport and for tourism called for by Glyptis (1982) have not been widely established (see Chapters 6 and 7), with agencies responsible for sport and for tourism still being generally reluctant to work together or showing a lack of appreciation of the nature and extent of the relationship between sport and tourism. Such lack of appreciation and reluctance to work together is mirrored, as noted by Gibson (1998), in some areas of academia. Some academics feel that sports tourism is not an appropriate area of specific study, and that it should be understood as a tourism market niche or a subset of sports management. However, such an approach fails to understand the unique experience of sports tourism as an interaction of activity, people and place that cannot be reduced to a mere tourism market niche or sports activity away from home. Furthermore, examining sports tourism as a part of the tourism or the sports industry focuses attention on providers and neglects the development of understanding of the motivations and behaviours of the sports tourists themselves. This area has been addressed in Chapters 3, 4 and 5 of this book, which make an initial contribution to the third 'need' identified by Glyptis (1982) in an area that has received little attention in the literature to date.

The historical and cultural separation of sport and tourism by both policy-makers and academics is a key area that needs to be addressed in the future development of both research and practice in the area. In relation to practice, even if Jackson and Weed's (2003) conservative estimation, drawn from previous work by Collins and Jackson (1999), Mintel (1999) and Standeven and De Knop (1999), of 'around' 10 per cent of tourists having sport as a main or significant activity within their travel is used, then 'sports tourism is a multi-billion-pound sector worldwide, and significant too within individual national economies' (Jackson and Weed, 2003: 247). Furthermore, the role sports tourism plays as a travel and activity motivator cannot be ignored. It has long been the case that sport and tourism have been linked in the minds of sports tourists and commercial providers and, to a lesser extent, by public sector providers seeking to use sports tourism as a tool in economic, social and community development. However, such links have not permeated policy, nor those areas of public sector provision, particularly in the sports area, that do not see any relationship between their activities and the developing area of sports tourism. The continued and predicted future growth of sports tourism

(Delpy-Nierotti, 2003; Gibson 1998; 2002; Jackson and Weed, 2003; Standeven and De Knop, 1999; WTO, 2002) means that such links cannot be ignored by these organizations for very much longer.

The lack of links among policy-makers and some providers gives rise to considerations of how educational curricula might best serve the future development of sports tourism. As noted in the prologue, there is a trend, possibly driven by the financial concerns of universities that see sports tourism as a lucrative area of provision, towards the development of specific undergraduate degree courses in sports tourism. A number of courses exist in both Europe and North America, and others are planned for the future. However, there must be some question about the need for such specialized courses. Is sports tourism as an industry sufficiently well developed to provide employment opportunities for cohorts of graduates? Will policy-makers and providers that have yet to recognize the extent of the sport-tourism link be prepared to employ sports tourism graduates? At the present point in time it would seem unlikely. A more productive route in relation to sports tourism curricula, therefore, may be to ensure that tourism students graduate with some knowledge of sport, and that sport graduates have some knowledge of tourism. This would ensure a broader range of employment opportunities for the graduates themselves, and would also locate graduate level staff in policy-making agencies and provision organizations that have some knowledge of the links between sport and tourism. This is the approach taken at Loughborough University, where students on the BSc Sport and Leisure Management course may take a year two option in tourism that provides a grounding in the industry and its issues, and a further final year tourism option that has a considerable sports tourism content. Further development of specific sports tourism knowledge is perhaps more appropriate at postgraduate level, and the development of Masters courses in sports tourism would appear to be a more useful educational provision strategy in the current climate.

Of course, any development of curricula for sports tourism assumes and requires a base of supporting knowledge and research activity. The aim of this volume has been initially to draw together current knowledge about the development, impacts and extent of sports tourism (Chapters 1 and 2), before discussing in detail themes and issues, grounded in empirical research, related to the motivations and behaviours of sports tourism participants (Chapters 3, 4 and 5), policy-makers (Chapters 6 and 7) and providers (Chapters 8 and 9). These issues were then illustrated in a range of extended case studies (Chapters 10, 11, 12 and 13). Many of the issues in the substantive chapters (3 to 9) are related to research findings that are presented together for the first time in this text. As such, many of the discussions raise a number of issues for future research development.

An initial observation, related to Gibson's (1998) discussion of the continued separation of sport and tourism in academia, is that the vast majority of sports tourism research takes place from the perspective of either sport or tourism. One of the key themes of this volume has been that not only can sports tourism not be fully understood from the single perspective of either sport or tourism, but that an analysis that neglects the unique nature of sports tourism as derived from the interaction of activity, people and place will also be limited. Gibson (2002: 122) notes the comment of Gartner (1996: 317) that 'sport tourism will probably develop its own cadre of researchers', and while this has been the case the subject still tends to be approached from the perspective of one of the subject areas. This is evident in the way Glyptis (1982) expressed her first 'need' for the field as, 'a recognition of the tourist potential of sport and the sports development potential of tourism'. Similarly, Jackson and Glyptis (1992) included substantial separate chapters examining 'sport in the development of tourism' and 'the role of tourism in generating sports participation', while Standeven and De Knop (1999) discussed in separate chapters 'sport in the development of tourism' and 'tourism in the development of sport. This approach has even been taken to a certain extent in examining the effects of linking sport and tourism in Chapter 2 of this text. It would therefore appear to be the case that in relation to a discussion of impacts it is difficult to avoid an approach that examines the impact of sport on tourism and vice versa. However, in examining the motivations and behaviours of participants, policy-makers and providers a more holistic approach is needed. In proposing a research framework for sports tourism, Hinch and Higham (2001: 48) describe such research as being about 'the relationship between sport, as a motivation to travel, and tourism'. Not only does this dismiss the role of tourism as a sports activity motivator, but it also relegates one of the areas to a subordinate role as a motivator in the generation of the other. What emerged as a key theme from Chapter 3 is that motivations for sports tourism are related to the unique experience derived from the interaction of activity, people and place, rather than being about motivations for sport or for tourism that happen to manifest themselves in the form of sports tourism. As such, it is the contention of this volume that sports tourism needs to be understood as a unique social, economic and cultural phenomenon, that is not simply derived from sport or from tourism, nor from some simple aggregation of the two.

However, notwithstanding the above, there are obviously some issues germane to sports tourism that are also significant within the individual sectors of tourism and of sport. Perhaps most obvious among these is the need for sustainable development of sports tourism. While there have been some references to the need for sustainable approaches in this text, the review chapter by Jackson and Weed (2003) discusses this issue in greater detail. Standeven and De Knop (1999: 330) raise the issue of 'democratization' in relation to sports tourism and call for the promotion of greater access by 'less privileged classes'. This call for 'sports tourism for all' is clearly derived from sports development programmes that promote 'sport for all', although it has perhaps been a less prominent issue in the sports tourism literature than concerns surrounding sustainability.

There are, of course, many other issues that are more specific to sports tourism. Despite the discussions in Part Two of this book, knowledge about the motivations and needs of sports tourists is limited, and this is a clear area for further research. More studies are needed that specifically take motivation as their central construct, and the Sports Tourism Participation Model developed in Chapter 5 may provide an organizing framework for such studies. One of the strengths of this model is the potential to build individual participation profiles across a range of sports tourism activities. The development and understanding of such profiles, and the relationship between individual motivations for a range of different activities, would seem to be an area that is ripe for further study. In relation to policy, it would appear that the most pressing need is to educate policy-makers about the potential of linking sport and tourism. While sports tourism activity by policy-makers does sometimes take place, genuine strategic collaborations between the sports and tourism sectors are few and far between. The Policy Area Matrix for Sport and Tourism presented in Chapter 7 provides a useful overview of the areas in which it might reasonably be expected that sports and tourism agencies should collaborate, and this might be a useful tool in any work that seeks to develop understanding about the sport-tourism link among policy-makers in the respective sectors.

Providers, particularly commercial sector providers, are perhaps most comfortable with promoting and developing sports tourism. Commercial provision has been far more advanced than policy development in this area, and in many cases has led demand. However, policy support for sports tourism provision is still required, as is greater knowledge about the wants and needs of sports tourists. The discussions in this text would seem to indicate that market segmentation on the basis of demographic information is less useful in relation to sports tourism than in other areas. Sports tourism markets would appear to be best provided for on the basis of motivations and behaviours rather than along more traditional demographic or socioeconomic lines. This is, again, a potentially fruitful area for further research.

Some final remarks are perhaps useful on the use of theory in the study of sports tourism. At an international conference in 2002, a keynote speaker was asked in a plenary session about what theoretical perspectives and concepts underpinned the study of sports tourism. While the speaker was able to point to one or two areas in which theory was prominent, this question highlighted a problem for the field of sports tourism related to some of the comments made earlier in this epilogue and in the prologue. The large amount of unconnected small-scale sports tourism case studies, and the continued preoccupation with advocacy work, have meant that there is a perception among academics in sport, tourism and leisure studies that sports tourism research is not theoretically informed. Consequently, a challenge for the developing 'cadre' of specialist sports tourism researchers is to ensure that the theoretical aspects of their work are clearly highlighted in any publications. Such theory may be drawn from a number of disciplines – in this text perspectives from psychology, geography, sociology, policy studies, marketing and management have all been used. In such cases the application of theoretical perspectives previously applied to other areas of sport, tourism and leisure studies is useful, as long as careful consideration is given to the way in which the unique nature of sports tourism might affect their application. A further strategy is to use a grounded theory approach, building theory based on primary empirical research. In this text, the Sports Tourism Participation Model (Chapter 5), the Model of Cross-Sectoral Policy Development (Chapter 6) and the Policy Area Matrix for Sport and Tourism (Chapter 7) have each been developed in this way, while the Model of Sports Tourism Types (Chapter 8) builds on and updates earlier empirical work. Furthermore, these models, concepts and approaches are the result of a range of linked but separate empirical work spanning more than a decade. They have been underpinned by the conceptualization of sports tourism as a social, economic and cultural phenomenon arising from the unique interaction of activity people and place. This conceptualization provides a useful context for future sports tourism research, the framework for which might be supplied by the thoroughly grounded and validated concepts and models discussed and developed in this volume.

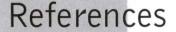

References

Agne-Traub, L. (1989). Volkssporting and tourism: something for the working class. *Leisure Information Quarterly*, 15 (4), 6–8.

Agyeman, J. (1990). Black people in a white landscape: social and environmental justice. *Built Environment*, 16 (3), 232–236.

Albert, E. (1991). Riding a line: competition and cooperation in the sport of bicycle racing. *Sociology of Sport Journal*, 8 (4), 341–361.

Amarcal, C. B. and Corrough, J. C. (1994). Two case studies of marine parks and marinas as economic and tourism activity stimulators. Proceedings of the International Conference, Marinas, Parks and Recreation Developments, ACSE, New York, pp. 565–572.

Anderson, J. and Edwards, C. (1998). Sport in the port: leisure and tourism in the maritime city. Proceedings of the Sport in the City Conference, 2–4 July, Leisure Industries Research Centre, Sheffield.

Anthony, D. (1966). *Sport and Tourism.* London: CCPR.

Ap, J. and Crompton, J. L. (1993). Residents strategies for responding to tourism impacts. *Journal of Travel Research*, 32 (1), 47–51.

Armstrong, G. (1998). *Football Hooligans: Knowing the Score.* Oxford: Berg.

Astrand, P.-O. (1978). *Health and Fitness.* New York: Skandia Insurance Company.

Astrand, P.-O. (1987). Setting the scene. In *Exercise Heart Health* (Coronary Prevention Group, eds) pp. 5–20. London: Coronary Prevention Group.

Baade, R. A. and Dye, R. F. (1988). An analysis of the economic rationale for public subsidation of sports stadia. *Annals of Regional Science*, 22 (2), 37–47.

Bailey, P. (1987). *Leisure and Class in Victorian England: Rational Recreation and the Contest for Control, 1830–1885*. London: Methuen.

Baker, M. J. and Gordon, A. W. (1976). *Market for Winter Sports Facilities in Scotland*. Edinburgh: Scottish Tourist Board.

Baker, W. J (1982). *Sports in the Western World*, Totowa, NJ: Rowman and Littlefield.

Bale, J. (1989). *Sports Geography*. London: E. and F. N. Spon.

Bale, J. (1994). *Landscapes of Modern Sport*. Leicester: Leicester University Press.

Bale, J. (2003). *Sports Geography* (2nd edition). London: E. and F. N. Spon.

Barker, M. L. (1982). Traditional landscape and mass tourism in the Alps. *Geographical Review*, 72, 395–415.

Barnard, C. L. P. (1988). *Sport Tourism . . . For You? A Guide to Develop a Sport Tourism Strategy*. Victoria: Ministry of Tourism, Recreation and Culture (Recreation and Sport Branch).

Bartram, S. A. (2001). Serious leisure careers among whitewater kayakers: a feminist perspective. *World Leisure Journal*, 43 (2), 4–11.

Beedie, P. (2003). Adventure tourism. In *Sport and Adventure Tourism* (S. Hudson, ed.). New York: Haworth Hospitality Press.

Bennet, T. (1991). The shaping of things to come: Expo '88. *Cultural Studies*, 5 (2), 30–51.

Benson, J. K., (1982). Networks and policy sectors: a framework for extending intergovermental analysis. In *Inter-Organisational Co-ordination* (D. Roger and D. Whitten, eds), Des Moines, IA: Iowa State University.

Boissevan, J. (1993). Some problems with cultural tourism in Malta. Unpublished paper presented at the International Conference on Sustainable Tourism in Islands and Small States, Foundation for International Studies – Malta.

Bone, V. (1995). Culture club. *The Leisure Manager*, 13 (4), 16–17.

Boon, M. A. (1984). Understanding skiing behaviour. *Society and Leisure*, 7 (2), 397–406.

Bourdieu, P. (1978). Sport and social class. *Social Science Information*, 18 (6), 820–833.

Bramwell, B. (1997a). A sport mega-event as a sustainable tourism development strategy. *Tourism Recreation Research*, 22 (2), 13–19.

Bramwell, B. (1997b). User satisfaction and product development in urban tourism. *Tourism Management*, 19 (1), 35–47.

Bramwell, B. (1998a). Strategic planning before and after a mega-event. *Tourism Management*, 18 (3), 167–176.

Bramwell, B. (1998b). Event tourism in Sheffield: a sustainable approach to urban development. In *Sustainable Tourism Management: Principles and Practice* (2nd edition) (B. Bramwell, I. Goytia Prat, I. P. Henry, G. A. M. Jackson, G. Richards, and J. van der Straaten, eds), Tilburg: Tilburg University Press.

Bratton, R. D. (1988). Amateur sport and the tourism industry in Calgary: a progress report. Post-Olympic Sociology Colloquium, Calgary.

Briggs, S. (2001). *Successful Tourism Marketing: A Practical Handbook* (2nd edition). London: Kogan Page.

Brincat, I. (1995). Sport tourism. *Cobweb, Business Journal*, special issue on Sustainable Tourism in Malta, AIESEC.

British Tourist Authority (1981). *Tourism, the UK – the Broad Perspective*. London: BTA.

Broek, M. van den (1997). Nature-based activity travel and its potential to the eastern part of Europe – a case study of Slovenia. *Tourism Recreation Research*, 22 (2), 21–27.

Brown, G. (2000). Emerging issues in event sponsorship: implications for host cities. *Sport Management Review*, 3 (1), 71–92.

Buckley, P. and Witt, S. (1985). Tourism in difficult areas: case studies of Bradford, Bristol, Glasgow and Hamm. *Tourism Management*, 6 (3), 205–213.

Bull, C. J. and Weed, M. E. (1999). Niche markets and small island tourism: the development of sports tourism in Malta. *Managing Leisure*, 4 (2), 142–155.

Bull, C. J., Hoose, J. and Weed, M. E. (2003). *An Introduction to Leisure Studies*. Harlow: Financial Times Prentice Hall.

Bull, P. (1997). Mass tourism in the Balearic Islands: an example of concentrated dependence. In *Island Tourism: Trends and Prospects* (D. G. Lockwood and D. Drakakis-Smith, eds), London: Pinter.

Burbank, M., Andranovich, G. and Heying, C. H. (2001). *Olympic Dreams: The Impact of Mega Events on Local Politics*. Colorado: Lynne Rienner.

Burke, V. and Collins, D. (2002). Outdoor management development: the provider's perspective on optimising the process of skills transfer'. In *Proceedings of the 10th European Congress on Sport Management* (K. Laaksonen, P. Lopponen, E. Nykanen and K. Puronaho, eds), Jyvaskyla: EASM.

Burkhart, A. J. and Medlick, S. (1992). *Tourism: Past, Present and Future*. Oxford: Butterworth-Heinemann.

Burton, R. (1995). *Travel Geography*. London: Pitman.

Busby, G. and Rendle, S. (2000). The transition from tourism on farms to farm tourism'. *Tourism Management*, 21 (6), 635–642.

Buswell, R. J. (1996). Tourism in the Balearic Islands. In *Tourism in Spain: Critical Perspectives* (M. Towner and M. Newton, eds), Wallingford: CAB International.

Butler, R. (1998). Rural recreation and tourism. In *The Geography of Rural Change* (B. Ilbery, ed.), London: Longman.

Butler, R. W., Hall, C.M. and Jenkins, J. M. (eds) (1997). *Tourism and Recreation in Rural Areas*. Chichester: John Wiley.

Butts, S. L. (2001). 'Good to the last drop': understanding surfers' motivations. *Sociology of Sport on Line*, 4 (1).

Cabinet Office (Enterprise Unit) (1985). *Pleasure, Leisure and Jobs: The Business of Tourism*. London: HMSO.

Canadian Geographer Special Edition (1991). West Edmonton Mall. *Canadian Geographer*, 35 (3).

Canadian Tourism Commission (CTC) (1999). *The Canadian Sports Tourism Initiative*. www.travelcanada.ca/en/ctc/partner_centre/partnering/sports-initiative.htm.

Carmichael, B. (1996). Conjoint analysis of downhill skiers used to improve data collection for market segmentation. *Journal of Travel and Tourism Marketing*, 5 (3), 187–206.

Carnibella, G., Fox, A., Fox, K., McCann, J., Marsh, J. and Marsh, P. (1996). *Football Violence in Europe*. Oxford: Social Issues Research Centre.

Carpenter, G. and Priest, S. (1989). The adventure experience paradigm and non-outdoor leisure pursuits, *Leisure Studies*, 8, 65–75.

Carron, A. V. and Hausenblaus, H. L. (1998). *Group Dynamics in Sport*. Morgantown, VA: Fitness Information Technology.

Center for South Australian Economic Studies (1992). Estimated economic impact of the 1994 Commonwealth Games (review of a report prepared by Coopers and Lybrand Consulting Group). *Sports Economics*, 3, 10–12.

Centre for Applied Business Research (CABR) (1986). *Americas Cup Economic Impact: Final Report*. Nedlands: CABR.

Cha, S., McCleary, K. and Uysal, M. (1995). Travel motivations of Japanese overseas travellers: a factor-cluster segmentation approach. *Journal of Travel Research*, 34 (1), 33–39.

Chalkley, B., Jones, A., Kent, M. and Sims, P. (1992). Barcelona: Olympic city. *Geography Review*, 6 (1), 2–4.

Chapin, T. S. (1996). A new era of professional sports in the northwest: facility location as an economic development strategy in Seattle, Portland and Vancouver. Paper presented to the Sport in the City Conference, Sheffield.

Chesterton Chartered Surveyors (n.d.). *Metrocentre*. Gateshead: Chesterton.

Chivers, B. (1976). Friendly games: Edmonton's Olympic alternative. In *The City Book: The Politics and Planning of Canada's Cities* (J. Lorimer and E. Ross, eds), Toronto: James Lorimer.

Chubb, M. and Chubb, H. (1981). *One Third of Our Time? An Introduction to Recreation Behaviour and Resource*. New York: Wiley.

Clark, G., Darrall, J., Grove-White, R., Macnaghten, P. and Urry, J (1994). *Leisure Landscapes, Leisure Culture and the English Countryside: Challenges and Conflicts*. Lancaster: Centre for Environmental Change, Lancaster University/CPRE.

Clark, J. and Critcher, C. (1985). *The Devil Makes Work: Leisure in Capitalist Britain*. London: Methuen.

Clawson, M, Held, R. and Stoddard, C. (1960). *Land for the Future*. Baltimore, MD: Johns Hopkins University Press.

Clements, C. J., Schultz, J. H. and Lime, D. W. (1993). Recreation, tourism and the local residents: partnership or co-existence. *Journal of Park and Recreation Administration*, 11 (4), 78–91.

Clowes, J. and Tapp, A. (1998). From the 4 Ps to the 3 Rs of marketing: using relationship marketing to retain football club supporters and improve income. *Managing Leisure*, 3 (1), 18–25.

Cockerell, N. (1994). Market segments: the international ski market in Europe. *EIU Travel and Tourism Analyst*, 3, 34–55.

Cohen, E. (1983). The social psychology of tourist behaviour. *Annals of Tourism Research*, 15 (1), 29–46.

Collins, M. F. (1991). The economics of sport and sports in the economy: some international comparisons. In *Progress in Tourism, Recreation and Hospitality Management* (vol. 3) (C. P. Cooper, ed.), pp. 185–214, London: Belhaven Press.

Collins, M. F. (1995). Sights on sport. *Leisure Management*, 15 (9), 26–28.

Collins, M. F. and Jackson, G. A. M. (1999). The economic impact of sport and tourism. In *Sport Tourism* (J. Standeven and P. De Knop, eds), London: Human Kinetics.

Collins, M. F. and Jackson, G. A. M. (2001). Evidence for a sports tourism continuum. Paper to Journeys in Leisure, Leisure Studies Association Conference, Luton, July.

Cooper, C. P., Fletcher, J., Wanhill, S., Gilbert, D. and Shepherd, R. (1998). *Tourism: Principles and Practice* (2nd edition). Harlow: Pitman.

Council for the Protection of Rural England (CPRE) (1991). *Sport and Recreation*. London: CPRE

Countryside Recreation Network (CRN) (1995). *Sport in the Countryside: Planning and Management for Sport and* Active *Recreation*. Proceedings from a workshop held at Aston Business School, Birmingham, 27 April.

Countryside Recreation Research and Advisory Group (CRAAG) (1991). *Young People, Adventure and the Countryside*. Bristol: CRRAG.

Critcher, C. (1991). Sporting civic pride: Sheffield and the World Student Games of 1991. In *Leisure in the 1990s: Rolling Back the Welfare State* (C. Knox and J. Sugden, eds). Brighton: Leisure Studies Association.

Croall, J. (1995). *Preserve or Destroy: Tourism and the Environment*, London: Calouste Gulbenkian Foundation.

Crompton, J. L. (1979). Motivations for pleasure vacation. *Journal of Leisure Research*, 6, 408–424.

Crompton, J. L. and Lee, S. (2000). the economic impact of 30 sports tournaments, festivals, and spectator events in seven US cities. *Journal of Park and Recreation Administration*, 18 (2), 107–126.

Cross, G. (1990). *A Social History of Leisure Since 1600*. State College, PA: Venture Publishing.

Crosset, T. and Beal, B. (1997). The use of 'Subculture' and 'Subworld' in ethnographic works on sport. *Sociology of Sport Journal*, 14 (1), 73–85.

Crozier, M. (1964). *The Bureaucratic Phenomenon*. Chicago: University of Chicago Press.

Cunningham, H. (1975). *Leisure in the Industrial Revolution, c. 1780–1880*. London: Croom Helm

Cushman, G., Veal, A. J. and Zuzaneck, J. (1996). Cross-national leisure participation research: a future. In *World Leisure Participation: Free Time in the Global Village* (G. Cushman, A. J. Veal and J. Zuzaneck, eds), London: CAB International.

D'Abaco, G. (1991). Marketing parks and recreational facilities as tourism attractions – experiences from the Victoria Tourism Commission's 'Melbourne Now' campaign. In *Who Dares Wins – Parks , Recreation and Tourism*. Conference proceedings, vol. 2. Canberra: Royal Institute of Parks and Recreation.

Dahl, R. A., (1956). *A Preface to Democratic Theory*. University of Chicago Press, Chicago.

Dalton, M. (1959). *Men Who Manage*. New York: Wiley.

Davies, N. (1997). *Europe: A History*. London: Pimlico.

De Knop, P. (1990). Sport for all and active tourism. *Journal of the World Leisure and Recreation Association*, Fall, 30–36.

Delpy, L. (1999). Disney's approach to sports tourism: developing sports facilities to increase tourism. In *Sport Tourism* (J. Standeven and P. De Knop, eds), Champaign, IL: Human Kinetics.

Delpy-Neirotti, L. (2003). An introduction to sport and adventure tourism. In *Sport and Adventure Tourism* (S. Hudson, ed.). New York: Haworth Hospitality Press.

Department of Culture, Media and Sport (DCMS) (2001). *Staging International Sporting Events*, Government Response to the Third Report from the Culture, Media and Sport Committee Session 2000–2001, Presented to Parliament by the Secretary of Culture, Media and Sport By Command of Her Majesty, October 2001.

Department of National Heritage (DNH) (1995). *Sport: Raising the Game*. London: DNH.

Department of the Environment (DoE) (1990). *Tourism and the Inner City*. London: HMSO.

Department of the Environment (DOE)/Welsh Office (1991). *Planning Policy Guidance 17, Sport and Recreation*. London: HMSO.

Destination Sheffield (1995). *An Event-Led City and Tourism Marketing Strategy for Sheffield*. Sheffield: Destination Sheffield.

Devetta, M. (2002). Temporary fixes: supplying temporary seating for global events. *Stadia*, S1, 92–94.

Dillard, E. M. (1995). Indoor workouts – top quality fitness centers satisfy hotel guests. *Aquatics International*, 7 (2), 29–31.

Dobson, N. and Gratton, C. (1995). From 'city of steel' to 'city of sport': an evaluation of Sheffield's attempts to use sport as a vehicle for urban regeneration. Paper presented at the Recreation in the City Conference, Staffordshire University, Stoke-on-Trent.

Dobson, N. and Gratton, C. (1997). *The Economic Impact of Sports Events: Euro '96 and VI Fina World Masters Swimming Championship in Sheffield*. Sheffield: Leisure Industries Research Centre.

Dobson, N., Gratton, C. and Holliday, S. (1997). The economic impact of sports events: Euro '96 and the VI FINA World Masters Swimming Championships in Sheffield. *The Regional Review*, 16–19.

Donnelly, M. P., Vaske, J. J., DeRuiter, D. S., Loomis, J. B. (1998). Economic impacts of state parks: effects of park visitation, park facilities, and county economic diversification. *Journal of Park and Recreation Administration*, 16 (4), 52–72.

Donnelly, P. (1993). Subcultures in sport: resilience and transformation. In *Sport in Social Development* (A. G. Ingham and J. W. Loy, eds), Champaign, IL: Human Kinetics.

Doorne, S. (1998). Power, participation and perception: an insider's perspective on the politics of the Wellington Waterfront redevelopment. *Current Issues in Tourism*, 1 (2), 129–166.

Dowding, K. (1995). Model or metaphor? a critical review of the policy network approach, *Political Studies*, 43 (1), 136–158.

Dowling, M. (Development Director – South East England Tourist Board) (1996). Personal communication.

Downey B. (1993). Major sports events in Victoria: the economic impacts and related tourism opportunities. *Leisure Options*, 3 (3), 28–32

Downs, A. (1967). *Inside Bureaucracy*, Boston, MA: Little Brown.

Dulac, C. and Henry, I. (2001). Sport and social regulation in the city: the cases of Grenoble and Sheffield. *Society and Leisure*, 24 (1), spring, 47–78.

Dunning, E., Murphy, P. and Williams, J. (1988). *The Roots of Football Hooliganism: An Historical and Sociological Study*. London: Routledge and Kegan Paul.

Edwards, J. A. (1996). Waterfronts, tourism and economic sustainability: the UK experience. In *Sustainable Tourism? European Experiences* (G. K. Priestley, J. A. Edwards and H. Coccossis, eds), Wallingford: CAB International.

Elson, M. J., Heaney, D. and Reynolds, G (1995). *Planning and Management for Sport and Active Recreation in the Countryside*. London: the Sports Council and Countryside Commission.

English Tourism Council (ETC) (2001). *Foot and Mouth Disease and Tourism*. www.englishtourism.org.uk.

English Tourist Board (1987). *A Vision for England*. London: ETB.

English Tourist Board/Countryside Commission (ETC/CC) (1993). *Principles for Tourism in the Countryside*. London: ETB/CC.

Erlinger, P., la Louveau, C. and Metoudi, M. (1985). *Practiques Sportives des Francais*. Paris: Ministere de Jeunesse et Sports.

European Commission (1995). *Tourism and the European Union: A Practical Guide*. Luxembourg: Office for Official Publications of the European Communities.

Everden, N. (1992). *The Social Creation of Nature*, Baltimore, MD: Johns Hopkins University Press.

Ewart, A. and Hollenhorst, S. (1994). Individual and setting attributes of the adventure recreation experience. *Leisure Sciences*, 16 (3), 177–191.

Ewin, D. (2000). Two court school/community sport and recreation centres – the long haul: the Trangie experience. In *Planning and Developing Rural Sports Facilities*, Official Forum Proceedings, New South Wales: Department of Sport and Recreation.

Fache, W. (1990). Splash out. *Leisure Management*, 10 (9), 26–28.

Farmer, R. J. (1992). Surfing: motivations, values and culture. *Journal of Sport Behaviour*, 15 (3), 241–257.

Fayos-Sola, E. (1998). The impact of mega events. *Annals of Tourism Research*, 25 (1), 241–245.

Ferras, R., Picheral, H. and Vielzeuf, B. (1979). *Languedoc Roussillon*. Paris: Flammarion et Editions Famot.

Finley, M. I. and Pleket, H. W. (1976). *The Olympic Games*. Edinburgh: R. and R. Clark.

Fitzgerald, H. F. (1993). Farm tourism and recreation in Stoke-on-Trent. Unpublished MSc thesis, Loughborough University.

Fogelman, B. (1992). Golf tourism: opportunities and strategies. *World Travel and Tourism Review 1992*, 129–134.

Fox, K. (1999). *The Racing Tribe: Watching the Horsewatchers*. London: Metro Books.

Fraser, K. (1998). The hosts with the most. *Marketing and eBusiness*, December, 29–35.

Freeman, J. L. (1955). *The Political Process*. New York: Doubleday.

Friel, E. (1990). Tourism as an aid to improving the economy of Glasgow. Paper to the Conference: Tourism and Job Creation, Edinburgh: Centre for Leisure Research.

Galloway, G. (2002). Psychographic segmentation of park visitor markets: evidence for the utility of sensation-seeking. *Tourism Management*, 23 (6), 581–596.

Gammon, S. (2002). Fantasy, nostalgia and the pursuit of what never was. In *Sport Tourism: Principles and Practice* (S. Gammon and J. Kurtzman, eds), Eastbourne: LSA.

Gammon, S. and Kurtzman, J. (2002). Editors' introduction. In *Sport Tourism: Principles and Practice* (S. Gammon and J. Kurtzman, eds), Eastbourne: LSA.

Garrigues, P. (1988). *Evolution de la Practique Sportive des Francais*. Coll. De l'INSEE, 134 M., October, Paris: Institut National de Statistique et d'Etudes Economiques.

Getz, D. (1991). *Festivals, Special Events and Tourism*. New York: Van Nostrand Reinhold.

Getz, D. (1997a). *Event Management and Event Tourism*. New York: Cognizant Communication Corporation.

Getz, D. (1997b). Trends and issues in sport event tourism. *Tourism Recreation Research*, 22 (2), 61–62.

Getz, D. (2003). Sport event tourism: planning, development and marketing. In *Sport and Adventure Tourism* (S. Hudson, ed.), New York: Haworth Hospitality Press.

Gibson, H. J. (1998). Sport tourism: a critical analysis of research. *Sport Management Review*, 1 (1), 45–76.

Gibson, H. J. (2002). Sport tourism at a crossroad? Considerations for the future. In *Sport Tourism: Principles and Practice* (S. Gammon and J. Kurtzman, eds), Eastbourne: LSA.

Giulianotti, R. (2002). Supporters, followers, fans and flaneurs: a taxonomy of spectator identities in football. *Journal of Sport and Social Issues*, 26 (1), 25–46.

Glyptis, S.A. (1982). *Sport and Tourism in Western Europe*. London: British Travel Education Trust.

Glyptis, S.A. (1991a). Sport and tourism. In *Progress in Tourism, Recreation and Hospitality Management* (vol. 3) (C. P. Cooper, ed.), London: Belhaven Press.

Glyptis, S. A. (1991b). *Countryside Recreation*. Harlow: Longman.

Glyptis, S. A. (1992). The changing demand for countryside recreation. In *Contemporary Rural Systems in Transition, Vol. 2* (I. R. Bowler, C. R. Bryant and M. D. Nellis, eds), Wallingford: CAB International.

Goldsmith, M. J. and Rhodes, R. A. W. (1986). *Register of Research and Research Digest on Central–Local Government Relations in Britain*: London: ESRC.

Goring, R. A. (1987). Why invest in leisure? In *Hotels: Profiting from Leisure*, Sports Council Recreation Management Seminar, workshop report, pp. 10–17. London: Sports Council.

Gouldner, A. W. (1954). *Patterns of Industrial Bureaucracy*. New York: Free Press

Government of Malta (1990). *Structure Plan for the Maltese Islands*, Valletta: Government of Malta.

Graburn, N. H. H. (1983). The anthropology of tourism. *Annals of Tourism Research*, 10 (1), 9–33.

Graburn, N. H. H. (1989). Tourism: the sacred journey. In *Hosts and Guests: The Anthropology of Tourism* (2nd edition) (V. Smith, ed.), Philadelphia, PA: University of Pennsylvania.

Grant, W., Patterson, W. and Whitson, C., (1989). *Government and the Chemical Industry: A Comparative Study of Britain and West Germany*. Oxford: Clarendon Press.

Gratton, C. and Henry, I. P. (eds) (2001). *Sport in the City: The Role of Sport in Economic and Social Regeneration*. London: Routledge.

Gratton, C. and Taylor, P. (1985). *Sport and Recreation: An Economic Analysis*. London: E. and F. N. Spon.

Gratton, C., Dobson, N. and Shibli, S. (2000). The economic impacts of major sports events: a case-study of six events. *Managing Leisure*, 5 (1), 17–28.

Grcic-Zubcevic, N. (2001). Swimming and other water activities in tourist centres. In *Sport for All and Health Tourism* (M. Bartoluci, ed.), Zagreb: CESS.

Green, B. C. (2001). Leveraging subculture and identity to promote sport events. *Sport Management Review*, 4 (1), 1–19.

Green, B. C. and Chalip, L. (1998). Sport tourism as the celebration of subculture. *Annals of Tourism Research*, 25 (2), 275–291.

Green, M. (2002). Western approaches to sport policy. Unpublished review paper. Loughborough University.

Green, S. (1982). *Cricketing Bygones*. Princes Risborough: Shire Publications.

Gregory, A. (1991). *The Golden Age of Travel, 1880–1939*. London: Cassell.

Gunn, C. A. (1990). The new recreation–tourism alliance. *Journal of Park and Recreation Administration*, 8 (1), 1–8.

Guttmann, A. (1992). Chariot races, tournaments and the civilizing process. In *Sport and Leisure in the Civilizing Process* (E. Dunning and C. Rojek, eds), Basingstoke: Macmillan.

Hall, C. M. (1992a). Adventure, sport and health. In *Special Interest Tourism* (C. M. Hall and B. Weiler, eds), London: Belhaven Press.

Hall, C. M. (1992b). *Hallmark Tourist Events: Impacts, Management and Planning*. London: Belhaven Press.

Hall, C. M. (1994). *Tourism and Politics: Policy, Power and Place*. London: Belhaven Press.

Hall, C. M. (2000). *Tourism Planning*. Harlow: Prentice Hall.

Hall, C. M. (2001). Imaging, tourism and sports event fever. In *Sport in the City: The Role of Sport in Economic and Social Regeneration* (C. Gratton and I. P. Henry, eds), London: Routledge.

Hall, C. M. and Jenkins, J. M. (1995). *Tourism and Public Policy*. New York: Routledge.

Hall, C. M. and Page, S. J. (2002). *The Geography of Tourism and Recreation: Environment, Place and Space* (2nd edition). London: Routledge.

Hargreaves, J. (1982). Sport, culture and ideology. In *Sport, Culture and Ideology* (J. Hargreaves, ed.), London: Routledge and Kegan Paul.

Harrison, C. (1991). *Countryside Recreation in a Changing Society*. London: TMS Partnership.

Harrison, J. (1990). *Leisure Facilities in Shopping Centres*. London: Royal Institute of Chartered Surveyors.

Hay, B. (1989). Leisure day trips: the new tourism. In *Tourism and Leisure*

(Part Two): Markets, Users and Sites (D. Botterill, ed.), Eastbourne: Leisure Studies Association.

Haywood, L. (1994). Community sports and physical recreation. In *Community Leisure and Recreation* (L. Haywood, ed.), Oxford: Butterworth-Heinemann.

Haywood, L., Kew, F.C., Bramham, P., Spink, J., Capenerhurst, J. and Henry, I. P. (1995). *Understanding Leisure* (2nd edition). Cheltenham: Stanley Thornes.

Hearne, J. (2003). A stakeholder analysis of Nottingham Forest Football Club. Unpublished BSc dissertation, Loughborough University.

Heclo, H. and Wildavski, A. (1974). *The Private Government of Public Money*. London: Macmillan.

Henderson, K. A. and Frelke, C. E. (2000). Space as a vital dimension of leisure: the creation of place. *World Leisure Journal*, 42 (3), 18–24.

Henry, I. P. (1993). *The Politics of Leisure Policy*. London: Macmillan.

Henry, I. P. (2001). *The Politics of Leisure Policy* (2nd edition). London: Palgrave.

Henry, I. P. and Matthews, N. (1998). Sport policy and the European Union: the post-Maastricht agenda. *Managing Leisure*, 3(1), 1–17.

Hetherington, K. (1996). Identity formation, space and social centrality. *Theory, Culture and Society*, 13 (4), 33–52.

Higgins, P. (2000). Outdoor recreation, outdoor education and the economy of Scotland. *Horizons*, 7/8, 24–29.

Hill, E., O'Sullivan, T. and O'Sullivan, C. (1995). *Creative Arts Marketing*. Oxford: Butterworth-Heinemann.

Hinch, T. D. and Higham, J. E. S. (2001). Sport tourism: a framework for research. *International Journal of Tourism Research*, 3 (1), 45–58.

Hinch, T. D. and Higham, J. E. S. (forthcoming). *Sport Tourism Development*. Clevedon: Channel View Publications

Holloway, H. (1995). Farm based tourism: an alternative farm exercise – a case study of South West Kerry. Unpublished paper, Swansea Institute of Higher Education.

Holloway, J. C. (2003). *The Business of Tourism* (6th edition). Harlow: Financial Times Prentice Hall.

Holt, R. (1988). Football and the urban way of life in nineteenth-century Britain. In *Pleasure, Profit and Proselytism: British Culture and Sport at Home and Abroad, 1700–1914* (J. A. Mangan, ed.). London: Frank Cass.

Holt, R. (1989). *Sport and the British: A Modern History*. Oxford: Oxford University Press.

Horne, J., Tomlinson, A. and Whannel, G. (1999). *Understanding Sport: An Introduction to the Sociological and Cultural Analysis of Sport*. London: E. and F. N. Spon.

Houlihan, B. (1991). *The Government and the Politics of Sport*. London: Routledge.

Houlihan, B. (1994). *Sport and International Politics*. London: Harvester Wheatsheaf.

Houlihan, B. (1997). *Sport, Policy and Politics: A Comparative Analysis*. New York: Harvester Wheatsheaf.

Houlihan, B. (2002). Personal communication to the author.

Houlihan, B. (ed.) (2003). *Sport and Society*. London: Sage.

House of Lords (1973). *Select Committee on Sport and Leisure*. London: HMSO.

Hudson, S. (1998). There's no business like snow business! Marketing skiing into the 21st century. *Journal of Vacation Marketing*, 4 (4), 393–407.

Hudson, S. (2000). *Snow Business*. London: Cassell.

Hudson. S. (ed.) (2003a). *Sport and Adventure Tourism*. New York: Haworth Hospitality Press.

Hudson, S. (2003b). Winter sport tourism. In *Sport and Adventure Tourism* (S. Hudson, ed.), New York: Haworth Hospitality Press.

Hudson, S. (2004, forthcoming). Winter sport tourism in North America. In *Sport Tourism: Interrelationships, Impacts and Issues* (B. Ritchie and D. Adair, eds). Clevedon: Channel View Publications.

Hughes, H. L. (1993). Olympic tourism and urban regeneration. *Festival Management and Event Tourism*, 1, 157–162.

Hunt Report (1989). *In Search of Adventure: A Study of the Opportunities for Adventure and Challenge for Young People*.

Hutchings, C. (1996). Trouble in paradise. *The Geographical Magazine*, January, 20–22.

Inglis, F. (2000). *The Delicious History of the Holiday*. London: Routledge.

Inskeep, E. (1994). *National and Regional Tourism Planning*, ch. 11. London: Routledge.

International Tourism Reports (1996). Malta Report No. 4, Travel and Tourism Intelligence.

IPK International (2001). *Sport Activities during the Outbound Holidays of Germans, the Dutch and the French*. Madrid: WTO.

Iso-Ahola, S. E. (1980). *The Social Psychology of Leisure and Recreation*. Dubuque, IA: William Brown.

Iso-Ahola, S. E. (1982). Toward a social psychological theory of tourism motivation: a rejoinder. *Annals of Tourism Research*, 9 (2), 256–262.

Iso-Ahola, S. E. and Wissingberger, E. (1990). Perceptions of boredom in leisure: conceptualisation, reliability and validity of the leisure boredom scale. *Journal of Leisure Research*, 22 (1), 1–17.

Iso-Ahola, S. E. (1984). Social psychology foundations of leisure and resultant implications for leisure counselling. In *Leisure Counselling: Concepts and Applications* (E. T. Dowd, ed.). Springfield, IL: C. C. Thomas.

Iso-Ahola, S. E. (1989). Motivation for leisure. In *Understanding Leisure and Recreation: Shaping the Past, Charting the Future* (E. L. Jackson and T. L. Burton, eds), State College, PA: Venture Publishing.

Jackson, C. (1999). Pedalling in the parks. *National Parks*, March/April, 34–36.

Jackson, G. A. M. and Glyptis, S. A. (1992). Sport and tourism: a review of the literature. Unpublished report to the Sports Council, Recreation Management Group, Loughborough University.

Jackson, G. A. M. and Reeves, M. R. (1996). Conceptualising the sport-tourism interrelationship: a case study approach. Paper to the LSA/VVA Conference, Wageningen, September.

Jackson, G. A. M. and Reeves, M. R. (1998). Evidencing the sport-tourism interrelationship: a case study of elite British athletes. In *Leisure Management: Issues and Applications* (M. F. Collins and I. Cooper, eds), London: CABI.

Jackson, G. A. M. and Weed, M. E. (2003). The sport-tourism interrelationship. In *Sport and Society* (B. Houlihan, ed.), London: Sage.

Jeffries, D. (2001). *Governments and Tourism*. Oxford: Butterworth-Heinemann.

Jenner, P. and Smith, C. (1992). The tourism industry and the environment. London: EIU.

Jennings, G. (2003). Marine tourism. In *Sport and Adventure Tourism* (S. Hudson, ed.), New York: Haworth Hospitality Press.

Johansson, S. (2000). Selecting the team: how to get the best value when planning and developing rural sports facilities. In *Planning and Developing Rural Sports Facilities*, Official Forum Proceedings, New South Wales: Department of Sport and Recreation.

Johnson, B. R. and Edwards, T. (1994). The commodification of mountaineering. *Annals of Tourism Research*, 21 (3), 459–478.

Jones, I. (2000). A model of serious leisure identification: the case of football fandom. *Leisure Studies*, 19 (4), 283–298.

Jordan, A. G. (1990). Sub-governments, policy communities and networks: refilling old bottles? *Journal of Theoretical Politics*, 2 (3), 319–338.

Jordan, A. G. and Richardson, J. J. (1987). *British Politics and the Policy Process*. London: Allen and Unwin.

Judd, D. R. (ed.) (2002). *The Infrastructure of Play: Building the Tourist City*. New York: M. E. Sharpe.

Katz, E. et al. (1992). *The Culture of Leisure in Israel: Changes in Patterns of Cultural Activity, 1970–1990*. Jerusalem: Israel Institute of Applied Social Research.

Keith, J., Fawson, C. and Chang, T. (1996). Recreation as an economic development strategy: some evidence from Utah. *Journal of Leisure Research*, 28 (2), 96–107.

Keller, P. (2001). *Sport and Tourism: Introductory Report*. Madrid: WTO.

Kelly, J. R. (1985). *Leisure Identities and Interactions*. London: Allen and Unwin.

Keogh, B. (1980). Motivations and the choice decisions of skiers. *Tourist Review*, 35 (1), 18–22.

Kerr, J. H. (1994). *Understanding Soccer Hooliganism*. Buckingham: Open University Press.

Keynote (2001). *Market Review: UK Travel and Tourism*. London: Keynote Market Information.

Keynote (2002). *Market Report – Health Clubs and Leisure Centres*. London: Keynote Market Information.

King, J. (1996). *The Football Factory*. London: Vintage.

King, L., Crabtree, R. and Alexander, E. (2002). a critical appraisal of relationship marketing: the effectiveness of a professional UK football club at retaining and developing loyalty of customers. In *Proceedings of the 10th European Congress on Sport Management* (K. Laaksonen, P. Lopponen, E. Nykanen and K. Puronaho, eds), Jyvaskyla: EASM.

King, R. L. (1982). Southern Europe: dependency or development. *Geography*, 67, 221–234.

Kitchen, T. (1994). *Manchester's Olympic Bid Review and Proceedings*. Manchester: Town and Country Planning School.

Knopf, R. C. (1998). The emerging convergence of recreation and tourism systems: implications for policy, management and research. In *Outdoor*

Recreation: A Reader for Congress (R. C. Knopf, ed.), Washington, DC: United States Government Printing Office.

Kolsun, J. (1988). The Calgary Winter Olympics visitor study. *The Operational Geographer*, 16, 15–17.

Koorey, G. (2001). National cycle touring routes: some thoughts on where to go from here. Paper to the New Zealand Cycling Conference: Transport for Living, Christchurch, New Zealand, September.

KPMG/Tourism Company (1994). *Activity Holidays in Scotland*. Edinburgh: STB.

Kretchmarr, A. S. (1994). *Practical Philosophy of Sport*. Champaign, IL: Human Kinetics.

Kreutzwiser, R. (1989). Supply (outdoor recreation). In *Outdoor Recreation in Canada* (G. Wall, ed.), Toronto: John Wiley.

Laaksonen, K., Lopponen, P., Nykanen, E. and Puronaho, K. (2002). *Proceedings of the 10th European Congress on Sport Management*. Jyvaskyla: EASM.

Laffin, M. (1986). Professional communities and policy communities in central–local relations. In *New Research in Central–Local Relations* (M. Goldsmith, ed.), Aldershot: Gower.

Lambton, D. (2001). Changing times on the top table. *Sports Business International*, 61, 54–56.

Landes, C. (1989). Volkssporting: the sport for everyone. *Parks and Recreation*, 24 (8), 38–41.

Larner, C. (1994). Interview with Peter Moore, Center Parcs managing director. *Leisure Management*, 14 (9), 20–23.

Laumann, E. O. and Knoke, D. (1987). *The Organisational State*. Madison, WI: University of Wisconsin Press.

Law, C. M. (1992). Urban tourism and its contribution to economic regeneration. *Urban Studies*, 29 (3–4), 599–618.

Law, C. M. (1993). *Urban Tourism, Attracting Visitors to Large Cities*. London: Mansell.

Law, C. M. (2000). Regenerating the city centre through leisure and tourism. *Built Environment*, 26, 117–129.

Law, C. M. (2002). *Urban Tourism: The Visitor Economy and the Growth of Large Cities*. London: Continnum.

Law, S. (1967). Planning for outdoor recreation. *Journal of the Town Planning Institute*, 53, 383–386.

Lee, S. (1999). *Investigating the Japanese Sports Travel Market: A Comparison of Golf and Ski Travelers*. Eugene, OR: University of Oregon, Microform Publications.

Leiper, N. (1990). *Tourism Systems: An Interdisciplinary Perspective*. Occasional Paper 2, Department of Management Systems, Massey University, Auckland, New Zealand.

Leiper, N. (1984). Tourism and leisure: the significance of tourism in the leisure spectrum. *Proceedings of the 12th New Zealand Geography Conference*. Christchurch: New Zealand Geography Society.

Leisure Consultants (1992). *Activity Holidays: A Growth Market in Tourism*. Sudbury: Leisure Consultants.

Lentell, R. (1997). Sport: origins, transformation and the growth of knowledge. In *Sport and Recreation Information Sources: Proceedings of a Seminar*

Organised by the Sport and Recreation Information Group (M. Scarrot, ed.), Sheffield: SPRIG.

Leslie, D. (2001). *An Environmental Audit of the Tourism Industry in the Lake District National Park*. Report commissioned by Friends of the Lake District.

Leung, Y. F. and Marion, J. L. (1999). Spatial strategies for managing visitor impacts in national parks. *Journal of Park and Recreation Administration*, 17 (4), 20–38.

Lewis, R. and Wild, M. (1995). *French Ski Resorts and UK Ski Tour Operators*. The Centre for Tourism Occasional Papers, Sheffield Hallam University.

Lilley, P. (1991). World class. *Tourism Enterprise*, February, 10.

Lilley, W. and DeFranco, L. J. (1999). The economic impact of the European Grands Prix. Paper presented to the FIA European Union and Sport Workshop, Brussels, February.

Lockhart, D. and Drakakis-Smith, D. (eds) (1997). *Island Tourism: Trends and Prospects*. London: Cassell.

Lockhart, D. G. (1997a). Islands and tourism: an overview. In *Island Tourism: Trends and Prospects* (D. Lockhart and D. Drakakis-Smith, eds), London: Cassell.

Lockhart, D. G. (1997b). Tourism to Malta and Cyprus. In *Island Tourism: Trends and Prospects* (D. Lockhart and D. Drakakis-Smith, eds), London: Cassell.

Lockhart, D. G. and Ashton, S. E. (1987). Recent trends in Maltese tourism. *Geography*, 72, 255–258.

Lockhart, D. G. and Ashton, S. E. (1991). Tourism in Malta. *Scottish Geographical Magazine*, 107 (1), 22–32.

Logan, C. (1991). Young people and the countryside: setting the scene. In *Young People, Adventure and the Countryside* (Countryside Recreation Research and Advisory Group), Bristol: CRRAG

London Marathon Ltd (2003). *Marathon Info*. www.london-marathon.co.uk/marathoninfo/racehistory.shtml (accessed 13 March 2003).

Long, J. (1990). Leisure, health and wellbeing: editor's introduction. In *Leisure, Health and Wellbeing* (J. Long, ed.), Conference Papers, No. 44, Eastbourne: Leisure Studies Association.

Longhurst, B. (1995). *Popular Music and Society*. Oxford: Polity Press.

Lowerson, J. and Myerscough, J. (1977). *Time to Spare in Victorian England*. Hassocks: Harvester Press.

MacCannell, D. (1976). *The Tourist*. London: Macmillan.

MacCannell, D. (1996). *Tourist or Traveller?* London: BBC Education.

Mannel, R. C. and Kleiber, D. A. (1997). *A Social Psychology of Leisure*. State College, PA: Venture Publishing.

Mannell, R. and Iso-Ahola, S. E. (1987). Psychological nature of leisure and tourism experience. *Annals of Tourism Research*, 14 (3), 314–331.

Marsh, D. (1983). Interest group activity and structural power: Lindblom's politics and markets. In *Capital and Politics in Western Europe* (D. Marsh, ed.), London: Frank Cass.

Marsh, D. and Rhodes, R. A. W. (1992). Policy communities and issue networks: beyond typology. In *Policy Networks in British Government* (D. Marsh, D. and R. A. W. Rhodes, eds), Oxford: Oxford University Press.

Marsh, J. (1984). The economic impact of a small city annual sporting event:

an initial case study of the Peterborough Church League Atoms Hockey Tournament. *Recreation Research Review*, 11, 48–55.

Marsh, N. R. (1987). Planning better tourism: the strategic importance of tourist–resident expectations and interactions. *Tourism Recreation Research*, 12 (2), 47–54.

Marsh, P., Rosser, E. and Harre, R. (1978). *The Rules of Disorder*. London: Routledge and Kegan Paul.

Martin, P. and Priest, S. (1986). Understanding the adventure experience. *Journal of Adventure Education*, 3 (1), 18–20.

Maslow, A. H. (1954). *Motivation and Personality* (2nd edition). New York: Harper and Row.

Mason, T. (1980). *Association Football and English Society 1863–1915*. Brighton: Harvester.

Mason, T. (ed.) (1989). *Sport in Britain: A Social History*. Cambridge: Cambridge University Press.

Mathieson, A. and Wall, G. (1989). *Tourism: Economic, Physical and Social Impacts*. Harlow: Longman.

McDonald, M. A. and Milne, G. R. (1999). *Cases in Sport Marketing*. Sudbury, MA: Jones and Bartlett.

McIntosh, R. W. and Goeldner, C. R. (1986). *Tourism Principles, Practices, Philosophies* (5th edition). Columbus, OH: Grid Publishing.

McKie, L. (1994). Signs of activity. *Leisure Management*, 15, 33–34.

McKoy, C. M. (1991). The role of sport at Butlins. Unpublished MSc thesis, Loughborough University.

Meler, M. (2001). Sports and recreation tourism – marketing a tourism destination. In *Sport for All and Health Tourism* (M. Bartoluci, ed.), Zagreb: CESS.

Mintel (1996). *Leisure Intelligence – Snowsports*. London: Mintel.

Mintel (1998). *The Sports Market*. London: Mintel.

Mintel (1999). *Leisure Intelligence: Activity Holidays*. London: Mintel.

Mintel (2000). *The Sports Market*. London: Mintel.

Mintel (2002a). *Leisure Intelligence: Holiday Centres*. London: Mintel.

Mintel (2002b). *Leisure Intelligence: Snowsports*. London: Mintel.

Mintel (2002c). *Leisure Intelligence – Hotels in the UK*. London: Mintel.

Mintel (2003a). *Leisure Intelligence: Golf*. London: Mintel

Mintel (2003b). *Leisure Intelligence: Health and Beauty Treatments*. London: Mintel

Morgan, D. (1998). Up the wall: the impact of the development of climbing walls on British rock climbing. In *Leisure Management: Issues and Applications* (M. F. Collins and I. Cooper, eds), London: CABI.

Morgan, G. (1986). *Images of Organisation*. London: Sage.

Morgan, G. (1997). *Images of Organisation* (2nd edition). London: Sage.

Morgan, N. and Pritchard, A. (2000). *Advertising in Tourism and Leisure*. Oxford: Butterworth-Heinemann.

Mortlock, C. (1984). *The Adventure Alternative*. Cumbria: Cicerone Press.

Moutinho, L. (1987). *Consumer Behaviour in Tourism*. Bradford: MCB University Press.

Mules, T. (1998). Events tourism and economic development in Australia. In *Managing Tourism in Cities: Policy, Process and Practice* (D. Tyler, Y. Guerrier and M. Robertson, eds), Chichester: John Wiley.

Myerscough, J. (1974). The recent history of the use of leisure time. In *Leisure Research and Policy* (I. Appleton, ed.), Edinburgh: Scottish Academic Press.

National Ski Areas Association (2000). *1998/99 Economic Analysis of United States Ski Areas*. Colorado: NSAA.

National Tourist Organization – Malta (1997). *Malta Sports Calender*. Valletta: NTO – Malta.

Nelson, J. G. and Scace, R. C. (eds) (1968). *Canadian Parks in Perspective*. Calgary: University of Calgary.

Neulinger, J. (1991). *The Psychology of Leisure* (2nd edition). Springfield, IL: Charles C. Thomas.

Nixon, H. L. and Frey, J. H. (1995). *A Sociology of Sport*. London: Wadsworth.

Office of Population Censuses and Surveys (OPCS) (1999). *Family Expenditure Survey*. London: OPCS.

Ousby, I. (1990). *The Englishman's England: Taste, Travel and the Rise of Tourism*. Cambridge: Cambridge University Press.

Owen, E., Bishop, K. and Speakman, C. (1999). The Northern Snowdonia study – an innovative approach to sustainable development. *Countryside Recreation*, 7 (2), Cardiff: Countryside Recreation Network.

Padfield, S. (Regional Officer, Sports Council South East) (1995). Personal communication

Page, S. (1990). The role of sport tourism: arena development and urban regeneration in the London Docklands. *The Geographer*, 8 (4), 18–25.

Page, S. (1999). *Transport and Tourism*. Harlow: Longman.

Page, S. J. (1988). Tourists arrive in the docks. *Town and Country Planning*, 57 (6), 178–179.

Page S. J. and Getz, D. (1997). *The Business of Rural Tourism: International Perspectives*. London: International Thomson Business Press.

Patmore, J. A. (1983). *Recreation and Resources*. Oxford: Blackwell.

Pearce, D. G. (1987). *Tourism Today: A Geographical Analysis*. Harlow: Longman.

Pearce, D. G. (1993). Comparative studies in tourism research. In *Tourism Research: Critiques and Challenges* (D. G. Pearce and R. W. Butler, eds), London: Routledge.

Persey, R. (Senior Regional Officer, Sports Council West Midlands) (1995). Personal communication.

Petrick, J. F. (2002). An examination of golf vacationers' novelty. *Annals of Tourism Research*, 29 (2), 382–400.

PGL (2002). www.pgl.co.uk/online/moreinformation/corporate/profile.asp (accessed, 6 November 2002).

Pigeassou, C. (2002). Contribution to the analysis of sport tourism. Oral presentation to the 10th European Sport Management Congress, Jyvaskyla, September.

Pigram, J. (1983). *Outdoor Recreation and Resource Management*, Beckenham: Croom Helm.

Pimlott, J. A. R. (1947). *The Englishman's Holiday*. London: Faber and Faber.

Priest, S. (1992). Factor exploration and confirmation of the dimensions of an adventure experience. *Journal of Leisure Research*, 24 (2), 127–139.

Readman, M. (2003). Golf tourism. In *Sport and Adventure Tourism* (S. Hudson, ed.), New York: Haworth Hospitality Press.

Reasons, C. (1984). Real estate: the land grab. In *Stampede and City: Power and Politics in the West* (C. Reasons, ed.), Toronto: Between the Lines.

Redmond, G. (1991). Changing styles of sports tourism: industry/consumer interactions in Canada, the USA and Europe. In *The Tourist Industry: An International Analysis* (M. T. Sinclair and M. J. Stabler, eds), Wallingford: CAB International.

Reeves, M. R. (1995). Sports tourism: review of fundamental research. Unpublished review paper, Loughborough University.

Reeves, M. R. (2000). Evidencing the sport-tourism interrelationship. Unpublished PhD thesis, Loughborough University.

Regan, M. (1999). Commonwealth gains. *The Leisure Manager*, 17 (12), 20–22.

Reznick, J. R. (2003). Health tourism in action – a best practice case study from France. Paper presented to the English Tourism Council Insights Seminar, Health Tourism – The Future, at the British Travel Trade Fair, Birmingham, March.

Rhodes, R. A. W. (1981). *Control and Power in Centre–Local Government Relations*. Farnborough: Gower/SSRC.

Rhodes, R. A. W. (1986). *The National World of Local Government*. London: Macmillan.

Rhodes, R. A. W. (1988). *Beyond Westminster and Whitehall*. London: Unwin Hyman.

Rhodes, R. A. W. and Marsh, D. (1992). Policy networks in British politics: a critique of existing approaches. In *Policy Networks in British Government* (D. Marsh and R. A. W. Rhodes, eds), Oxford: Oxford University Press.

Richardson, I. (2000). Developing shared community/school facilities: models, budgets and loan servicing. In *Planning and Developing Rural Sports Facilities*, Official Forum Proceedings, New South Wales: Department of Sport and Recreation.

Richardson, J. J. and Jordan, A. G. (1979). *Governing Under Pressure*. Oxford: Martin Robertson.

Ripley, R. and Franklin, G. (1980). *Congress, The Bureaucracy and Public Policy*. Homewood, IL: Dorsey Press.

Ritchie, J. R. B. (1984). Assessing the impact of hallmark events: conceptual and research issues. *Journal of Travel Research*, 23 (1), 2–11.

Ritchie, J. R. B. (1988). The Seoul Olympics as a tourism management: understanding and enhancing long term impacts. Paper to Korean National Tourist Organisation, Seoul.

Ritchie, J. R. B. (1990). Promoting Calgary through the Olympics: the mega-event as a strategy for community development. In *Social Marketing: Promoting the Causes of Public and Nonprofit Agencies* (S. H. Fine, ed.), Toronto: Allyn and Bacon.

Robertson, M. and Guerrier, Y. (1998). Events as entrepreneurial displays: Seville, Barcelona and Madrid. In *Managing Tourism in Cities: Policy, Process and Practice* (D. Tyler, Y. Guerrier and M. Robertson, eds), Chichester: John Wiley.

Robinson, H. (1976). *A Geography of Tourism*. Plymouth: Macdonald and Evans.

Robinson, T., Gammon, S. and Jones, I. (2003). *Sports Tourism: An Introduction*. London: Continuum.

Roche, M. (1992). Mega events and micro modernisation: on the sociology of the new urban tourism. *British Journal of Sociology*, 43 (4), 22–29.

Roche, M. (1994). Mega-events and urban policy. *Annals of Tourism Research*, 21 (1), 1–19.

Roche, M. (2001). Mega-events, Olympic Games and the World Student Games 1991 – understanding the impacts and information needs of major sports events. Paper Presented at the SPRIG Conference, UMIST Manchester, 1 May.

Rosentraub, M. S. (2000). Sports facilities, redevelopment and the centrality of downtown areas: observations and lessons from experiences in the Rustbelt and Sunbelt City. *Marquette Sports Law Journal*, 10 (2), 219–235.

Rossi, B. and Cereatti, L. (1993). the sensation seeking in mountain athletes as assessed by Zuckerman's sensation seeking scale. *International Journal of Sport Psychology*, 24 (4), 417–431.

Rotter, J. B. (1966). Generalised expectancies for internal versus external control of reinforcement. *Psychological Monographs: General and Applied*, 80 (1), 1–28.

Rozin, S. (2000). The amateurs who saved Indianapolis. *Business Week*, 10 April, 126–130.

Ryan, C. (1991). *Recreational Tourism: A Social Science Perspective*. London: Routledge.

Ryan, C. (2002). *The Tourist Experience: A New Introduction*. London: Continuum.

Sandiford, K. A. P. (1994). *Cricket and the Victorians*. Aldershot: Scholar Press.

Schreiber, R. (1976). Sports interest: a travel definition. *The Travel Research Association 7th Annual Conference Proceedings*. Boca Raton, FL: TRA.

Schroeder, T. (1993). Making a case for tourism. *Parks and Recreation*, 28 (9), 92–95.

Schuett, M. A. and Holmes, T. P. (1996). Using a collaborative approach to developing a regional bicycle tourism plan. *Journal of Hospitality and Leisure Marketing*, 4 (1), 83–95.

Schumacher, D. (2000). Personal communication to Donald Getz, noted in Getz, D. (2003). Sport event tourism: planning, development and marketing. In *Sport and Adventure Tourism* (S. Hudson, ed.), New York: Haworth Hospitality Press.

Schutt, A. M. (1998). Trails for economic development. *Journal of Applied Recreation Research*, 23 (2), 127–145.

Scott, A. (1995). Gearing up. *Sunday Times*, 19 November.

Selin, S., Uysal, M., Fesenmaier, D. R. and Uysal, M. (1993). Collaborative alliances: new interorganizational forms in tourism. *Journal of Travel and Tourism Marketing*, 2 (2/3), 217–227.

Selman, P. (1992). *Environmental Planning*. London: Paul Chapman.

Seward, K. (1994). Jewel in the crown. *Leisure Management*, 14 (9), 22–23.

Shakespear, W. (2002). Developing sustained high performance services and systems that have quality outcomes. In *Proceedings of the 12th Commonwealth International Sport Conference*. London: Association of Commonwealth Universities.

Sharpley, R. and Craven, B. (2001). The 2001 foot and mouth crisis – rural economy and tourism implications: a comment. *Current Issues in Tourism*, 4 (6), 527–537.

Sharpley, R. and Sharpley, J. (1997). *Rural Tourism: An Introduction.* London: Thompson Business Press.

Shaw, G. and Williams A. M. (1994). *Critical Issues in Tourism: A Geographical Perspective.* Oxford: Blackwell.

Shaw, G. and Williams, A. M. (2002). *Critical Issues in Tourism: A Geographical Perspective* (2nd edition). Oxford: Blackwell.

Sheffield Children's Festival (SCF) (1994). *Sheffield's Youth Festival – a Five Year Plan.* Sheffield: SCF.

Sheffield City Council Sports Development and Event Unit (SCCSDEU) (1995). *Major Sports Events Strategy.* Sheffield: SCCSDEU.

Sheffield City Liaison Group (SCLG) (1994). *The Way Ahead – Plans for the Economic Regeneration of Sheffield.* Sheffield: SCLG.

Shibli, S. and Gratton, C. (2001). The economic impact of two major sports events in two of the UK's national cities of sport. In *Sport in the City: The Role of Sport in Economic and Social Regeneration* (C. Gratton and I. P. Henry, eds), London: Routledge.

Short, J. R. (1991). *Imagined Country: Society, Culture and Environment.* London: Routledge.

Sidaway, R. (1988). *Sport, Recreation and Nature Conservation.* London: Sports Council/Countryside Commission.

Sidaway, R. M. (1991). *Good Conservation Practice for Sport and Recreation, Study 37.* London: Sports Council.

Sidaway, R. M. (1997). Recreation pressures on the countryside: real concerns or crises of the imagination? In *Leisure Management: Issues and Applications* (M. F. Collins and I. S. Cooper, eds), Wallingford: CAB International.

Sidaway, R. M. and O'Connor, F. B. (1978). Recreation pressures in the countryside. In *Countryside for All? Proceedings of Countryside Recreation Research Advisory Group Conference.* Cheltenham: CRRAG.

Simmons, I. G. (1994). *Interpreting Nature: Cultural Constructions of the Environment.* London: Routledge.

Skinner, Q. (1978). *The Foundations of Modern Political Thought* (volumes I–II). Cambridge: Cambridge University Press.

Slusher, H. S. (1967). *Men, Sport and Existence: A Critical Analysis.* Philadelphia, PA: Lea and Febiger.

Smith, C. P. and Jenner, P. (1990). *Travel and Tourism Analyst: Activity Holidays in Europe.* London: Mintel.

Smith, M. J. (1993). *Pressure, Power and Policy.* Hemel Hempstead: Harvester Wheatsheaf.

Smith, S. (1989). *Tourism Analysis: A Handbook.* Harlow: Longman.

Smith, S. L. (1998). Athletes, runners and joggers: participant-group dynamics in a sport of 'individuals'. *Sociology of Sport Journal*, 15, 174–192.

Smith, S. L. J. (1983). *Recreation Geography.* Harlow: Longman.

Smith, V. L. (ed.) (1977). *Hosts and Guests: An Anthropology of Tourism.* Philadelphia, PA: University of Pennsylvania Press.

Snyder, E. (1991). Sociology of nostalgia: halls of fame and museums in America. *Sociology of Sport Journal*, 8, 228–238.

Sonstroem, R. J. (1982). Attitudes and beliefs in the prediction of exercise participation. In *Sport, Medicine, Sport Science: Bridging the Gap* (R. C. Cantu and W. J. Gillepsie, eds), Toronto: Callamore Press.

Sonstroem, R. J. and Morgan W. P. (1989). Exercise and self esteem: rationale and model. *Medicine and Science in Sports and Exercise*, 21, 329–337.

Speakman, L. and Speakman, C. (1999). Car-dependency and countryside recreation – the need for an alternative culture. *Countryside Recreation*, 7 (2), Cardiff: Countryside Recreation Network.

Sport England (1999). *The National Lottery Sports Fund Strategy*. London: Sport England.

Sports Business Market Research Inc. (SBMR) (2000). *The 2000 Sports Business Market Research Handbook*. Norcross, GA: Richard K. Miller and Associates.

Sports Council (1988). *Sharing Does Work*. London: Sports Council

Sports Council (1988). *Sport in the Community: Into the Nineties*. London: Sports Council.

Sports Council (1990). *Sport and Urban Regeneration*. London: Sports Council.

Sports Council (1992). *A Countryside for Sport*. London: Sports Council.

Sports Council (1994). *Community Use of Sports Facilities on School Sites – a Review of the 1992/93 Management Awards*. London: Sports Council.

Standeven, J. (1992). Sport and tourism: a global desire or dilemma? Unpublished paper, Brighton Polytechnic.

Standeven, J. (1993). Sport and tourism in the South of England. Unpublished paper, University of Brighton.

Standeven, J. and De Knop, P. (1999). *Sport Tourism*. Champaign, IL: Human Kinetics.

Standeven, J. and Tomlinson, A. (1994). *Sport and Tourism in South East England: A Preliminary Assessment*. London: SECSR.

Stebbins, R. (1992). *Amateurs, Professionals and Serious Leisure*. London: McGill.

Stevens, T. (1987). Dallas. *Leisure Management*, 7, December, 26–27, 35.

Stevens, T. (1992). Barcelona: the Olympic City. *Leisure Management*, 12 (6), 26–30.

Stevens, T. and Wootton, G. (1997). Sports stadia and arena: realising their full potential. *Tourism Recreation Research*, 22 (2), 49–56.

Stewart, P. (1993). Corporate hospitality: are running events missing out on a valuable component for sponsors? *Road Race Management*, 137, 1–7.

Strange, I. (1993). Public–private partnership and the politics of economic regeneration policy in Sheffield, c. 1985–1991. Unpublished PhD thesis, University of Sheffield.

Swarbrooke, J. (2000). Tourism, economic development and urban regeneration: a critical evaluation. In *Reflections on International Tourism: Developments in Urban and Rural Tourism* (M. Robinson, R. Sharpley, N. Evans, P. Long and J. Swarbrooke, eds), Sunderland: Centre for Travel and Tourism.

Swart, K. (1998). Visions for South African sport tourism. *Visions in Leisure and Business*, 17 (2), 4–12.

Swimming Times (1991). Ponds Forge, Sheffield. *Swimming Times*, June, 10–11.

Tananone, B. (1991). International tourism in Thailand: environment and community development. *Contours*, 5 (2), 7–9.

Taylor, P. (1998). *Sports Facility Development and the Role of Forecasting: A Retrospective on Swimming in Sheffield*. Paper presented at the Sport in the City, Sheffield.

The Times (1988). Special report on Sheffield. *The Times*, 24 May.

The Times (2003). How Scottish fans fell out of love with Hampden and their team. *The Times*, 29 March 2003, p. 29 (Scottish edition).

Tischler, S. (1981). *Footballers & Businessmen – The Origins of Professional Soccer in England*. New York: Holmes and Meier.

Toh, R. S., Khan, H. and Lim, K. (2001). Singapore's tourism industry: how its strengths offset economic, social and environmental challenges. *The Cornell Hotel and Restaurant Administration Quarterly*, 4 (2), 42–49.

Tokarski, W. (1993). Leisure, sports and tourism: the role of sports in and outside holiday clubs. In *Leisure and Tourism: Social and Economic Change* (A. J. Veal, P. Jonson and G. Cushman, eds), Sydney: Sydney University of Technology.

Tomlinson, A. (1996). Olympic spectacles: opening ceremonies, and some paradoxes of globalisation. *Media, Culture & Society*, 18, 583–602.

Tomlinson, A. and Walker, H. (1990). Holidays for all: popular movements, collective leisure and the pleasure industry. In *Consumption, Identity and Style: Marketing, Meanings and the Packaging of Pleasure* (A. Tomlinson, ed.), London: Routledge.

Tourism Canada (1993). *Spectator Sporting Activities in Canada from a Tourism Perspective*. Ottowa: Tourism Canada.

Tourism Marketplace (1993). Olympian effort from Manchester, *Tourism Marketplace*, 94, 29.

Towner, J. (1985). The Grand Tour: a key phase in the history of tourism. *Annals of Tourism Research*, 12 (3), 297–333.

Towner, J. (1996). *An Historical Geography of Recreation and Tourism in the Western World 1540–1940*. Chichester: Wiley.

Train, P. (1994). Tourism and economic impacts of staging a special event: the Europa Cup, Birmingham 1994. Unpublished MSc thesis, Loughborough University.

Travel and Leisure (1995). Mission Inn Golf and Tennis Resort. *Travel and Leisure*, 23 (9), 10.

Trollope, K. (1986). Docklands aid tourism growth. *Caterer and Hotelkeeper*, 9 January, 23–25.

Tuppen, J. (1998). France. In *Tourism and Economic Development: European Experiences* (3rd edition) (A. Williams and G. Shaw, eds), Chichester: Wiley.

Turco, D. M., Riley, R. S. and Swart, K. (2002). *Sport Tourism*. Morgantown: Fitness Information Technology.

Tyler, D., Guerrier, Y. and Robertson, M. (eds) (1998). *Managing Tourism in Cities: Policy, Process and Practice*. Chichester: John Wiley.

Tyrer, B. (1990). *London Docklands 1990*. Reprinted from the *London Docklands Business Directory*.

UNDP and WTO (1989). *The Maltese Islands Tourist Development Plan*. Madrid: WTO.

Urry, J. (2002). *The Tourist Gaze* (2nd Edition). London: Sage.

Uyssal, M., McDonald, C. D. and Reid, L. J. (1990). Sources of information used by international visitors to US parks and natural areas. *Journal of Park and Recreation Administration*, 8 (1), 51–59.

Vamplew, W. (1988). Sport and industrialisation: an economic interpretation of the changes in popular sport in nineteenth–century England. In *Pleasure,*

Profit and Proselytism: British Culture and Sport at Home and Abroad, 1700–1914 (J. A. Mangan, ed.), London: Frank Cass.

Van Dalen, D. B. and Bennett, B. (1971). *A World History of Physical Education*. Englewood Cliffs, NJ: Prentice-Hall.

Veal, A. J. (1986). *People in Sport and Recreation 1980: Summary of Data from the 1980 General Household Survey for England and Wales*. London: Centre for Leisure and Tourism Studies, Polytechnic of North London

Vester, H.-G. (1987). Adventure as a form of leisure. *Leisure Studies*, 6, 237–249.

Vrondou, O. (1999). Sports related tourism and the product repositioning of traditional mass tourism destinations: a case study of Greece. Unpublished PhD thesis, Loughborough University.

Wahlers, R. G. and Etzel, J. (1985). Vacation preference as a manifestation of optimal stimulation and lifestyle experience. *Journal of Leisure Research*, 17 (4), 287–295.

Waitt, G. (1999). Playing games with Sydney: marketing Sydney for the 2000 Olympics. *Urban Studies*, 36, 1055–1077.

Waitt, G. (2003). Social impacts of the Sydney Olympics. *Annals of Tourism Research*, 30 (1), 194–215.

Wales Tourist Board (WTB) (2000). *Achieving Our Potential: A Tourism Strategy for Wales*. Cardiff: Wales Tourist Board.

Wales Tourist Board (2002a). *Best Foot Forward: A Walking Tourism Strategy for Wales*. Cardiff: Wales Tourist Board.

Wales Tourist Board (WTB) (2002b). *Saddling Up for Success: A Riding Tourism Strategy for Wales*. Cardiff: Wales Tourist Board.

Wales Tourist Board (WTB) (2002c). *Moving up a Gear: A Cycle Tourism Strategy for Wales*. Cardiff: Wales Tourist Board.

Wales Tourist Board (WTB) (2002d). *Time for Action – an Adventure Tourism Strategy for Wales (2002–8)*. Cardiff: Wales Tourist Board.

Walter, C. (2002). A winter's trail. *Skiing*, 54 (5), 106–107.

Walton, J. K. (1981). *The English Seaside Resort: A Social History, 1750–1914*. Leicester: Leicester University Press.

Walton, J. K. (2000). *The British Seaside*. Manchester: Manchester University Press.

Walton, J. K. and Walvin, J. (eds) (1983). *Leisure in Britain, 1780–1939*. Manchester: Manchester University Press

Wann, D. L., Melnick, M. J., Russell, G. W. and Pease, D. G. (2001). *Sports Fans: The Psychology and Social Impacts of Spectators*. London: Routledge.

Ward, J., Higson, P. and Campbell, W. (1994). *Advanced Leisure and Tourism*. Cheltenham: Stanley Thornes.

Weaver, D. B. and Lawton, L. J. (2001). Resident perceptions in the urban–rural fringe. *Annals of Tourism Research*, 28 (2), 439–458.

Weed, M. E. (1999a). Consensual policies for sport and tourism in the UK: an analysis of organisational behaviour and problems. PhD thesis, Canterbury, University of Kent at Canterbury/Canterbury Christ Church College.

Weed, M. E. (1999b). More than sports tourism: an introduction to the sport-tourism link. In *Proceedings of the Sport and Recreation Information Group Seminar, Exploring Sports Tourism* (M. Scarrot, ed.), Sheffield: SPRIG.

Weed, M. E. (2000). The social dynamics of sports groups: arguments for a meso-level analysis. In *Proceedings of the Fifth Annual Congress of the European College of Sport Science* (J. Avela, P. V. Komi and J. Komulainen, eds), Jyvaskyla: LIKES Research Centre.

Weed, M. E. (2001a). Developing a sports tourism product. Paper to the 1st International Conference of the Pan Hellenic Association of Sports Economists and Managers, The Economic Impact of Sport, February.

Weed, M. E. (2001b). Tourism and sports development: providing the foundation for healthy lifestyles. Paper to the 1st International Congress, Sport and Quality of Life, Villa Real, Portugal, December.

Weed, M. E. (2001c). Ing-ger-land at Euro 2000: how 'handbags at 20 paces' was portrayed as a full-scale riot. *International Review for the Sociology of Sport*, 36 (4), 407–424.

Weed, M. E. (2001d). Towards a model of cross-sectoral policy development in leisure: the case of sport and tourism. *Leisure Studies*, 20 (2), 125–141.

Weed, M. E. (2002a). Understanding cricket crowd behaviour: a note of caution for event managers. Paper to the 12th Commonwealth International Sport Conference, Manchester, July.

Weed, M. E. (2002b). Football hooligans as undesirable sports tourists: some meta analytical speculations. In *Sport Tourism: Principles and Practice* (S. Gammon and J. Kurtzman, eds), Eastbourne: LSA.

Weed, M. E. (2002c). Organisational culture and the leisure policy process in Britain: how structure affects strategy in sport-tourism policy development. *Tourism, Culture and Communication*, 3 (3), 147–164.

Weed, M. E. (2002d). Sports tourism and identity: developing a sports tourism participation model. In *Proceedings of the 10th European Congress on Sport Management* (K. Laaksonen, P. Lopponen, E. Nykanen and K. Puronaho, eds), Jyvaskyla: EASM.

Weed, M. E. (2003a). Mediated and inebriated: the pub as a sports spectator venue. Paper to the Leisure Studies Association Conference, Leisure and Visual Culture, Roehampton, July.

Weed, M. E. (2003b). Emotion, identity and sports spectator cultures. Paper to the 11th European Congress of Sports Psychology (FEPSAC), Copenhagen, July.

Weed, M. E. (2003c). Why the two won't tango: explaining the lack of integrated policies for sport and tourism in the UK. *Journal of Sports Management*, Special Edition on Sports Tourism, forthcoming.

Weed, M. E. (2003d). Sports tourism services: understanding provision strategies. Paper to the 11th European Association of Sport Management Congress, Sport Management in a Changing World, Stockholm, September.

Weed, M. E. (2003e). Healthy holidays? Motivations, intentions and perceptions of health/spa tourists – a pilot study. Paper to the 17th Annual Conference of the European Health Psychology Society, Kos, September.

Weed, M. E. and Bull, C. J. (1997a). Integrating sport and tourism: a review of regional policies in England. *Progress in Tourism and Hospitality Research*, 3 (2), 129–148.

Weed, M. E. and Bull, C. J. (1997b). Influences on sport-tourism relations in Britain: the effects of government policy. *Tourism Recreation Research*, Special Edition on Sport and Tourism.

Weed, M. E. and Bull, C. J. (1998). The search for a sport-tourism policy network. In *Leisure Management: Issues and Applications* (M. F. Collins and I. S. Cooper, eds), Wallingford: CAB International.

Weiler, B. and Hall, C. M. (eds) (1992). *Special Interest Tourism*. London: Belhaven Press.

Weinberg, R. S. and Gould, D. (1995). *Foundations of Sport and Exercise Psychology*. Champaign IL: Human Kinetics.

Weiss, O., Norden, G., Hilschers, P. and Vanreusel, B. (1998). Ski tourism and environmental problems. *International Review for the Sociology of Sport*, 33 (4), 367–379.

Whannel, G. (1985). Television spectacle and the internationalisation of sport. *Journal of Communication Enquiry*, 2, 54–74.

Wheaton, B. (1998). The changing gender order in sport? The case of windsurfing subcultures. *Journal of Sport and Social Issues*, 22 (3), 252–274.

Wheaton, B. (2000). 'Just do it': consumption, commitment and identity in the windsurfing subculture. *Sociology of Sport Journal*, 17 (3), 254–274.

Whitson, D. and Macintosh, D. (1993). The hosting of international games in Canada: ecological and ideological ambitions. Unpublished paper, Loughborough University.

Whitson, D. and Macintosh, D. (1996). The global circus: international sport, tourism and the marketing of cities. *Journal of Sport and Social Issues*, 20 (3), 278–295.

Wickers, D. (1994). Snow alternative. *Sunday Times*, 27 November, p. 9.

Wilkinson, P. F. and Murray A. L. (1991). Centre and periphery: The impacts of the leisure industry on a small town. *Society and Leisure*, 14 (1), 235–260.

Wilks, S. (1989). Government–industry relations. *Public Administration*, 67, 329–339.

Wilks, S. and Wright, M. (eds) (1987). *Comparative Government–Industry Relations*. Oxford: Clarendon Press.

Williams, C. (1994). Exercise and well-being. Unpublished paper to the Sports Science Research Group, Loughborough University.

Williams, J., Dunning, E. and Murphy, P. (1989). *Hooligans Abroad* (2nd edition). London: Routledge

Williams, P. and Dossa, K. (1990). *British Columbia Downhill Skier Survey 1989–90*. British Columbia: Centre for Tourism Policy and Research, Simon Fraser University and Canada West Ski Areas Association.

Williams, P. W. and Basford, R. (1992). Segmenting downhill skiing's latent demand markets. *American Behavioural Scientist*, 36 (2), 222–235.

Williams, T. and Donnelly, P. (1985). Subcultural production, reproduction and transformation in climbing. *International Review for the Sociology of Sport*, 20 (1–2), 3–16.

Wilson, A. (1991). *The Culture of Nature*. Toronto: Between the Lines.

Wilson, J. Q. (1973). *Political Organisations*. New York: Basic Books.

Withey, L (1997). *Grand Tours and Cook's Tours: A History of Leisure Travel, 1750 to 1915*. London: Aurum Press.

Wöber, K. (1997). International city tourism flows. In *International City Tourism* (J. A. Mazanec, ed.) 39–53, London: Pinter.

Woodward, S. (1990). Lucky dip. *Leisure Management*, 10 (6), 36–39.

World Alliance of YMCAs (1998). *YMCA Directory*. Geneva: WAYMCA.

World Tourism Organization (WTO) (1963). *United Nations Conference on International Travel and Tourism*. Madrid: WTO.

World Tourism Organization (WTO) (1988). *Special Interest Tourism*. Madrid: WTO.

World Tourism Organization (WTO) (1991). *Tourism to the Year 2000: Qualitative Aspects Affecting Global Growth*. Madrid: WTO.

World Tourism Organization (WTO) (2002). *Sport and Tourism*. Madrid: WTO.

Wright, B. (2000). An arm and a leg: how climbers' and mountaineers' money can benefit rural communities. *Climber*, November, 88–89.

Wright, M. (1988). Policy community, policy network and comparative industrial policies, *Political Studies*, 36 (4), 593–612.

Yardley, J. K., MacDonald, J. H. and Clarke, B. D. (1990). The economic impact of a small, short-term recreation event on a local economy. *Journal of Park and Recreation Administration*, 8 (4), 71–82.

Index